WHAT I'VE ALWAYS KNOWN

Also by Tom Harmer

Going Native

WHAT I'VE ALWAYS KNOWN

Living in Full Awareness of the Earth

TOM HARMER

HARMONY BOOKS

NEW YORK

Published by Harmony Books, New York, New York.
Member of the Crown Publishing Group, a division of Random House, Inc.
www.randomhouse.com

Harmony Books is a registered trademark and the Harmony Books
colophon is a trademark of Random House, Inc.

Printed in the United States of America

Design by Leonard Henderson

Library of Congress Cataloging-in-Publication Data

Harmer, Tom.
What I've always known : living in full awareness of the earth / Tom Harmer. — 1st ed.
1. Harmer, Tom.   2. Spiritual biography—Washington (State).   3. Salish Indians—
Religion—Miscellanea.   4. Salish Indians—Social life and customs—Miscellanea.   I. Title.
BL73.H35A3   2003
299'.789—dc21   2002154325

ISBN 1-4000-4855-9

10 9 8 7 6 5 4 3 2 1

First Edition

For my mother,
Dorothy Mae Harmer

NOTE

THE EVENTS DESCRIBED HERE are a continuation of the story I told in my first book, *Going Native*. I've written this book so it can stand on its own, but certainly a richer understanding could be gained by knowing in more detail what went before.

I've re-created here to the best of my memory the words of elders no longer living that I heard twenty years ago. Nothing of importance was ever said to me just once, and so much was repeated in the same words over a period of years that I have no reservations about passing them on as they appear here. The stories about nature power have been presented word-for-word as I memorized them and told them back to the elders who taught them to me.

Everyone but myself has been disguised with a fictional name, and some of those not central to the experiences I've told about were collapsed into single persons to make things simpler. In the desire to protect other people's privacy, I've moved certain events to other locations and been vague about where some people lived. Some events and conversations were shifted in time to make them more understandable, but as in *Going Native,* everything in this book actually happened.

Instead of inflicting the unfamiliar symbols of linguists on the reader, I have used my own phonetic way of spelling the Salish Indian words used in this book. The usual English pronunciations apply, except for *x* (a guttural "h" sound like *ach* in German), *tl* (which is one sound like the "tl" in "bottle"), and the apostrophe, which is either a glottal stop or used to separate syllables usually run together in English. Salish consonants are more complex than I've represented them here, and vowels without stress accents are usually barely sounded.

The terms "Native American" and "First Nations People" do not appear in this book because nobody used them in actual conversation. Instead, "Indian," "Native," "Okanogan," "Salish," and *Sḵélux* are used interchangeably because those are the words they used for themselves, their language, and their way of living in the world.

WHAT I'VE ALWAYS KNOWN

1

IT DIDN'T FEEL THAT cold to me at first. I remember miles of packed powder crumping underfoot as I walked along in the vast silence of forest. Winters are the real thing along the U.S.–Canada border in the interior of British Columbia and Washington state, so I carried matches and a knife and was dressed in layers. In those days it was a down vest over a wool coat, over a sweater, over a flannel shirt with flap pockets. Probably jeans and those military black leather gloves with wool inserts I liked to wear. Leather boots, of course, and a knit cap pulled down over my ears. Definitely not a parka, which shows how unprepared I was for what happened.

Maybe it had to do with no longer working outdoors in the cold every day. For years I'd spent the winters pruning apple trees, repairing fences, even feeding cattle during the worst blizzards. But ever since I'd taken a job with a local social services agency and moved into town, all I did was interview people and shuffle papers in overheated offices. And the days when I would spend every spare moment off in the hills with my Okanogan Indian friends to hunt deer, cut firewood, or search for stray horses were just a memory.

I was already having second thoughts about my new life of small town, indoor tameness. It bothered me that there was no need to pay attention to what my senses were telling me. Indoors, it was always the same—if it got cold, you just turned up the heat. Maybe a kind of atrophy had set in, because coming out of the mountains on foot in snow that day, I failed to read the obvious signs of danger.

It wasn't as if I was breaking trail through the deep snows of the back country. It was a Sunday afternoon visit with old friends, and then an easy walk down the forestry road from their cabin on Cecile Creek to the town of Loomis, a distance of only seven miles. I'd driven the road hundreds of times, and when snow closed it, walked it out many times. Like a stroll down memory lane, every turn in the road reminded me of the life I'd left behind. The spot under towering tamarack and fir where a herd of deer milled around on the road one summer morning, fearlessly blocking my way as I drove a stock truck up to a rancher's cattle permit in the high country. The cobbled cutbank where I parked to gather rocks for the sweatlodge. The open, rocky slopes where chukar partridges would burst into flight when I passed. The pullout where cowboys would sit in pickup trucks, looking through binoculars at a herd of bighorn sheep across the valley, on the open side of Aeneas Mountain.

It was there at the pullout, where the road emerged from timber and curved back and forth steeply down to the Sinlahekin Valley below, that the cold really hit me. Smoothed and rounded in snow, the open slopes were broken here and there with brush and solitary ponderosa pines. Out in the open I could see for miles and feel the flow of frigid air from the north. The sky was undecipherable—not clear, not really cloudy, just a northern interior steel-gray blur, indistinct but solid overhead. The winter birds that had been so noisy on the morning walk up were noticeably absent, yet I failed to interpret what that might mean. No crows sailing overhead, no chickadees calling from groves of trees, no bluejays or magpies shattering the silence with their raucous cries. Just a hissing, vacant, brittle solitude—the world asleep under snow and only the sound of my steps to keep me company.

The afternoon light was fading, and it got colder and colder the farther down I went. I hoped to get to Loomis before nightfall, and could see the cluster of houses in the far distance, under a pall of woodsmoke. Without giving thought to anything else, I kept on.

I should have known better. I was walking steeply downhill, barely generating any body heat into an arctic outflow imperceptibly fingering its way into the lowlands under the relatively milder air higher up. (It had been maybe 20 degrees F in the mountains. By the time I finally made it, long after dark, to Sully's Store where I'd left my car, the thermometer outside in the glare of neon light read minus 28.)

Somewhere below Apricot Flat I began shivering uncontrollably. I couldn't fathom why I was so suddenly freezing, and walked faster, breathing deeply and swinging my arms to still the muscular spasms. After a time, my shivering stopped, and I had the disconcerting sensation that I had no clothes on, that my skin was bare to the cold air. I found out later that this was a signal my body temperature had dropped dangerously low, but at the time, since it was followed by a deceptively pleasant warmth and sense of well-being, I thought I'd succeeded in warming myself up. After that, things became vague.

I remember slowing down and beginning to wander, my steps leading me back and forth between the rows of rabbitbrush lining the road. Eventually, my looping line of walk became so erratic and directionless, I stepped off the road in such a daze that although I was aware of drifting aimlessly through the brush, it didn't seem to mean anything. Barely conscious of what I was doing, only the faint memory of wanting to get somewhere keeping me going, I stumbled around in the snow wherever my feet took me.

When I came upon fresh tracks, it dawned on me that they were my own, that I was walking around in circles on an open flat somewhere. It seemed oddly humorous. Since it was useless to go on, my befuddled mind turned to what seemed the only alternative—to stop and rest. As I was already drowsy, the urge to give in was irresistible, but I kept plodding on because I didn't want to sit in the snow. I couldn't remember why it was such a bad idea, and eventually my dwindling ability to keep putting one foot in front of the other led me to wonder why I was persisting to look for somewhere free of snow. My last thread of conscious thought was something like: Hey, there's nothing wrong with sitting down in the snow. . . . With no further resistance, I felt the relief of giving in and slowed to a stop.

At that moment, I heard a loud screeching noise that was like a gun going off next to my ear. I was startled out of deep nothingness into the instant recognition that it was my mother calling me. It was so familiar, so impossible to ignore, so exactly how she called me when I was a boy—"Tommy!"—that I looked around to see what she was doing out there. In a moment of anguish and uneasiness, it came to me that she couldn't be there, that something had to be wrong—and I suddenly came back to myself, aware of my actual situation.

The realization was awful. I couldn't feel my hands or feet or face, and trying to walk again was like trying to move with my body encased in concrete. There was so little coordination between what I intended and how I tottered around, barely able to stay on my feet, that my rising fear approached panic. I was like a tiny spark of awareness high up in a stiff robot taking its clumsy first steps. Unable to see the road anywhere, I couldn't figure out where I was or what to do. Stumbling around aimlessly again, I could feel my body weakening, my knees buckling at the effort. I began to feel hopeless. Then I heard another voice.

"Build a fire or you're going to die."

It wasn't my voice, but it spoke as if inside my mind, as clearly as if by someone standing beside me. The voice was familiar, calm, and imperative, and instantly quieted my panic. Everything narrowed to how.

I remembered the matches in my pocket. A ponderosa pine not far away gave direction to my feeble steps. As I came closer, I saw how thin the snow was underneath the tree and how dead branches hung low enough to reach. Long practice in firemaking outdoors kicked in, guiding me like an instinct in what to do. Scuffing aside the snow and breaking branches directly overhead so they'd fall on the bare pine needles, I went through the motions in a kind of single-minded daze, my gloves and boots like blocks of wood. When I finally sat down before the pile of branches, I fell over sideways, face into the snow, and realized how pathetic I'd become. It seemed to take forever pushing myself back up into a sitting position.

Breaking off the tiniest twigs into a little pile was slow work, but how I built a fire was deeply ingrained. Years of experience starting fires had taught me the best results came from a careful preparation of the kindling, so despite how hard it was with unfeeling gloved hands, I took my time. Once things were ready to light, I tried to take off my gloves, but it was so impossible, I had to drag them off with my teeth. Then the endless task of digging out the small box of wooden matches from my shirt pocket. Exposed to the air, my fingers quickly lost whatever dexterity they had left, and as I tried to open the box and extract a match, it was demoralizing to discover I couldn't do it. I fumbled with what I could see but not feel and the box fell apart onto my lap. I poked around in the strewn matches, suddenly struck with how useless they were since I couldn't feel or pinch enough to pick one up. It was a desolate moment.

But somehow in my desperation, my hands figured out a way: A stick match could be picked up by my fingertips clenched flat against my palm, and likewise, the striking part of the box by clasping it flimsily the same way in the other fist. I had no strength to hold them tightly, so I lightly brushed the head of the match on the strike strip. Time after time nothing happened. When I tried to rub harder, the match turned aside and dropped out of my grasp. Finally, a match ignited. Dropping the box and cradling the tiny flame, I discovered I couldn't get it under the kindling, sticking out of my closed fist like that. I had to drag the pile of twigs over my fist while it rested on the ground, and wait until a thin thread of flame rose up through the kindling enough for me to extract my hand.

Fortunately the fire took off with only one match, and as the flames shot up, so did my hope. Little by little I added larger and larger branches until I had a roaring bonfire. My relief was immense, but tempered by the excruciating pain of my hands and face thawing out in the blast of heat. When my hands had regained enough feeling to untie my bootlaces, I bared my feet to the flames and went through more agony. With a return to warmth and movement came strength and a kind of furious delight. I would live! There was suddenly nothing sweeter than this roaring fire that was keeping me alive. Heating my boots and socks until they smoked, I pulled them on and leaped up, amazed at how much energy I had. Breaking more branches off the pine tree with a noise like gunshots, I built the fire up even bigger, and then looked around, wondering where the road was.

It was almost dark. When I stepped away from the fire to get away from the glare and see farther, I could really feel the cold, and it was brutal. Then I started to laugh. The road was no more than twenty feet away from the pine tree. I was on a little flat where the road curved around on three sides, and the lone pine tree was one I'd driven by so many times, I knew exactly where I was. I was almost to the bottom of the valley.

Suffering from unbearable thirst, I held snowballs close to the flames and sucked the water that melted out. Nobody was out there in the dark night of winter to hear me sing songs or see me dance in the swirling pine smoke. My thoughts turned to going on as the fire burned down to coals. Loomis was maybe three miles away, and I wasn't going to underestimate the cold again. I needed to make a dash for town, and this time remember it was bad news if I no longer felt the cold. House lights glimmered in the distance, where apple orchards lined the paved road into town. If I couldn't make it, I could always knock on some orchardist's door.

Bundled tightly, down the road I went at a jog. So fit and renewed and sure of myself after a brush with death, the world was unthreateningly beautiful again, even in the dark, buried in snow, the air so cold it hurt to breathe. There was no moon, but a few pallid stars showed through the veil overhead. In no time, I made it to the paved road, plowed clear and sanded. There wasn't a single car on the road as I dogtrotted all the way to town.

2

B Y THE TIME IT dawned on me to wonder where the old man might be heading, I'd been following his footprints in fresh snow for an hour. All the way from the house where he was staying and up into the timbered heights swathed in icy fog, his tracks showed he walked without pause or hesitation toward somewhere definite he had in mind. The wet soaked through my pants and boots as I slogged upward through deeper and deeper snow, hoping I could catch up to him before it got dark and I had to turn back.

At least the weather was holding. Once the cold snap had given way to days of snow, things had been milder. Now it was one of those still, dim afternoons after the snow stopped falling when the narrow mountain valleys were socked in under low clouds. There had even been a sunbreak at noon when the snow melted into churned-up pudding on the highway. Driving home from work earlier than usual, I'd been thinking about what happened to me when I almost froze to death. Only when the edge had worn off in the familiar routine of going to work did I remember the voices I'd heard, and how they came at critical moments to wake me up and get me to build a fire. Something momentous had happened, something that made me feel different. On a whim, I'd turned off the highway to drive up in the mountains and see if I could find my old friend, the Okanogan Indian elder Clayton Tommy, Jr. He was the one person who'd always made sense of my strange experiences.

Miles of plowed county roads even my old Ford Falcon could nego-
tiate without having to chain up brought me to the old homestead
where Clayton's sister, Annie, told me he'd gone off shortly before, on
foot into the hills. Even though I was dressed for work, I dug out my
boots and set off following his tracks. The snow was so fresh his prints
stood out sharply in every detail. It was easy at first, stepping in his deep
footprints, following where his trail led over the still sleep of snow on
the land.

Grateful to be outdoors and doing something physical after another
week of mindwork in stuffy offices, I was reminded again how much I
missed my old life. The steady tramp along game trails showing tracks
of deer and coyote, the shadowless forest of fir and pine hidden under
heavy snow, the ever-upward line of Clayton's trail drawing me closer
to the low roof of clouds—I was waking up again and wondering why
I'd ever moved to town. And it was new country to me, somewhere I
hadn't hiked into before, the steep and bouldery ascent up the east side
of Chopaka Mountain. Such a maze of switchbacking passageways
through timbered slides, I had to step carefully as I entered the frigid
mist drifting down from above.

I marveled at the old man's unerring route following what had to be
a trail he knew well, but which was invisible to my eye. His tracks led
through openings between rocks bigger than houses and up a steep-
walled draw where the snow became so deep I floundered up to my
waist. Before long I was wet through and beginning to chill. Once
again I wasn't dressed for the conditions, I thought, and wondered if I
should turn back. Where was he going? Looking back the way I'd
come, I saw the distant valley of the Similkameen River far below,
through a veil of ice fog. Then I smelled woodsmoke. Figuring it had
to be Clayton, that he'd stopped just ahead to build a fire, I went on.

The smell of smoke got stronger and the fog thinned out as I entered
a deep ravine. Clayton's trail became no more than the sign of where
something had waded through waist-deep powder, and I forced myself
on into the deepest part where a narrow chute came down from the
mountain hidden above. I heard a strange sound, like a continuous,
muffled hiss. Then I saw where it was coming from: A thirty-foot-high

column of ice about six feet wide, and hollow inside. It was the frozen sheath of a waterfall where a creek came over a sheer drop, the muted roar of water on rock held in the grip of translucent blue I could faintly see through. I was in a hidden grotto of enormous trees where the sun probably never penetrated and the cold was numbing. I looked around, shivering in awe. On the far side, beyond the ropy pedestals of ice stepping down like buttresses at the base of the ice column, I saw a dark, cavelike rock overhang, and deep inside, a yellow glimmer of flame.

I found Clayton sitting by a hot fire of pine branches, sheltered from the cold and wet under the sloping ceiling of rock. Once inside the low, wide opening in snow, I could see it was the bottom of an ancient avalanche pile of enormous angular granite slabs, with passageways leading off to other hidden recesses. As my eyes grew accustomed to the dim firelight, I saw the walls were covered in weathered pictographs, the red ocher paintings of nature spirits Clayton's people left behind in the old days, after quests for power in remote spots like this.

Since I hadn't seen him in a long time—maybe six months—I was a little self-conscious about blundering into his presence, invading what looked like a sacred place for elders like him. Fortunately there was an etiquette for chance meetings in the bush, and Clayton predictably made no sign of noticing me as I moved to warm myself at his fire. Long used to the Native preference for easing indirectly into meeting someone, I sat down across from him and stayed quiet, too, holding my bare hands up to the welcome heat.

He looked older in the flickering light, his wide face creased and worn after such a hike in snow, but there was the same clearheaded alertness that always animated his eyes. Hat off and cropped gray hair standing out in clumps, he sat cross-legged, staring into the flames, the same self-possessed old man who'd meant so much to me in years past. He wore an insulated snowmobile suit with beaded edging around the collar and pocket flaps, and with the side zippers open, I could see he wore only long johns underneath. After the usual minutes of feeling things out, he finally glanced up at me.

"So . . . you still comin' around, eh?" he said indifferently, stirring the fire with a stick.

"Yeah, well, barely made it." My jeans began to steam.

"What for?" His eyes inspected my unlikely clothes for traipsing around the mountains in snow.

"Been a long time, Clayton," I said, wondering why he sounded so harsh after our years of friendship. "Got off work early and drove up to see if you were around. Annie said you just took off somewhere, so I tracked you. Somethin' happened to me and . . . well, I wanted to ask you about it."

"Ah, that some nice lookin' getup for the busy White man who go about his important business!" The tie I'd taken off and stuffed into my coat pocket was hanging out, a florid seventies thing I wore to mock having to wear a tie at all.

"Thrift store specials," I said, and tried to tell him about my job interviewing people who applied for government money to pay utility bills. But he wasn't listening. I stopped talking and listened to the muted hiss of the frozen waterfall, how the rock overhang made it sound like it was all around us, enveloping us in a blur of white noise. Clayton sighed.

"This how they do. Come to the old-time Indian to get what they need, then go away. Go back to be the same as all the rest."

"Huh," I mumbled, stunned. Then lamely, "I'm not stayin' away. It's just . . . this job, livin' in town. It takes a lot."

"The Whites, they still strangers. Why is that? Seem like forever they been here. All my life they been here, and I keep wonderin', when they goin' to ground? When they gonna feel the earth, how she take care of us? But no, they still strangers."

Clayton was like I remembered him in winters past—inward, thoughtful, disconnected. His every word colored by concentration on the round of winter spirit dances that would soon begin. But there was something else, too, something dismissive toward me personally. He didn't seem like the same man who'd taken the time over the years to sponsor me in traditional sweatlodge and spirit quest practices he called "self-training" (*k'ulsht* in Okanogan Salish).

"Just strangers," he repeated, musing at the flames. "I wonder what happen to that White man who come to live with us? Years ago, come across the line. The hunter, the bush man, the one with that fierce love for our mother?"

"I'm still here!"

"Yah, he still out there, ain't it? He still out there roamin' the hills!" Clayton gave a short, ironic laugh, his face turned toward the misty world of snow outside, as if his words were directed at someone listening out there.

Everything he'd said since I first sat down sounded as if phrased for some other listener, someone offended by my presence and involvement with him. I had an eerie sensation that someone really was outside, even though I would have seen other tracks. Then everything clicked in my mind. He'd come up here to this place of solitude to call on his power, to look into something, to prepare himself for the grueling all-night dances in longhouses. To ready himself for this winter's public display of how the powers of earth and sky still helped those who lived in the old way. For the first time I noticed the open pouch of tobacco at his side, the cloth pipe bag tucked under one knee.

"No, I don't get up in the hills much anymore," I said. "Last week was the first time in a long time, and I had a bad experience. That's what I wanted to talk to you about."

Clayton looked directly at me. He said nothing, just studied me, then sighed again.

"Been a long time I wonderin' what happen with you, Tom. And here you come drag up, the sharp dresser out for a stroll in the timber. The smart mouth who have that want to know, find out how the Indian know the world. Well, other Whites find this place, too. Where the Native paint the picture of his power, what come to him in life . . ." and he waved toward one panel, vandalized with spray-painted initials. "This where they come in the old days to tell the stories, teach the young how to seek for somethin' in life. Only one thing matter in a place like this. Whether you still got somethin'. That one earth power, come to you in life, in childhood, give you somethin' to live by. Just like I always tellin' you about, teach you what I know, the years past. So you can live that way, use that power. Maybe what I'm thinkin', you have somethin' to say about that?"

"I don't know. Maybe. I heard voices."

"Aaaa," he said, encouraging me with a nod.

I told him about my experience of almost freezing to death. It was the first time I'd tried to put into words what had happened. I faltered at certain points, correcting myself to be more exact. Talking about it made me aware how disturbed I was at how real my mother's voice had been, and how familiar the other voice had seemed. I finished by saying how dismayed I was that I could miscalculate the weather so badly.

"Well, that maybe happen to anybody, get caught out in the hard cold comin' on," Clayton said. "But not to be saved like that. Not anybody be warned and told what to do. Only the power man." He seemed surprised and pleased by what I'd told him.

"I don't get it."

"They do that, the *shumíx,* the spirit partners. This how they do, speak in the voice of someone close, like your parent. When things are bad, to save your life. Make you listen, wake you up. Many stories handed down tell how they done that. And then, when you see how bad it is, how pitiful you are, tell you what to do. What you got don't fool around, say, 'Don't die, make a fire!' So this show you still got somethin'. That power still stickin' with you. Maybe I figure wrong about you after all."

He piled more pine branches on the fire, then stared off thoughtfully.

"But now, my want to know, you just another stranger like all the rest, or you maybe an earth person after all?"

"What can I say, Clayton? I don't know what you're getting at."

"Tiskélux ḳul temxúlaux, somebody who come alive on this earth, wake up here, live like a natural person. You know what I mean—White or Indian don't matter. How all people used to know how to live here." He patted the ground at his side.

"I don't know. I think I'm trying to. That's why I like to learn from you. How would I know?"

He shook his head slowly, staring into the fire, rubbing the stubble of hair on the back of his wrinkled neck. A flock of chickadees came flitting and peeping from limb to limb in the lower branches of a fir tree just outside, foraging in the snow-heavy tips of needles, displacing the burdens in cascades of glittery powder drifting down. Clayton watched them going about their ancient business, then spoke with unexpected sadness.

"There's a war going on. A war against the earth, against mother earth. I wonder whose side you on?"

I didn't know what to say.

"Ever since your people come here. But now, everybody in on it. Not many left to be on the earth's side. Just the few."

One of the chickadees flew down and landed just under the overhang, on the tip of a dry limb in Clayton's pile of firewood. A tiny black and white ball of fluff tamely studying us.

"You either on the earth's side, or you not. One or the other. If you are, everything in the world knows it, eh? Every animal, every tree, they know it. And they show themself to you. Open things up to you, watch over you, make things happen for you. Whisper in your ear so you feel in your heart what to do.

"But if you not on the earth's side, why, the earth don't even know you here. Don't even see you, feel your steps, know you breathin'. Just like you don't mean nothin' to her, ain't it?"

The chickadee fluffed out its feathers and continued to perch, watching us in profile. Clayton turned to the bird and said gently, "*Aaaa, sits'ḳaḳána, alá ch'xóoyux uhl ḳwu asḳ'amútem* (So, chickadee, you came here to sit with us)." Then to me: "Yah, this one listen to what we sayin', eh? Can carry the message to the whole world. Wonder whose side you on? Wonder if you livin' in the same world I am. Where this not just some little birdie that come to the bird feeder in the back yard, but is someone powerful and can know what we say."

"I want to be on the earth's side," I said with sudden conviction.

"*Aaaa,*" Clayton said.

I felt a flutter in my chest at how immediately the chickadee flew up into the fir tree with the others. A clear song burst out, "Chick chick chick-a-dee-dee-dee!" There was a cloud of snow powder as they all flew off.

"But what can I do?" I added, feeling the same desperate impotence I always felt in the face of how the modern world was relentlessly eating up nature. "What difference does it make if I am?"

"You think you got somethin' from the earth just so you can feel powerful?" he said sharply. "This kinda thing come to a person for a reason. The earth know who you are. The wind, the snow, the rocks, the whole world know how you feel. And they know you feel bad how the earth is hurtin'. They know you feel bad how they make war on our mother. What you gonna do—turn your eyes away from this war, act like nothin' happenin'? You think some earth power gonna help somebody who hide like that?"

His words reminded me of a dream I had after I left the back country and moved into town. It bothered me at the time, but then I forgot about it. Now it leaped back to mind as somehow just what he was talking about. In the dream, I was looking at somewhere like the main Okanogan Valley where I'd come to live, at a vast expanse of irrigated, industrialized agriculture. A whole valley in arid country that had been transformed into lush, tamed farmland with towns and highways and power lines. I hiked uphill into the open, untouched hills of native brush and grass, where I felt more at home. I noticed a deep canyon off to the right, and felt drawn to go look down into it. When I got to the bare rock rim, the canyon opened up below, even more beautiful than I expected because there was a deep, clear river rushing down it. Not far upriver, around a sharp bend, I stumbled onto the source of the river, where it emerged fully formed from a huge cave. But then I noticed, hidden inside, back from the mouth of the cave, some kind of elaborate industrial works. To one side of the opening was a door and concrete steps leading down to a road. With a sense of pain and revulsion, I realized "they" had already ruined the place, already installed some kind of industrial power plant right at the source. In the dream, I dimly understood this as how "they" do things—tap into the very source of things wild and free on earth, channeling the power away to fuel the tamed and controlled modern world, like this place did for the developed valley down below. I started to turn away when the door opened and a security guard came out. He looked up at me and said, "I'm just watching you, to make sure you don't do anything!"

When I related the dream to Clayton, he laughed grimly and said, "Yah, there it is. You see it just like it is. Give to you in the dream. And you see how the ones make war on the earth, they just guards. They stand guard over what they doin'. This dream the same for anybody who follow what's real back to where it come from, and find how they got a stranglehold on it, tame it and turn it into somethin' else. They see a man like you, who don't want no part of that, just go straight to the earth. They see you know what they doin', see you don't need 'em, don't want 'em. They have to watch out for you, for anybody who on the earth's side.

"Must be that power, that one helpin' you, give you that dream. Take you to see that. But what he show you is how they got you scared off, ain't it?"

"Scared off?"

"Yah, right there at the last, your want to turn away, get away from how they ruin even that wild place. Maybe go on, farther, find where they not come yet. That how they got you."

He was right. It had been the most unsettling part of the dream, the urge to run off even from how they were going into the wildest and most awesome places remaining, the very sources of things on earth.

"But I don't get it," I said. "How do they keep me scared of doing something?"

"Hah! They got you right where they always get 'em. You want to *be* somebody!"

"Be somebody?"

"Why you suppose I teach you about the old power way? Not to go off and be the big man who think he so important! Get the big desk in the county building, sit there chewin' on the end of his tie! Who you tryin' to be somebody for? The ones makin' war on our mother? Whose side you on?"

"Oh."

"To have that want to be somebody, why not be somebody for the earth? Be her man. Stand up for her. Be her grandson, one who is true to her, who she feel for as one of her own. When I instruct you in the years past, that who I see. The White man who want to know how he can be the earth person, how he can live here like the Native. How the Native know the world. But then, you just go away. Stop in the middle of it, don't finish. Go off *waí'payem* (like a White person, like White people do)."

"Huh?" I said, surprised. "I thought that was it. All I remember, you said you'd help me with the sweatlodge and then fasting in the mountains. Is there more?"

He laughed, shaking his head in disbelief.

"You just barely got the horse saddled, nephew!"

It was the first time he seemed genuinely amused since we started talking.

"I thought you just had enough," he added in a soft voice. "Too hard, and you have a change of heart."

"No, I thought this is what I was supposed to do. Go make something of my life."

"Yah, but now, how somebody gonna be on the earth's side, if a person don't know how the power work? How to live in the world with what she give? Somebody want to know somethin' like that, they gotta train for it. Like my elder before me, show me how the power come, he say to me, many times, "*Chak̓ sxi'míux k̓s'mai'mia'enchoót'ax wai k̓ut k̓'ulshtíux* (If you want to know something, you have to train yourself for it)."

"What kind of training would that be?" I asked.

"Like I said, how to use the power, how to call on what you got. Then, for the kinda power you got, the old way is to send 'em on the long wander in the bush, see if they can find things."

"Find things?"

"Yah, like hard to just tell. Some places we know, still left out there, where nobody go. Where the spirits are still awake, still waitin' for the ones who got somethin', who can see 'em, learn somethin' from 'em. Like sent on a mission, like I send you that time, but real long, *xooy lek̓uuut* (go very far)."

His words awoke an old passion in me for being off in the hills learning from him again. But I had to be back to work the next day, had to be thinking about heading down the mountain.

"When can I see you again?"

Clayton laughed. "Well, now. You sure that horse is broke to ride?" He told me he was heading to the coast and then up to British Columbia to attend winter dances. He'd be back in a month or two, "when the Chinook wind blow again."

"You ponder on what you say to the earth this day. They always waitin' for us to make up our mind, hear what we say, words from the heart. Then maybe they show themselves, come and look at you, see if you mean what you say."

"Who?"

"*Chip'choptíkxwl,* the Animal People, the ones the old stories tell about. One of 'em already done it. Maybe you remember? That time we comin' back from Wenatchee, and we stop at the dam on the river. Go down where we see the fish go by. Maybe you remember that one salmon, the chief of all the salmon, how he come and look at you that time, eh?"

I remembered we stopped at Rocky Reach Dam on the Columbia River one afternoon, and went down to a dimly lit public-viewing room with rows of benches. We sat with tourists watching a long window, the glassed-in side of where the fish ladder opened out to the lake. It was like looking into a huge, long aquarium, the greenish water rushing by left to right, with occasional salmon, in ones or twos, darting quickly across from right to left. There were long lapses of nothing to see between the infrequent, sudden appearances of fish that made it up the ladder from the river below and swam by toward open water. The tourists would ooh and ahh when a fish or two went by, then get bored and leave. Only Clayton and I remained while tourists came and went.

The dams on the Columbia had decimated what once had been one of the world's largest salmon runs. Clayton sat brooding and uncommunicative beside me, sighing occasionally at what had become of the run since his childhood. At one point, all the other visitors left and we were alone in the viewing room for about five minutes. It was silent and dim, and the only thing to look at was the rush of water behind glass. Something big appeared from the right, the biggest salmon I'd ever seen, maybe three feet long. It was so thick around the middle it looked like the granddaddy of all salmon compared to all the smaller, slimmer ones that had gone by. The salmon actually came to a halt just inside the glassed-in channel, as if warily looking things over before going on. The look of its great eye in profile was startling. Then with preposterous ease, as if the current was nothing to something so big and powerful, the salmon glided by slowly and effortlessly, and disappeared out the opening. Clayton said something to the salmon in Salish when it paused. After it was gone, he said, jokingly I thought at the time, "He come to check you out, see this White man who wanna be the Indian!"

Now he said, "That how they do. Come and show themself to somebody who want to be in the world like they are. Come to see what is in your heart. Maybe you watch for that. That bird, *sits'ḵaḵána*, he spread the word, eh?"

There seemed nothing more to say. I sat in silence with him as the fire burned and the light outside the rock overhang faded into evening. The white noise of icebound waterfall filling the whole chamber made me drowsy. Clayton's eyes closed and his head drooped, nodding slowly as if he were falling asleep. But then he sniffed sharply a few times, his face turned aside, and I recognized the familiar little ritual moves he always went through when he wanted to read the weather.

"You got any tire chains?" he asked abruptly, eyes still closed.

"Yeah, sure."

"You gonna need 'em," he said, sitting up and throwing more wood on the fire. He had enough wood gathered to last the night. I sensed that it was time for me to leave. I zipped up, pulled on my gloves, and stood up.

"*Wai, ḵn'xooy* (Well, I'm going)," I said. There were no formal hellos or goodbyes in the Native language.

"*Aaaa, en'xaschín* (Okay, sounds good)," he said without looking up.

Once I was out of the deep ravine, the fog was so thick, it took all my attention to stay on the trail. But going downhill was much faster than going up, and soon I came out from under the clouds and saw the lights of Annie's house in the distance. I wondered why Clayton thought I'd need chains. The weather report had called for continued cloudy and mild conditions, with no snow expected for another day or so. I laughed to myself. I knew better than to doubt Clayton when it came to knowing about the weather. Besides, he hadn't said it was going to snow, just that I'd need the chains.

I got to my car in the dark and started it. Laying the tire chains out in front of the rear tires, I drove over them and hooked them up. Then I went inside to warm up at Annie's woodstove and drink a cup of coffee with her.

She spoke very little English, but managed, "You see 'em?"

"Yeah."

Once on the snowpacked roads, driving slowly to keep down the deafening clatter of chains rolling underneath, I regretted putting them on. I'd driven up without chains, why should I need them going back? But I kept on, and when I came out into the open country between Spectacle Lake and Whitestone Lake, the wind was blowing hard. Around a curve, I drove into a complete whiteout of wind-driven snow drifting across the highway. For a few miles, it was like driving on a skating rink, and I never would have made it home without the chains.

3

With a clap of thunder, snow began to fall. Jerked awake from a vivid dream, I found myself home in bed at first light, staring at the snow blowing hard against my bedroom window. A sudden spring storm battering the little house, making me grateful to be alive somewhere else than where I was in the dream. With a start, I remembered it was the recurring nightmare I used to have when I was a boy, back when I was old enough to be afraid of the H-bomb but too young to have an interest in girls.

Clothed in a boy's language of the 1950s, I was out in some hilly, wooded country, wandering without a care under a bright, starry sky when I felt danger approaching. It was coming across the sky like an airplane, like the bomber my father flew over Germany during his war. But there was something else about it—it was looking for me, seeking me out, I could feel it. I had to hide, so I slipped under the shadows of thick vegetation, tried to blend with the earth by holding still, hoping the terrible thing in the sky couldn't find me buried under scented leaves. But it still knew where I was and raced at me, hitting me with something like the whole world exploding, jerking me awake somewhere else with a scream. Or like this time, more than twenty years later, startled awake by a single boom of thunder into a fallout of snow outside my window.

When I was older, dressed in the uniform of my own generation's war, I asked my father, "When you were flying over those German cities, dropping bombs, did you ever think about the people down below, the women, the little kids being killed by what you were doing?"

"No, I never thought about it," he said. "I was just doing my part in the war. I was twenty-three, off on a lark."

The sins of the fathers visited on the sons. As a boy I thought I'd been dreaming about the Russians dropping the bomb on us, and hey, this was how it felt to die like that. But then once when I did a few weeks' time in a military stockade, when I had plenty of time sitting in a six-by-ten holding cell to ponder this nightmare as an adult, I wondered if I was reliving what it was like for some German boy when my dad dropped bombs on him. Or even if I *was* that boy, reborn as the son of the man who killed him! Crazy thoughts, but the dream was that powerful, that real. And made even more so by the fact that I had never told anyone about it. For days I stared at the wall while they kept me under observation without shoelaces or a belt, like they did all first-time prisoners, just in case I tried to kill myself. When I wasn't entertaining myself imagining how anyone could string himself up with a belt and shoelaces, I gradually came to the conclusion that this dream was my memory of being born.

It was the music, the songs that did it. Late at night, bored stockade guards played the radio so far away I could barely hear it. Familiar popular rock songs I could recognize, but so faintly, all I received in my cell was the pure feeling, the insinuating rhythm, and maybe a key phrase—what the songwriter felt as a mysterious conviction coming through like a message from the unknown. How I was over there, wherever it is we come from, wandering invisibly in a beautiful landscape. How the power that does such things came for me and pushed me through the veil, the opening into somewhere bright and unfamiliar I didn't want to go. The soul suddenly clothed in a body and exposed to all that incoming sensation flooding a point of consciousness. Coming alive with such a start that a woman turns smiling to her husband and says, "Somebody is there, inside me. I just felt him arrive."

But now, ten years later, as the snow turned into sleet hissing against my windowpane, I wasn't so sure. Alone in my thirties with dark thoughts at dawn—maybe the dream was about how I would die after all. There was nothing that made me feel more alive than wandering in the hills as I did in the dream, moving over the wild earth on two legs, drinking it all in. Maybe there I'll be, one last walk under a starry sky, and sense my time approaching. Who will that be, coming for me from above? Such a sweet, familiar existence that having it taken away feels like the extinction of who I think I am.

Or maybe it was both. The experience of coming alive on this earth we all know, and of leaving it. They both seemed the same to me— going alone through the veil into something waiting for us. Did other people have this dream? Was I the only one who remembered coming through to here, and saw the same thing coming again when I left?

I am suddenly reminded of my son who was born and died on the same day. Is that how it was for him? My own sins as a father have been buried, just like the nightmare, in forgetfulness. But this time, somehow I'm able to remember without crying. Scenes from an earlier life lived with a woman long since gone from my life. . . . When I held our son as he gasped for air, born premature and not ready to be outside his mother, out in the world with the rest of us, all I could do was watch him die. So much blood all over the bed, I wrap him in a blanket and hope his mother can hold on to him as I carry her outside into another snowy dawn, to the ambulance trying to find where we live. Unable to leave her side in a hospital bed until the doctor says she'll make it okay, and waves me out. I try to find my son but none of the brisk, cold, efficient faces seem to know where he was taken. How I found him wrapped in a plastic bag like leftovers on a hospital cabinet and went a little crazy. . . .

Not a good way to start a day, a Saturday as it turns out, blowing so hard under the eaves that fat snowflakes stay suspended in a swirling holding pattern because the wind won't let them fall to earth and be done with it. I have to get out of here. Out of bed, into clothes, out the door. Out into the snow like a Viking who's glimpsed Valhalla and leaps into the fray with something broken inside. No longer caring, berserk, fey, inconsolable.

But it's no battleground with hacking swords—not even the clap-clap-clap of helicopter gunships in a jungle sky where so many high school buddies stopped bullets with their basketball muscles in the war that made us all crazy. No, it's the little apple-packing town of Tonasket on the Okanogan River in Washington. The month of March, 1982. Almost unbearable to still be alive and have to feel in a place like this. Bare trees and sturdy houses and snowblown Main Street and hardly anybody out to see a man in faded khaki campaign coat striding out of town like he'll never stop until maybe the border with Canada, twenty miles away.

This is all I know to do: Walk, eat up the miles, stay on the slushy shoulder of highway so I don't have to think about where I'm going. Watch how the storm is slowly passing and sunrise breaks through the fog, illuminating the farmed bottomlands glittering under fresh snow. It's supposed to be spring, but March is like that here behind the Cascade Range—a sudden hush of winter where sagebrush is pushed back to orchard fences and swollen apple buds are shrouded in white. Walking until I'm nothing but a body in motion, aware of moving over the earth, all the way to the bare granite steeps of Mount Hull looming to the right before a car pulls over to give me a ride.

It's Jim Woods in his hot yellow Barracuda, Mötley Crüe tank top as if it's summertime, heavyset Okanogan Indian good looks under a beaded baseball cap, and not able to hide a smile at picking me up on the side of the road. Because picking him up as a hitchhiker was how I met him almost six years before, and now here he is, returning the favor. Nothing is said, of course. No greeting, no small talk, no White man nonsense as I climb in and he takes off, shifting through the gears up the wet highway. Carried along in the yanking, V-8 power of his ride he calls *kurrílux in'kewáp*, his "yellow horse." Such small fists on such a big man. Heater blasting, the smell of mildew and horse leather, and no music on the stereo to intrude on the silent first miles of being together for the first time in months.

I don't have to be an Indian to appreciate how useless it is to try and hide behind words or distractions when it's more real just to be myself. So we're already through the border town of Oroville, turned left at all the tavern signs and winding up the Similkameen River canyon when the words come out of me from somewhere just under the surface:

"Just before my son died, he blew bubbles. He blew bubbles with his little mouth."

"*Aaaa,*" Jim murmurs.

"Why did he have to blow bubbles?"

"*Aaaa.*"

The stupid golf course to the left, the vandalized petroglyph rocks to the right. The long and winding road up into the mountains. The sun climbing higher in a clearing sky, melting the snow, making the dark timber stand out like soldiers massed on the ridgetops. And down below, the turquoise river in flood, swamping the willows, racing by in a thunderous mist.

Jim sighs.

"When my father died, I wanted to kill somebody, eh?" he says. "That's when I ran off to Wounded Knee. Militant! Guess I wanted to make somebody pay. I fit right in with all those dudes carryin' rifles, always talkin' about how it was a good day to die."

"Ah."

"Then after I came back, there was that Mexican guy, the young one, killed himself. Shot himself in the head playing Russian roulette with a pistol. You remember? He worked in that orchard next to where you used to live in that trailer on Palmer Lake."

"Yeah, the orchardist came and got me to translate. Tell the sheriff what the other Mexicans were saying how it happened," I say, remembering the squalid little picker's shack, the smell of beer and blood, the bloated body on the floor with one side of the head swollen and black. Just like so many times before, a young life snuffed out and nothing left but a gurgling body to zip up inside a black rubber bag. The coroner and sheriff making jaded jokes about one less Mexican the Border Patrol had to worry about while the dead man's friends looked on with blank eyes as if they couldn't understand English.

"Well, me and Kootch were having a beer at the Loomis Tavern the night he shot himself. He was there, drunk, flashing a pistol. He spoke pretty good English and came up to us at the bar to show us the gun in his waistband, under his coat. All he said was, 'Sometimes you feel like you just have to kill somebody!' "

"Huh."

"I could relate. The next day we heard how he shot himself, and Kootch turns to me and says, 'Well, if he just had to kill somebody, at least he killed the right person!' "

The canyon opens up to a wide, flat-bottomed valley and there's the log corral I built years ago down by the river. On the other side, there's the two rows of dilapidated wood buildings they call the town of Nighthawk. And there's the first glimpse of Chopaka Mountain so huge and high overhead and swathed in clouds and snow it's hard to believe something so pure and beautiful looks down on so much misery. Jim turns right, onto the road to the border crossing that winds through sagebrush overgrazed cow pasture hills, and I realize I have no idea where he's going. I guess I figured he was going home, but here we are heading up to British Columbia. Two solitary customs houses perched on a dryland alfalfa plain, each flying a different flag. The bored old Canadian in weekend whiskers recognizes Jim and waves us through. On into the realm of the other North Americans, but it's only cosmetic because it's the same mountains, the same fir trees, the same melting snow. The same Okanogan Indian homeland.

"*Wai, la'ḳín xooy awhá an'ḳewáp i ḳurrílux?* (So, where's this yellow horse of yours going?)" I mused out loud.

Jim laughed. I'd said it a little wrong, but he got the drift. I was taking evening classes in the Native language at the tribal center in East Omak. I was getting better.

("He's riding us double up to see somebody.")

("Nice day to a visit for to go.")

"White man speak with forked tongue!" he mocked, punching on the stereo. Led Zeppelin ascended the staircase to heaven at maximum, pounding volume as we hit the straightaway lined with orchard trees.

The sun was shining on the wet streets of Keremeos, British Columbia, when an ancient pickup truck pulled out of the Chevron station, barely moving as we passed. Jim waved to the elderly Indian couple inside, who waved back. There was something familiar about the woman with white braids pressed so tightly against the old man driving that they looked like teenagers, like young first-time lovers. Then it came to me—it was Margaret Sisencha, the outspokenly traditional grandmother who had told me so many stories from the before time, the Animal People stories called *chaptíkx*.

I'd heard how she got married again at almost seventy, after her husband died, to a man who'd been her first love when she was young. They'd married other people, arranged by their parents, and had raised families, raised grandchildren. And then when his wife died, they ran into each other again at his *sníxwam* where he gave away his wife's things as keepsakes to all who came. After her husband died, he'd discreetly waited out her time of mourning before he started coming around, courting her as if the intervening years hadn't even happened. That must be him, cowboy hat at a rakish angle on his bony head, a mask of wrinkles not hiding his grin of how good life was with his old flame Margaret pressed at his side.

"That's Margaret Sisencha, isn't it? And her childhood sweetheart?"

"Yeah, the new Mr. and Mrs. Puwalukin," Jim said. As for how closely the couple sat together, he observed dryly: "I guess it takes two to drive that pickup!"

And then I knew the gravel road we turned off on and where we were going. The old frame house with peeling paint squeezed between the river and the mountain rising up to timber so steeply behind. The wet scent of juniper trees dripping with melting snow planted around the screened-in front porch. Deer on the hillside above, browsing on the spring green with winter-starved preoccupation, their coats ratty with patches missing where thick hair had already sloughed off. A raven perched at the very tip of a spruce tree, croaking in the sun's warmth about something.

Inside the house smelling of cedar smudge, Margaret's brother, Old Willie the Indian doctor, looked up the way he always did from his favorite easy chair by the potbellied woodstove. No knock on the door, no greetings, just Jim and I walking in like family to join the few people sitting around the front room on old, secondhand furniture. Besides Old Willie looking more wispy-haired and fragile than ever, Clayton Tommy nodded hello, radiating such a muscular fitness after months of winter dancing that he seemed years younger than when I last saw him at the frozen waterfall. Across from them sat Clayton's stepdaughter, Rose, and a self-consciously uncomfortable White man in his twenties I'd never seen before. They stopped talking, but nobody showed any special interest in our arrival except the White guy in glasses and cardigan sweater, pen poised over a spiral notebook open in his lap. Jim went over to his uncle, Clayton, shook his hand, and with an impudent air, induced a round of hand-shaking by all of us. It was one of those silent, ceremonious and perfunctory touching of hands that Indians are so fond of in group gatherings. The other White guy revealed his unfamiliarity with the custom by pumping our hands in an iron grip, repeating, "Hi, pleased to meet you, eh?" We'd interrupted something, but Rose got up without a word and went into the kitchen, returning with two plates of food, which she set before us.

It reminded me I hadn't eaten that morning, but something bitter and unresolved sat heavily on my empty insides, making the thought of food repellent. Salish good manners made it deadly impolite to refuse to eat without good reason, so I tasted a little of the eggs and potatoes and toyed with my fork as Jim dug in with unrestrained pleasure.

"Well, um . . . as you were saying," the White man said, his cultured voice intruding on the prolonged silence. "The animals look different now, but, um, back in the beginning they were like people?"

"*Wai, ixí apená sḳulehát tlíḳ'wet ch'xilht i sḳélux enya'aíp s'ájits nax-emhl. . . .*" Old Willie said in measured, slurred Salish, his wrinkled eyes closed, his head tilted back.

"Yah, Kenneth," Clayton said when Willie finished, looking just as formal as the older man, just as worn by a life of hard work outdoors in the callused, wrinkled look of his gesturing hands. "Like he say, like now, today, they still people. Still like people. But they only show themself as the animal."

Still running on the dregs of the dream, the sadness of remembered death, the uselessness of blowing bubbles, I bristled at what was coming down. The two old men sitting like buddhas in cowboy shirts, feeding Kenneth little pieces of their knowledge as if they were feeding an infant just starting in on solid food. I knew Old Willie could speak English when he wanted to, but I also knew he didn't like to talk about the spirits of nature except in the *Sḳélux en'ḳwalikwaíltin,* the Native language, for fear of being punished by them. So Clayton interpreted his answers to Kenneth's questions. The questions sounded like he was an anthropology student gathering information on how Indians related to animals. I could tell Jim was stifling a laugh at Kenneth scribbling furiously while Clayton was talking.

Purposely distancing myself from Kenneth by refusing to speak English either, I responded to Rose and Jim's quiet asides in their language with my own lame command of conversational Salish. Rose sat in the chair beside Jim, a little younger than us both, her amused, brown-eyed self-possession softening the edges around my still being alive in the world. Few women I knew could be as quiet and yet as present and attentive to what was happening as she was. Very small and barely filling out the white restaurant waitress uniform she was wearing—ready to go to work when the time came—she seemed infinitely patient. Then she noticed I wasn't eating.

Rose: *"Ch'mai loot en'ahl'níls?* (Maybe somebody doesn't feel like eating?)"

Me: ("Very much it pleases me this food I don't eat.")

Jim: ("I think he's saying yes, little sister. But why don't you ask your older brother if he wants more to eat?")

Rose: ("Oh you! I already know you want more, big man.")

Me: ("Yes, I'm saying yes, not hungry, but he is, he did all the driving.")

Clayton smiled at overhearing our exchange. Kenneth looked startled at the novelty of a White man casually talking Indian, and a little uneasy, as if we were talking about him behind his back. But the elders would never tolerate such bad taste. Let him stew in it, I thought. He doesn't believe in what he's hearing from the two old men anyway. It's just data for his preposterous theories.

"Kwu'xwícht inchá lecaapi (Bring me some coffee)," Old Willie said to nobody, and Rose got up. She made the pot and I brought poured cups to everybody except Kenneth who sipped from a green bottle of mineral water. When Jim finally ate his fill and Rose took away my almost untouched plate, we listened to what Clayton was telling Kenneth about his own experience.

"Yah, I seen 'em. The animal look like us, only little bit different."

"You've seen them as people? What, like in a dream or vision, something like that?"

"Yah, maybe so. Like that. Another way of lookin'."

"Like another world? Like seeing into another world?"

"No, same world. All one world, only maybe wider. Bigger world than what the White people see."

Kenneth bit his lip to conceal a condescending smile. "So, um . . . How do they look when you see them?"

"Look like something that's alive ain't supposed to look like. Hard to look at, so much more than I ever see before. Make me afraid, have to drop my eyes."

Old Willie snorted.

"You disagree, Mr. Sisencha?" Kenneth asked. The old man just rolled his eyes and turned to stare out the window.

"It different for the Indian doctor," Clayton said. "They have the gift to command the animal. Make 'em do things like they family. But I don't know nothin' about that. . . ." He did know something about it, but I'd seen him lie this way before to inquisitive Whites who were only curious.

"But they resemble people? Animals look like us?" Kenneth went on doggedly.

"Yah, they just like us, Animal People, eat and talk and have family like the Indian do. We have the stories told, word by mouth, from all the way back. From those who were there. Tell how the Animal People put on the covers, dress up in the clothes of the animal, to be just like we see today. For the change, for when human people come alive on the earth. Once we here, they don't want us to see 'em like they really are. Only if they choose, only if they want us to know 'em, to give a gift . . ."

Kenneth interrupted with, "Why don't they want us to see them as they really are?" but Clayton ignored him.

". . . somethin' hard to know. Somebody can know 'em only if they can see the world like in a dream. Like a power, like the power come and you in a dream, but you still awake. Like that, like to see in another way. But what we see every day, maybe just the little bit they let us see of themself. The deer on the hill, show us the least little bit—just how they look as the animal. And not just the animal—everything in the

world like that. The tree, the mountain, the river, the stars, the wind.
All just show us the least little bit."

"*Aaaa,*" I said, moved by his words, and was joined by Jim and
Willie and Rose, all of us voicing the Salish affirmation that we were
listening, that we were feeling what he was saying, that we were hearing good talk. I'd never heard him give such a sensitive explanation of
how he looked at nature before. And it made me think of my own
experiences that he'd interpreted over the years as animals showing
themselves to me in human form. Kenneth's groping after something
that meant nothing to him personally was suddenly intolerable. Before
he could ask another question, I blurted out in Salish:

"*K'ast ispu'ús* . . . (My heart is bad . . . There's so much death, bad
dreams. Hard for me to want to live. I've seen one animal, one bird, as
the man. But who are they, the ones who wait for a person, out in the
mountains? Who show themselves, give instruction, do things for a
person?)"

("They're the ones who make the world shine when we sing their
songs!") Old Willie said with equal emotion, cutting off any response
Clayton might have had, and looking so directly at me I could feel his
eyes. ("They're the ones who take pity on us, who give us something we
can be good at, who show us how to live.")

Willie spoke slowly, using what had to be baby talk for someone like
him, patiently responding to my plea in words I could understand with
my limited grasp of Okanogan Salish. He'd never spoken to me this
way before, and I knew instinctively that this was the only way into his
knowledge—real need expressed with real feeling.

("They know what we're doing, how we live, everything. They go
everywhere. They see where the dead go. They see what's going to happen. They can see all of that, so then, they show us what they see, and
it's too big. Too wide. Too far. So much, it's hard to know it. Something
comes apart that we think doesn't have any insides. A mountain is hollow where they live, or down in the river they breathe and talk. We
don't live like they do, we're too feebleminded, so they help us. They
give us whatever we can learn well. The song, the thing to carry, something hidden that makes us strong, something we can be good at.")

"*Aaaa*," I said. ("So I remember that—somebody waited for me as a child, showed me something. But I'm a man now, and I don't know how to be good at doing that, whatever I was shown.")

Old Willie just looked in my direction for a minute, his eyes sunk into deep wrinkles, unfocused but seeming to inspect something in the air above my head. Kenneth tapped his pen on paper in irritation at being left out, but Clayton sipped his coffee and looked off into space, making no move to translate.

"*P'na ks'ksápi atlí ti swit kw'alenchóot il kwílsten* (Maybe it's been a long time since somebody warmed himself in the sweatlodge)," Old Willie finally said in a kind of singsong, his voice on a low register and fading away as if he was suddenly tired. He was right, I hadn't gone to a sweat in months.

"*Wai, ixí kwílsten . . . ixí kwailenchoóten!* (Well, that sweatlodge . . . that's God!)" he went on in the brusque certainty of Indian doctors. ("Not here, not like this will I talk about this matter. That one, that chicken hawk, I know him. That one who's been with you so long, he's still waiting for you. Somebody goes into the sweatlodge and wipes off all that bad clinging to him, then he can see and hear again.")

He'd said "chicken hawk" in English instead of *tl'tlak'w* for falcon, and I laughed out loud for the first time that day.

"What's he saying?" Kenneth finally ventured.

"He talkin' to Tom," Clayton said. Then to me in Salish: ("Out back by the river is where he has his sweatlodge. Somebody might go and build a fire and heat some rocks.")

"Okay," I said, standing up, pulling on my wet coat. Jim followed me out onto the screened-in porch.

"Hold up, dude. I'll give you a hand. Old Willie usually keeps an axe in here somewhere," he said, looking around behind boxes and stacked firewood lining the walls.

Rose came out with her coat and the beaded leather bag she used as a purse. "*Wai, kn'hooy kul sen'kúlmen* (Well, I'm off to work)," she said.

"Lucky you," Jim said with his back turned. "*We* have to go see *God*, eh?"

Rose smiled at his customary irreverence when out of Old Willie's earshot. She looked at me with brisk, assessing eyes. "Maybe you'll be hungry when you get done sweatin'. I'll be back too late to cook you somethin'. Willie has some elk in the freezer."

"Who's the other *Suyápi*?" I asked.

"From some university back east. He's been asking questions for hours! He said he'd pay Dad and Willie some money for their time . . ."

"Tom, on the other hand, will pay 'em with sweat, ain't it?" Jim said, turning around with the axe in his hands. "Blood, sweat, and tears—hey, we could be a rock group!"

Rose left in Clayton's old white Ford station wagon. Jim and I walked around the house and down through the cottonwoods toward the river, the afternoon sunshine already too warm to be wearing a coat.

4

THERE'S NOTHING LIKE THE work of preparing for a sweat to ground me again in the simple mechanics of doing life. Jim and I had done it many times together, but everything was unfamiliar at Old Willie's sweatlodge hidden from view in a tall thicket of riverside brush. The smell of the earth waking up after winter, the murmur of the river so swollen by snowmelt it lapped at the top of the bank— everything was wet and cold to the touch, with skiffs of melting snow still hiding in the shadows. It was that time of year when you could identify the different kinds of shrubs and brushy trees by the color and texture of their shiny wet bark. No leaves, no flowers, just the tangle of branches showing how the yellow smoothness of willow lived easily with the gray roughness of alder and the bright red of osier dogwood. A screen tall enough so nothing could be seen of the settled, farmed valley—only the river, the mountains all around, and the sky overhead.

Larger than most sweathouses I'd seen behind Indian homes, it was a familiar, dome-shaped framework of willow poles covered with blankets and tarps, and sat in front of an older, old-fashioned *kwílsten* dug into the cobbly hillside, whose rotten logs and boards stuck out of caved-in rocks and earth. Various cloth and leather items, some of them no more than faded shreds, were tied to branches or hung in the forks of shrubs or nearby cottonwood trees. The skull of a mountain goat and some rounded, white quartz rocks sat on top of the sweatlodge itself.

Carrying down armloads of firewood, splitting the resinous ponderosa pine into kindling, searching through the pile of used volcanic rocks for enough solid, unshattered ones for a sweat—building a fire and heating rocks was quiet, familiar, meditative work. Jim went back to the house, leaving me alone to tend the fire for the hour or so it took for the rocks to be ready. Alone to sit in the still perception of the world around me, so that thinking about nature faded away into the feel of nature, which was where I was actually alive and breathing.

Somebody came walking through the brush behind me and I looked up to see Kenneth in a bright blue windbreaker that rustled noisily with his every move.

"Hey," I said, and he nodded, warming his hands at the fire. Curiously subdued as he stared into the mystery of flames leaping up from the pit, I saw him for the first time as somebody like me, some-body's son, just another guy. I instinctively knew he had the kind of mind that clung to the surface of things in the world, and had no inter-est in the invisible fire that drove it. He looked around, then kneeled down at the open door to look into the sweatlodge like someone who'd never seen one before. He studied the cozy interior floored with a bed of fir boughs and the small pit in bare dirt just inside the opening to the right. When he stood up, he stared at the pitchfork in my hands, used to carry hot rocks to the pit inside.

"So, how long have you been doing it, eh?" he asked.

"Doin' what?"

"Uh, sweating."

"A few years, I guess."

"How hot does it get in there?"

I laughed. "I don't know. I never went in with a thermometer. What difference does it make?"

"I just want to know what it's like."

"Why? You don't have to know what it's like to have an education in order to go to school, do you?"

He shrugged. "I don't know if I could stand it, eh? I just, well . . . I don't know if I could take the heat. I think about it and I guess it scares me."

"Huh," I said, never having thought about it like that. "I guess that's honest. It can get pretty hot sometimes, but that's not what it's about. It's a good thing to do, just not easy. I guess I never felt afraid of it."

"Then what's it about?"

"It's not about anything," I said automatically, giving him the same answer I got years before. Why do we think we have to understand something before we dare to experience it? Then it came to me where he was coming from.

"They invited you to go in with us, did they?"

"Yeah," he said, still looking troubled. "So, uh, is it like a sauna?"

Jim walked up and joined us at the fire, looking suspiciously blank.

"Sort of. Look, maybe they suggested you talk to me about it, but I could say anything and it wouldn't help you decide."

"Yeah," Jim said. "Just be prepared to die, and you'll be fine, dude." He and I both laughed at Kenneth's sudden look of alarm. Jim had said the same thing to me years before when I was about to sweat for the first time. Now it seemed like the bluntest sort of truth, but utterly funny at the same time. There was no way for me to allay Kenneth's fearful groping.

"You have to do it to know what it is," I said, and he nodded solemnly.

Clayton and Old Willie came rustling through the brush carrying towels and a big plastic bucket. Kenneth abruptly turned around and went to meet them.

"You were supposed to tell him how you lived through the hundreds of times the Indians tried to kill you in the sweatlodge," Jim said with a straight face.

"Yeah, right. Seriously, how can someone be afraid of something that people have been doing for thousands of years to have a better life?"

Jim shrugged.

"It's like that White missionary who came to the rez. Gonna convert the Indians, save 'em from worshipping the devil. He hears about that sweatlodge thing—naked men crowding into a dark hole, burning hot for hours, and then they come out and say how good it feels! It had to be the work of the devil, eh? But he wanted to see for himself, so late one night he sneaks out there where the Indians were sweathousin', right? The very next Sunday he's preachin' from the pulpit that he had proof that the sweatlodge was devil worship. He'd seen it with his own eyes—a great big fire, and standing next to it, a man holding a pitch-fork!"

The sweat was a mild one, a "wipe-off" until the very end when it finally got real hot, but nothing like how Old Willie could burn us alive when he was calling his helpers to look into something, or getting ready to doctor someone. Kenneth had left without another word to me, and Jim stayed out to do the door, saying he'd eaten too much to sweat. The two old men joked and teased in the darkness as the steam worked on us between songs sung to the beat of Willie tapping the dipper handle on the rim of his plastic water bucket. It was sweating for the pure pleasure of it, and whatever it was that had been weighing so heavily on me before lost its hold in the singing of familiar sweatlodge songs.

The feel of sitting on a springy bed of fir boughs in burning dark-ness, the roar of glowing rocks splashed with dippers of river water, the sweat pouring from every part of my body, the loss of any normal thoughts—it all drove me deep into the core of my own feeble self. Deep inside where my breath came in and went out, where my heart thudded slowly, where I sensed as I always did when sweathousing, the mystery of being alive at all.

Jim lifted the doorflap for us, brought more hot rocks with the pitch-fork, and kept the fire burning on the remaining rocks. Four times we crawled out and bathed in the river, and each time the water felt less cold. Each time I returned from the icy dip in the Similkameen with a stronger sense of being alive in a beautiful world. Of having a right to be here, an upright, dripping human animal feeling fit and ready for anything. Back inside with the last of the hot rocks splashed and siz-zling, steam raced up and the heat intensified unbelievably. Head down, I drifted away into my own experience of how hot and unbear-able it was. The two old men gasping out grateful cries of pleasure didn't make it any easier, they just reminded me that this was some-thing I could endure. Letting go into the fiery breath of Sweatlodge, I thought only of how this was something good, something that would help us all, something so much more powerful than human beings that humbling myself to it was the only way to receive its blessing.

Then Willie sang one of his power songs, and Clayton and I joined in.

(Listen, I'm coming, I'm here
Listen, I'm coming, I'm here
Something drops down from above
Something drops down from above
Listen, I'm coming, I'm here.)

The verses alternated with spirit vocalizings in the same melody, and after four or five renditions, Willie's voice faded away. We sang on without him as it slowly began to cool down inside, and after about ten minutes, he came back in and ended the song. He sighed and began to speak in Salish in his faint, slurring sweatlodge voice that I could never follow. When he paused, Clayton translated:

"His want to tell you what he have to say. Those animals, those powers of earth, they know we so pitiful. If they don't help us, we just birds without wings, just foolish people. Barely awake, can't live very well, can't live very long. So they the ones who do the trainin', show us what the world is really like. They give us somethin' to look at, like a picture. They help us so we can know the mountain and the river. We can see who they are, the sun and moon, the dawn and night, the wind and clouds. They give that to us, like to be stronger. Strong, like they are, in the power way. Then the whole world shine, like to be so beautiful.

"So they come toward us, however they do that. Maybe a person will appear in front of us. Somethin' will be seen, somethin' bright and shiny to stare at. Somethin' like singin' will make us shiver, shake all over. Then we catch that, hold on to it, whatever it is. We know things because they keep doing that. Somethin' more, and we know that, too. That how they train us so we know somethin'. How to be good at doin' somethin'. Little by little, we call for someone to come, and they will come. Whatever they show us, we use it, we keep doin' it, then we get good at it."

My ears popped. In the pitch-dark, sweaty simplicity of pumping blood, breathing, feeling fit and renewed—the thoughtless silent just being there—I knew exactly what he meant. I tried to tell them about the dream I'd awakened from that morning. I stumbled and faltered with the Salish words, searching for some way to express how it felt. When I finished with ("something came and hit me and pushed me into somewhere very bright but with no sound . . .") they both said *"Aaaa."*

"That what he say, they show us things," Clayton said, continuing to translate. "Give us the picture to know somethin'. As we grow up, we just have the story of where we come from, where we goin' after we die. All we know is what right here, where we alive. Maybe see the child come into the world, take that first breath. See the person die, stop breathin'. Just gone, the dead body. Gets to be dark, to be the bad, when we see that. Like to be carryin' somethin', carryin' around a big pack of rocks, because all we know is the story that others tell. So they help us, show us somethin', take us where we don't remember. And you got somethin'. One of 'em come to you in life, in childhood—why else would you know a thing like this?

"For people who don't have no help from those powers, maybe just a story. But you go there and go through it. They teachin' you, they take you there, back to where you come alive on earth, and up ahead to where you leavin', where you goin' to the afterward. They do that for the one they choose, so he know what he doin'. How the world really is, *that* where he have to live! So he can use the power they give, so he can move in the world like they want.

"Same for any power man, power woman. Can't do what we have the gift for unless we see for ourself how the world really is, what we need to know, so the whole world shine again! They do that for us, give us somethin' to do, like the song to sing, so we can see the world light up again. So we can be in the world like they are, have that want to live. No matter how bad things get for a person, all his people die, he got nothin', no reason to live, well, he can turn to the earth, cry to the powers of this world for somethin' to make the world shine for 'em again. Like Willie say, they come to the one who so pitiful, and say, *'Ku'xílux ixí chuxwentsín uhl en'p'ap'áux i temxúlaux'* (Do what I say and the world will shine)."

Old Willie *aaaa*'d Clayton's words in Salish, then spoke some more in a barely audible murmur.

"He say all the same for the Indian doctor, they choose the one who can doctor. *Shox'púx'ent,* the one who blows over people, the person who doctor other people. They take the one they choose, they take 'em over to die like what you see in your dream. And they do die, just like they do with him when he young. Come and push him through. Then take 'em apart, like we butcher the deer, but put 'em back together again, put things together in a different way. Put things into 'em that only he can see. Then push 'em back into come alive again, back through to where we livin'. Only now the breath come from the heart. All covered over with what they done to 'em, like breathin' on him, breathin' through him. All that *xa'xá,* that power they have. So when the doctor sing, he blow all that over the sick one. All that power. Like you see, the tobacco smoke, blow that on the person. Because that smoke is theirs, their food they put here for us to offer to 'em. Make the breath what you can see. That how the doctor train for that, not like to be just the power person. Train more and more, years and years, maybe most of his life to get that breath movin' just right to doctor people later in life."

Old Willie went on, but this time his voice changed, switching between two ways of talking as if relating a conversation between two people. One voice was low, gravelly, and weary like his own usual voice, and the other high-pitched, excited, and so fast the Native words ran over each other in an incomprehensible blur. With each change of voice, Clayton responded with a loud *"Aaaa,"* each time sounding more moved by emotion and ending with a long groan of sadness. Willie finished by repeating a phrase over and over that I'd heard him say at other times when he'd revealed something clairvoyant he'd seen after calling his helpers to look into something. It was an odd construction using ordinary words in a strangely inflected way that roughly translated as "I hope this is not me lying."

After a long silence, Willie splashed more water on the rocks so cooled that very little steam was produced, and only a faint bubbling was heard from down deep in the bottom of the pit. Clayton sighed and told me what Willie had said.

"*Wai, choot,* he say they show 'em things even when he not askin'. Show the Indian doctor what the hurt is in the other person. Like in the pitch dark like this, give 'em a picture in his mind, show 'em what happen to cause the other person to have that hurt. Or maybe to hear what the dead say. Maybe the dead relative want to be heard, have somethin' to tell the person left behind on earth. Still care about 'em and maybe want to warn 'em about somethin'.

"So when we sing his song, we singin' his power song with him like we did, one of his helpers come and say to him, 'Look at that man, look at that man over there.' He look and he see my brother, Jim's dad, the dead one." Clayton's voice cracked, and he faltered, casting around for the right words. "That dead one, that dead, he say . . . he say, 'Tell my brother that time we broke the horses for the rancher, Old Man Cooksey, nobody know how he fix the cinch strap with baling wire but my brother. Nobody but my brother.' This so I know, this really him comin' to Old Willie. Then he tell somethin' . . . he tell somethin' that going to happen, to warn me . . ."

Again Clayton faltered and fell silent, sighing. Then without revealing what the warning was, he cleared his throat and went on.

"So then again his helper say, 'Look at that man, that White man over there.' Old Willie look and he see you, and you younger, maybe long time ago. 'Now look,' his helper say, and he see the little baby, born of the woman havin' a bad time, maybe bleed to death. That baby come alive for maybe just the few breaths of life, just the short time, and then stop breathin'."

I sobbed and felt a sharp pain in my chest that was relieved only by sobbing louder.

"And that helper say, 'Now look again,' and he see that child as the boy who can talk. Boy child, ain't it?"

"*Aaaa,*" Willie responded affirmatively in a low voice as if he were listening carefully to how Clayton was translating.

"And that boy child, he say, 'Tell my dad I'm a-comin' back. Just wait and he see me again. Come alive as the other child, another one to come. He know that's me because I do somethin' with my mouth. He remember me by what I do with my mouth.'"

By now my tears were flowing freely in the darkness, mingled with salty sweat still pouring down my face.

"Then that helper tell 'em, 'Look over there. Look at that White woman, the mother of that boy child.' They talk so fast, them spirits. They talk so fast and so high in the voice, you can't hardly grab onto what they say. Old Willie have a hard time, he can hardly follow what that helper sayin' to him." Clayton mimicked how the helper spoke in a garbled rush of words spoken in a high falsetto: "Lookatthatwomanwayoverthere. Overthereonthecoast. That'sthatbaby'smother."

For the first time in years I remembered how she looked, how she took so long recovering from her miscarriage, the sound of her voice. How she was never the same after our son died, and how she moved to the coast where the sound of the ocean and the smell of endless rain seemed to give her some peace. And I also marveled at the gift given to Willie in life. There was no way for him to have known—I'd never told anyone about our child that was born and died in another state, hundreds of miles away and years before, until I told Jim that morning, "When my son died, he blew bubbles with his little mouth."

"And that helper tellin' him that White woman have it hard," Clayton said. "Say, 'Tell that man sweatin' with you, she have it hard. Like to feel so bad, she not have the right to live good. She feel she not do the right thing and so her baby die. Now she feel she have to suffer. What a man and a woman do together that feel good, have relations, she feel now only the bad. Can't do nothin' about it.'

"So Old Willie say, too bad. Like we know, we pray for the other person, the loved one, to have the good life, be healthy, live long to enjoy. But maybe that person don't accept the prayer. Don't see how they bring on the sick. So the helper can't do nothin' for 'em, can't go and take away that sick, what hurt inside. The power can't touch 'em. For the power to work, we gotta remember how the world really is. That if we still alive, if we still breathin', then we have that right to be here. We have that right to a good life. No matter what we do, no matter what bad happen to us, to anybody we care about, we can give that away. Cry to the powers that know everything, get in our right mind again, and leave that bad here, in a place like this. Let 'em touch us with their power, their breath. And so we can come alive again, go on just renewed, just pure and not have any sick clingin' to us any more. Start over. Care for ourself again, care for others. This how we been doin' for the thousands of years, ain't it?"

Old Willie seemed done with what he had to say. After a long silence, Clayton spoke his own thoughts to me.

"The person, man or woman, who have somethin', have a spirit partner, why, the more he learn from that *shumíx*. The more he learn, the more they tame each other, the more the person change."

"Huh. Change, like, for the better?" I mused.

"Like to crave life more, more than ever before. The *shumíx* make 'em enjoy life better. Come to see how little he know, how much there is to see that he never notice before. How the world so full of power . . . how the world so beautiful to be alive."

("It's not for nothing they show us our death!") Old Willie interjected.

"Yah, they let you see that, take you where you feel you dyin', where you come away knowin' for sure your time is comin'—that so you not so full of yourself. So you let go of all that, what hold you back, keep you from livin' like they want. So you don't think you doin' everything on your own. So you don't think every little thing you doin' is important, eh? None of us doin' much but livin' a life they give. They give and they take away, and maybe that the only kind of knowin' that do any good.

"Can't be hide from your own death and have anything to do with power. That's where the power is for the come-alive person. They do that for us, show us our death, rub our face in it, make us look at the loved one, how they look when they dyin'. Feel that loss. Know what's real, and how only for a short time, for all of us. That way, we turn and we lookin' at the real thing in life, just go and look for it. Wonder at how we alive like this. Just let the power move in us. Not have to make anything happen, just sing and dance and laugh and wink at the women!"

Old Willie laughed helplessly, then coughed, cleared his throat, and spoke with strong feeling: "This my friend he learn to talk that hiiiiiigh English, and he the one you care to listen to. Aaaaaall that we look into from the relative in the past, and no relative as far back as we remember. But the relative anyway, maaaade that way, for in his heart to keep alive the way for who follow, even the White man. Not just grow old, the white hair, and feel sorry for hisself, just the dumb old-time Indian. No, he the one even the doctor have to look out—maybe steal my power. Then I just be the geezer in the old folks' home, growl at the pretty nurses tryin' to pet me!"

Clayton laughed softly.

"This the one," Old Willie went on. "This one know where the power hidin' out. Hide away from the White man, from the Indian that live *waí'payem* (like a White person). Hide from their great minds. But not hide from this one. He know better how to find somethin', chase after somethin' and show itself. You listen to his White man talk. My own just *en'chokchán,* broken-up way to say that English words. But this here man, he know how to chase after power, make 'em show their face."

"You maybe see what he gettin' at?" Clayton said. "The real Indian doctor, his want that everybody have somethin', have their own power, their own spirit partner. Then they have the better life, be healthy, live long, have things come easy. But maybe the doctor not have the gift to show how to do that. The others go off into the White man's world and he can't follow. Maybe don't have the words to say, now that everything in English. So he see how the power move, how they give the gift to the one who can say how in *Suyápi.*

"They always waitin' for us to be like they are, like things were in the before time. See if we gonna live by how things really are in the world. All that, what the *Suyápi* call Mother Nature, if we live by that, if we know a little bit about her, we can help her do her work. But train for whatever. The powers, they do the choosin'. They choose how they gonna work through a person, they show up to work through the person, then that how they work through the person. Like they do with you, the good hunter, the outstanding hunter."

Old Willie laughed softly. "Outstanding!" he repeated.

"Yah, you got the gift," Clayton went on. "Only you ain't been huntin' much for a long time, ain't it? You just work in town these days."

"Too long," I said.

"En'ahlna'kwáshkaitin!" Old Willie said, pronouncing the name he'd been calling me ever since the time I came down from fasting in the mountains and he'd advised me about what I'd experienced. Besides not understanding how "Something That Eats Bluejays" had anything to do with me, the similarity of the construction to the familiar Salish word for "cannibal" or "people-eater" made his name for me sound vaguely monster-like. Oh well, there was no accounting for the whims of Indian doctors.

Eating bluejays or having an old-time hunting power in the twentieth century—they both seemed equally preposterous from the point of view of the modern world. I voiced what had been in the back of my mind for a long time: Why would they give me something like this when nobody lived by hunting anymore?

"Wai, ixí ti'ch'maísts i shumíx!" Old Willie responded dismissively. ("Well, that spirit power definitely knows!")

5

WHEN I STARTED GOING hunting with Clayton Tommy again, I was never sure if it was food we were after or something else just as necessary to life. Another kind of time prevailed, another way of looking for something opened up. How the natural world appeared and moved—that was what held our attention and drew us on, two armed men wandering in the hills, doing the oldest thing men have done on earth.

It might be a deer, a mule deer. Not the white-tailed deer of lowland flatwoods, but one of the mountain deer, what Clayton called *stla'chínum,* "food someone goes looking for." The most important food animal in the old days before cattle ranching. So critical to making it through long, snowy winters that "looking for food" meant these long-eared, wide-antlered, strong-bodied creatures we find everywhere in the mountains along the British Columbia–Washington border.

Often enough it would be a deer that presented himself to be shot. To be "prayed over" with ancient words of gratitude, thanked for offering his body to us as food, in Clayton's high-pitched, oratorical sincerity, his complex Salish consonants punctuated by long, drawn-out vowels showing how deeply he felt. That moment when another living creature breathed his last, and how it felt to be the one who took his life. A deer we dragged by the antlers to lay on green fir boughs, a dead body we carefully gutted, skinned, and boned, the meat and organs wrapped in the greasy blood of his own skin, tied onto pack frames, and carried home.

But just as likely it would be to watch a herd of bighorn sheep grazing the rocky slopes above Vaseux Lake, or a family of mountain goats strung out along the cliff face of Chopaka Mountain. And Clayton identifying each member by size and behavior, speaking in a murmur that blended with the wind—his mountain voice, a certain low, pulsating tone that didn't sound or carry like human speech. Or it would be spending the better part of a morning observing how a certain trout lived in constant motion but went nowhere, fighting the current to stay behind a certain boulder in the Similkameen River.

Or stopped cold along a game trail just below timberline, both of us surprised by a "whistler"—a hoary marmot—running down the trail at us, completely unafraid. We instinctively froze in the face of such unnatural behavior—pondering what it could mean that this short, wide, shuffling animal was running right down to two men with rifles, her eyes looking directly at us. Marmots are usually heard, not seen, their sharp whistles of alarm a single, piercing note coming from jumbles of boulders or rockslides in high mountains. Sometimes they can be crept up on, basking sleepily on sun-warmed rocks, or surprised, nose down, gorging on the brief, high-meadow lushness they feed on for a few months between long winters of hibernation. But their first instinct is to dive for cover.

This one looked like she was going to come right up to us like a dog who knew us. We didn't move, didn't raise our guns, because the whistler wasn't offering herself as food—she was on some kind of mission. Behavior so out of the ordinary meant something else was afoot. What Clayton's people called xa'xá. What Lakota speakers call wakan. What every Indian language has a name for, but what our own scientists simply call "unbelievable" because they aren't hunting for sign of the power that animates all life. The mystery still moving in the world, there for those who haven't forgotten how to see it.

Came down toward us and veered to the left at the last moment, this whitish, furry whistler with black markings on her face, weaving expertly through boulders, not slowing down a bit as she passed us and ran downhill and out of sight. Clayton seemed indecisive for a minute. Then he cleared his throat.

"Maybe he tell us somethin' powerful, somethin' dangerous up ahead," he said. "Somethin' from the deep earth places he know about. See, he don't run across in front of us, warn us not to go on that way. And he don't run 'longside of us, goin' the way we goin', what might be the good sign, the lucky sign. No—he comin' right at us, no fear, right on the trail we walkin'. Somethin' *xa'xá* up ahead, some spirit, somethin' from the deep earth."

Neither of us had been so far up this particular creek valley, a tributary of the Ashnola River in British Columbia, way up in the headwaters where the dense spruce-fir forest was thinning out near timberline. We'd been following game trails generally upstream all morning, and up ahead of where we stood, I could see sunlight penetrating the heavy timber. We continued uphill more cautiously, pausing to study things, and eventually emerged from the thick forest, the last spruce trees battered and broken by falling rocks. We found ourselves at the spot where the creek flowed out full and fast like a small river from a cavelike overhang, the only opening in a sixty-foot-high wall of granite so bright and glittering in noonday sunlight I could hardly see through squinted eyes.

The creek simply sprang forth fully developed, deep and swift, from a pool half-hidden below the roof of rock disappearing far back in the darkness. We stood just inside the shade of the overhang, marveling at how so much water gushed continuously from the earth, forming in a few yards a stream too wide to leap, fringed with a riot of yellow monkeyflowers in bloom, and went rushing and roaring downhill into forest. Like my dream of finding the source of a river coming out of a cave, I was in the presence of something rare and extraordinary.

Clayton fumbled in his pockets and brought out a pouch of tobacco. He crumbled some in his fingers and spread the offering onto the shaded pool of water so pure and clear I didn't realize it was six feet deep until I saw the bits of brown leaf land on the otherwise invisible surface. The spring emerged down deep from a twisting tunnel that looked like a giant throat. Unknowable how far it went back into the earth, I thought, dabbling my hand in water so icy my fingers were numb in seconds.

"*En'xa'xa'ítux, ḵwun'ḵwanmínt!* (Something powerful sleeping here, take pity on us!)" Clayton said in a restrained voice, almost a whisper, squatting on his haunches beside me. Then he made a gesture with his chin, the way older Indians point something out, and I knelt lower to follow his look far back into the gloom. Off to one side, I could make out the flat top of a ledge just under the surface of water. Several fist-sized, rounded, milky-white quartz rocks had been placed on the ledge, a sure sign that this was a questing site, a place of power in the old world of the Okanogans.

Such stones were brought by fasting youths. Suffering for help in life from the spirits of nature, as their elders had done all the way back to the beginning. Praying to whoever lived deep in the earth here. Showing by their sleepless vigil, their concentration and courage, their willingness to endure solitude, lack of food, and frigid dives deep into that dark tunnel that they were worthy to "gain spirit"—to receive the lifelong power of a *shumíx,* or spirit partner. Diving over and over through the endless hours, and then dancing in place, shivering and naked, in front of a fire through the short summer night so they would never for a moment be inattentive to whatever might come, to whoever might show themself. A bit of something extra in life, a share of all that power unleashed at creation, long ago in the time of the Animal People.

And so much of it concentrated right here, Clayton and I back away, circle around counterclockwise where we cautiously avoid stepping on the charcoal remains of just such a fire disappearing under lush wild-flowers. A pole stands leaning back in some rocks, the remains of some-thing tied to it fluttering in the wind. Walking away, we're startled by piercing whistles—the sharp alarm whistles of marmots hidden in the rocks above suddenly announcing our presence. Announcing our departure.

We hiked for miles without saying anything to each other. Neither of us was hunting anymore, but we saw no animals anyway. Tramp, tramp, tramp, following game trails over a high saddle, down long ridges into more heavily timbered country, and down to another creek as daylight faded. Lowering our packs and leaning them against tree trunks, we chopped alpine fir boughs to lay our rifles on and for our beds. Setting up camp and breaking dry branches for a fire in a familiar routine that we'd shared so many times nothing needs to be said. Only when the pot of water bubbles for tea do I see the deep emotion showing on Clayton's weathered old face, the glow in his eyes looking over the flames at me.

"I hear about that spring from the old stories," he says softly. "But I never know where it is. All my life, and now I see where. That whistler come at us, he the one guard that power. Now I know why that old power woman who come here when she just a girl, who tell me a little bit about divin' here, why she do that whistle when she dance at the Winter Dance. Just like the whistler, sharp, two, three times. When she get up to dance, when that power come over her. She been gone the long time now, maybe thirty, forty years. Maybe that was her, comin' to warn us. Comin' to greet us."

And another time, we were sitting side by side, rifles resting across our laps. Looking out over the rounded grassy slopes and deep timbered ravines of Swakane Canyon, a long creek valley that empties into the Columbia River near a rock formation in Washington called Lincoln Rock. This rock actually does look like the profile of Abe Lincoln from a certain angle as seen from the main north-south highway near Rocky Reach Dam, but its older name is *Shwa'ḳain,* "Cougar Head," more easily recognizable from a boat on the river as the head of a huge mountain lion of ancient lore. It was a place where boys quested for help hunting the deer that still were so numerous up Swakane Canyon that Clayton and I had been jumping dozens of them in our long day's wander. But as sometimes happened, none of them presented themselves to be killed for food, and Clayton started singing to the deer, the handgrip of his old single-shot rifle pressed to his cheek so his voice came out through pouty lips. Hilarious, short tunes in Salish that I'd heard before around campfires at night, from hunters wryly congratulating the deer people on staying away from the business end of their weapons.

(This won't hurt
Why do you run away?

Long legs carrying my food away
And still I'm hungry.)

Like Native hunters in the old days, Clayton had a full complement of hunting technology on hand, only now it's rifles and shotguns of various makes and ages, cleaned and smudged and fondled until they were like extensions of his arms. He carried his favorite, a turn-of-the-century, British military training rifle that had an outdated sliding-block breech, and the barrel bored out so he could use modern .38 Special pistol cartridges. So underpowered compared to the high-velocity rifles he and Jim also had, I could detect the blur of the bullet when he fired. But Clayton knew how to compensate for its limited range and light impact by stalking closer to game animals than other hunters had to, in the same way I had to, using my dad's hand-me-down .22.

"Well, now you've done it," I said when he seemed to be done singing. "They all know we're out here gunnin' for 'em after that!"

"Bambi musta been up here and warned 'em anyway," he said, shrugging.

He settled us on a grassy perch high up where we looked out over the very tops of enormous Douglas fir and ponderosa pine trees. He was in a playful, talkative mood, naming in Salish each of the kinds of trees and bushes we could see and giving humorously unlikely translations, as if their names were body parts of animals. The light of a cloudy autumn afternoon was beginning to fade—a perfect time to hunt when the deer get up to feed and go for water, but Clayton talked and laughed, other things on his mind.

Clayton was one of the few men I knew at his age, almost seventy, who still roamed the mountains on foot. Actually more lean and fit than I was since I'd quit ranch work and got a desk job, he nonetheless was beginning to slow down, resting longer and talking more than he used to. He wore his white hair cropped short and kidded me about my long hair, saying it was good for attracting women, not deer. His face was wide and expressive, his eyes shining out from deep wrinkles, and his hands moved like small brown animals in gestures that caressed the features of the land around us as if they were close enough to touch. And he spoke English with the same chin-lifted, facially controlled attention to singing out his words that accomplished Salish storytellers used speaking the Native language.

"We see the tall trees, so much older than us, even me, close to the end of life," he said. "But I just a young guy to these elders. Up high like this, we see the tip-tops up close, the oldest ones, how up at the very tip they just like the young tree. All that wood they build up, thick, tall. Their skin to be so wrinkled, so rough, so many scars. Like to live as long as many men live, one after the other.

"That one there, now," he said, pointing with his chin at a truly ancient Douglas fir leaning a little before straightening up to a dense crown of massed branches reaching out over the empty shadows below. "Not any different from when I see 'em when I just a boy. My grandpa leave me here one time. This a power place for me. Up huntin' with other men, he say, 'You rest here and we hunt a ways. After while, we come back this way.' All alone, just me and this tree. *Ch'k'ilhp* we call 'em, fir tree, the one we lay down, place the green on the ground. He got a lotta relatives that point up like that. But this kind, *x'it,* the *real* one, he the boss over all the others that point up. The one we pull on. Break off the arms."

"*Aaaa,*" I said, letting him know I was listening, that I was content to sit beside him and hear another of his rambling monologues—take in what good he always had to say.

"Well, anyway, even maybe my grandpa see this one, lookin' as old as she lookin' now, when he just a boy. But now, there at the top, we see the young fir tree just as soft and fresh as the little ones just comin' up. Just tender, reachin' for the sky. Same for us come-alive people. To look like the old fir tree in the face, but I don't live in that crumpled old bark. No, I'm up at the top! Still the same boy who walkin' all day in the hills. I stroll far in life—but I just the same boy!"

Clayton sighed. "The old trees, they give that to us, ain't it? How they disguise theirself. How their blood move so slow and they stay in one place, never move away from one spot. Live there all their life. And we ponder on how they live. We sit and watch. Not ever change while we watchin'. But they know we watchin'. Then maybe the old one decide to take pity on the come-alive person, speak to him. Say, 'You like my clothes? All these other ones scattered around here, they my children, my grandchildren. They just like me. We all the same tree person. Whatever touch my green, then I be there. Touch me and it just like at the beginning of time! I livin' here before you come alive, and I livin' here after you gone. This green, this the same green that smell good and give power in legend time!' " He sighed again.

"But nowadays all people tell about is how they screamin' when they fall. Cut 'em down, cut 'em down! Make a lot of frogskins, big wad of dollar bills burnin' a hole in somebody's pocket. Scream so loud you hear 'em even when the chain saw so loud. And don't ever ask 'em to take their body like that. Just knock 'em down, chop off the green, the arms, leave 'em layin' all around, drag out the log. Well, so, that how it is now. . . ."

I told him how I'd worked as a logger in my younger days, when I'd try anything to make a living and still stay out in the hills. Setting chokers, trimming behind a diesel shear that laid trees down in rows, even falling trees for the top dollars you could earn when you were skilled and fast with a chain saw—I'd done well, but hated it, too. The roar of machinery in the mountains, dozers churning up the earth dragging logs to landings, the smell of sappy stumplands. Log trucks carrying the wood away to build houses in cities.

"Nobody ask, so nobody know," he said. "But they people. Trees don't look like us, don't go anywhere but where they always live in one spot. But so old. To still remember the before time, and yet at the top, to be the youngest of all. And these here ones, *xa'xa'ílhpelux* ('power trees' like Douglas fir, juniper, alpine fir), they the ones give us the most to live in the power way. The oldest way.

"You askin' that time at Old Willie's house, how to do what you been showed, whatever that power is you got. How it work to be the power man. And I been thinkin' about that, how it must be for the White man tryin' to live with nature power and he don't know things like how we do. But somebody like you, been around so long, talk Indian, just listen and take it all in like the one of us, so we forget you don't know. And like Willie tell about how the power make the world shine, you listen to whatever he say when he talk like that, because he talkin' to *you*. We already know this stuff—me, Rose, Jim, whoever. We grow up with it and we already know how it go.

"So now I'm thinkin', your want to know how it go, and so we come to this tree, sit here with this power at a place like this, and I have words to say about that."

He paused long enough for me to be aware that he expected something more than my occasional *aaaa*'s. So I said, "*Wai, xast ispu'ús awhá ḵwu'm'aixítux* (My heart is good about this, what you're telling me for my own good)."

"See, the power man, *tlaḵwílux,* his want to be where the power move. This how they talk about it, my grandpa, my elders. The power man, his want to live the *shumíx tu'últ,* the power way. Can't be layin' around the house, watchin' television, scratchin' hisself. Have to be out in the hills, the timber, train hisself for how to do it. Out here like this, study how the world move, go to a place good for the spirit. Sweathouse, not eat much, wander alone. Dive in the cold water, river or lake. *Xwist'lwís il muḵ'máḵw* (Roam around in the mountains).

"First, he tame the *shumíx,* do what bring him closer, make 'em want to be around. He tame that power by what he do, how he live, how he concentrate on 'em and follow what little sign he get from 'em. Do what they do for the thousands of years to attract their attention, make 'em want to hang around. Get so we say about a man like that, *en'pix-um'tíls i xa'xá,* want to hunt power, always feel like seein' the spirit move, can't see no other way to live no more. Then, that *shumíx* want to tame that man, so he tame him, and that man is tamed. Start to come on, maybe when he don't expect it. But he been trainin' for it, so he watchin' for it now. Always have in his mind, his heart, that he want to live in the power way. So what he got start to tame the man, come on him, like a wind rushin' through his ears. Like he hear him comin', that sound they make, like buzzin', like somebody whistle in his ears. And he suddenly don't feel so good, feel pitiful, and he start to cry, he have the big sob that come outta nowhere. You remember that? How he come on you like that?"

I thought back to the early days when I first started running around with him, and remembered two times when something like that happened to me. I nodded yes.

"That first time I see you cryin', we all standin' out by the river at night, and I think this not good. You don't know nothin' and maybe you just hurt yourself, so I wipe 'em off. Me and Johnny Stemilt, we feed that *shumíx*. We say, 'Yah, we see you tryin' to work through this man, we see what we can do with 'em.' And we do what make 'em back off. Then that other time, I show you my power at Omak Lake, to have the rain fall just a little. And you get sick when the spirit come on you. I figure maybe that happen, that if you got somethin', what you got will come on you when you touched by the power, when you so moved by how the power work. And when you thinkin' about maybe you got somethin' too, you remember how somebody tell you in life, 'Only wind is real.' So I ready for that, and I do what we do to help the new power person, to welcome that spirit comin' on, that power comin' over you. I rub you with the sagebrush so you can see and feel in the power way, and make you like sweeter to how they want us, like more attractive to them. And I rub your neck below the ears, what we call 'pullin' the thoughts out,' so you don't think about nothin', just let go into the power. Because that Omak Lake, that a good place, like this, good for the *shumíx* to show hisself. Just the time and place for the power to come on you. But then that power back off, what you got back off on his own. You start talkin' like nothin' happen, and I wonder about that, ponder what that might mean.

"I see what they say, no good for the power to come over the man if he not ready. If he don't really know about the power way, *shumíx tu'últ*. So I take the time in life to help you learn about that, how we train ourself with the sweatlodge, with the dive in water, with the wander in the mountains. And with the eye trainin', *wík'wst,* how we take in more of what is out there, what is movin' in the world. And I send you on the mission so you know how to do things, be just pitiful without the food or water, no sleep, wander alone in the mountains. Nothin' left in life but make yourself good for the power to take pity on you, help you remember what come to you when you just a boy, give you new life.

"So now we see the power man, have that want to hunt power. He know enough now for that power to come on 'em. Like we say, he put hisself right in the middle, in between. He do life where everything is ordinary, common, natural, but he keep his eyes on how the power move in everything, how the power show hisself in what happenin'. He try to stay right there, in the middle, in the center, *en'ḳaḳ'a'íus*. Put hisself there where it all happen. Like we see the hawk in the sky, always huntin', always watchin' for what move. See, the power man, his want to be like the hawk, to have that way of movin'—how the power move. *Tlaḳwílux,* you could say, maybe, 'move like the hawk huntin'.'

"And the power man learn about the power by what he do, not how he think about hisself, or how he show hisself to others. He know somethin' because he do things the way his power train him. Maybe others notice that, how he do different than other people, set him apart, but he don't pay attention. Don't say nothin' about it. Don't say why he do that. Like to sleep under the pine branches at night like Louis Pilliken do when he go huntin'. Or like some carry somethin' with 'em all the time, or talk a certain way, or can't be around somethin' that don't bother nobody else—like Old Willie can't be have no radio, no TV be on where he come around, say what he got don't like that. Or like Johnny Stemilt, talkin' to cars the way he do. He don't want to stand out, but he know if he don't do what the power show him, whatever it is, he won't have nothin'. Leave 'em. Because they test you like that with what they care about, see if you really mean it, you want them as the partner in life.

"Time pass, the power man livin' the power way," Clayton said. He gestured with a slow wave of his arm. "Out there in the world, huntin' power, and he begin to see things, know things. See things in dreams. Hear little whispers, like. Have strong feelings that he have to do somethin', or not do somethin.' He see things comin', what goin' to happen. If he get hurt or scared or thrown in jail, he do what he shown to do and things turn out good. He show up to help where somebody was just thinkin' about him, wishin' he was there to help. He see he have the gift to do what others can't, or he have it easy at somethin' hard for others. He feel how what he need in life just come and find him, so he have whatever to share with others, give away what come so easy to him.

"And now he ready to call on that power, and that power will come.

He do things he been taught to do, and he wait for that *shumíx* to come on him again. Now he ready, he know enough, he want to live. And so we out here like this, do things in the old way, keep doin' 'em, little by little, until he start comin' on you again, and you can learn how to handle it.

"The power, when the power come over us, not like anything we know how to do. Like when we first learn to walk, or we first learn to ride a horse, we keep fallin' down, fallin' off. But we keep at it, not know how to do it, but keep at it, until we get good at it. And the power does the trainin', we just learn to follow how it go. Have to be just ready, live the power way, and do what come. You see, in time, you do like I been showin' you, he have to come.

"The new power man, see, he just waitin' for that. He keep huntin' for power because he have a taste for that, now. Can't ever go back unless he throw it away, run away from it. Get drunk and feel sorry for hisself. Stay in town and don't look at nothin'. Try to find a lot of frogskins, chase around and be crazy, be nobody. No, the power man, he see somethin' else. He been to where he gonna die, and see how short his time is, how sweet life can be.

"The power man want that, to be alive again, the pure little child with wonder in the eye. To see it all movin' behind everything, like shadows. How the world still move like in the before time. So we pull off that tree's green, we ask and we thank 'em, and we take that sweet-smellin' clothes of this here *ch'k'ilhp*. We do like that, lay down a bed. Like in the sweathouse, we sit on that, we touchin' that green. Just dark—you know, you the power man, you sweat a lot now. To sit on that green in the dark. Sufferin', rub ourself with that green. And he do that for us, to see again like the child, how all those old ones comin' around, show themself in the dark. Give us the picture of what we askin' about. Just like eyes open in legend time.

"Well, now, who know about that, eh? Who want to live like the real come-alive person nowadays? Who want to live with power?"

I wanted to know about it because ever since I came to live in the Okanogan country and started roaming around with Clayton Tommy and other Indians, my life had changed. It wasn't just that the way of life I was learning was something I'd always vaguely longed for, though after years with him I marveled how I ever lived not knowing such things. Or even that Clayton Tommy was just the kind of older man I always wanted to learn from—so alive to the natural world around us that I loved him more than was sensible. It was because everything he said turned out to be true. Even that I'd been given a gift of power as a child, that I had "gained spirit" as he called it, and had only to awaken to it and live it consciously.

It's no wonder we completely forget the magical experiences that define our lives through child's eyes. Coming from a culture that lives a materialist dream of never looking deep, that invalidates children's reports of encountering otherworldly beings as fantasies they need to grow out of, I almost instantly forgot what nobody but I had seen. So absorbed in the vast adult reality around me and thirsting for knowledge of how it worked—how I could share in it once I grew up—I was left with only a longing for something I couldn't identify. Despite what schoolteachers said, growing up wasn't about mastering some increasingly esoteric lore that adults possessed so I could embark upon an adventure of unlimited potential. It was by narrowing the possibilities, by excluding so much personal experience that only the agreed-upon game plan of the "real world" mattered. I became a fully operational adult, ready for the serious business of war, work, and mastering technology. And I was afflicted with the same amnesia as other modern adults—the vague sense that I used to know something even more important.

To help me remember, Clayton had years before sponsored me and guided me in traditional practices that for thousands of years were how his people approached the forces of nature, seeking gifts of unusual ability and knowing. Practical, time-honored, ritualized ways of sacrifice and suffering for a better life, undertaken in the solitude of the natural world. A ten-day sweatlodge retreat in late autumn when each day I sweated and dived in the Similkameen River. A long, wandering fast in the Pasayten Wilderness the following summer that finally brought back the memory of my childhood encounter with a man who grabbed a robin out of the air as it flew by. That lined up with a lifetime of uncanny experiences with peregrine falcons.

The fact that I was a White man and had no living tradition for understanding or making use of such things meant little to Clayton. The *shumíx* or spirit partners were the backbone of his religious feelings and practical accomplishments in life. The lore of spirit powers that he and others shared with me was something that they took for granted, that they lived by, and they knew I would lose my power (and maybe my life) if I didn't know how to handle it.

"What you got won't stay with you, if you don't live like he want you to. If you don't use him, do what he say," Clayton said more than once. Elders like Clayton still living the old ways never worried why a gift was given. It wasn't something casual or ego-feeding. It was serious business, life-threatening if I didn't acknowledge the attention and desire of the "spiritual" to live through me. Living without power was perfectly acceptable, but lamentable—nothing to write home about. "Ordinary" was the word I heard a lot. But *k'stím,* "having something"—living with the influence and protection of a spirit partner, having a direct relationship with something out in nature that tied me to the source—that was what really made life sweet and exceptional.

6

WORKING A REGULAR nine-to-five and living in a rented cottage in town meant I didn't see Clayton Tommy, or for that matter Jim Woods or Old Willie, very often. Occasional weekends in the mountains, hanging out at the Omak Stampede, meeting for lunch in a cowboy restaurant, sitting with them at spirit dances in the dead of winter—it wasn't much. As the summer of 1982 wore on, I knew I was dragging my feet.

"What you waitin' for?" Clayton asked me out of the blue late one night when we were driving home from Dry Falls, and crossing the bridge at Grand Coulee Dam.

The Columbia River is big, but the dam is enormous, looming high above, filling the whole canyon. Lit up at night with garish, pastel-colored floodlights, it was like a city skyscraper wedged into the gorge, backing up a lake all the way to Canada. It always made me uneasy to get so close to the thrumming monster at night, as if it was something alien forced on the world that might not let someone like me pass without something bad happening. People who live in cities may not know what I'm talking about, but for those who live out in the open, where the night is stars and dark hills and the scent of sagebrush, coming upon the dam is like finding a city crammed into the Grand Canyon.

Anyway, I was concentrating so hard on making it across the bridge that it wasn't until we were out of harm's way and onto the dark sagebrush benches beyond that I said, "What?"

"What you waitin' for? You think they gonna stop here, with what they got?"

"Who?"

"They put that dam in when I just young, and don't listen to the Indian. Don't care what my elders say, that this is wrong to take the life of the river. Never listen. Another dam, another, another. Cut down the trees. Dig the mines, take down the whole mountain. They never stop. See, they can't stop themself. That White man's madness, makin' war on our mother. Whose side you on? What you waitin' for?"

"It just seems so hopeless. Look at that thing back there!" I saw the pastel glare of the dam receding in my rearview mirror.

"Your heart is bad about that dam, maybe?" he asked softly.

"Yes."

"But then, maybe you think, how the Native know the world, to go and learn that, how that gonna do any good, eh?"

I admitted having such doubts.

He laughed. "Well, you stuck then. But not me. Maybe all you can see is what's wrong. What bad things are happenin' to the earth, to all of us. Maybe just stuck on that, what you don't want to see happenin', eh?"

"Well, it's hard not to. Like you say, they never stop."

"Yah, but to be stuck there, well, they got you. Like the bear, to be surrounded, cornered by the pack of dogs. So many on their side, to wear you down, little by little until nothin' left. Hopeless. What kind of life is that?"

"What's the alternative? They seem to be the ones who have the power, like nothin' can stop 'em from eating up the world!"

"They eat up the earth like that because they live the story that the earth is somethin' dead. So they have a power, yah, but not the power of earth and sky. Power over people, maybe, because of the story they tell, the yarn they spin, that human people the only ones really alive. So that kinda power is somethin' else, like givin' candy to children. Keepin' people like children in the mind, that they don't know their teeth go bad, only taste the sweet how it is right now. Everything they do is like candy, just to feel good. Well, why they don't feel the good to begin with? Maybe all along, they growin' up all the way to the old age, how they have to live to keep gettin' that candy, and well, maybe not really livin'. Sweet maybe. Safe. Nice. Easy. But not the real thing. Your want to have the real thing, what the earth and sky give to anybody who know what is true, that the world is alive and know what we doin'."

Then he spoke for a long time about a numinous, knowing feel for the earth that was disappearing from people's hearts in the face of how things like the dam were justified and accepted. He said the old way of being on the earth's side was a better way, a more real way that gave a person a *xast pu'ús*, a "good heart" for whatever needed doing in life. He spoke with quiet authority about keeping alive in his own life what he called the "oldest way of knowin' the earth. What a pity," he said, "that those others don't know the world as it really is!" Instead of going at things only with what the mind understood, a person acted on what they knew in their heart, and for someone like him, that meant he had the river in his heart.

"The big river, that's alive. The river, that's forever. The river know my heart, know what side I'm on. Those dams, they not gonna last. The river is old, old as time, and will run free again someday. The river, that old man who is a power on this earth, he someone I can know with my heart because we the same. And so, that dam not make me bad in the heart, not make me feel hopeless. See, to hold the river in my heart, that dam not have any power over me."

He talked about how the old way kept the natural world going, how any person could be a part of that, by training for that kind of knowledge in practices that were how his people had lived for thousands of years in harmony with nature. And how my own people had their minds on other things than what their hearts felt, which left someone like me with a sense of being powerless and complicit in the continuing destruction of the earth. What my people could never seem to see, he said, was that the Native way was not some alien mystical sense only Indians had that was always out of reach and never grasped by outsiders. It was something any human being could learn if they truly came to see who was supposed to be in charge—the earth and sky who gave us all life. His words left me feeling he knew something I couldn't even imagine, a secret I was denied having for my own only because I couldn't stop looking at the world in the way I'd been conditioned most of my life.

"Can I really know like you know, Clayton?" I asked.

"You and me, we both human people, both walk on two legs, both can drive the car down the road," he said. "What the big difference?"

"I don't know. My people just spell things out. Say what they know. Like, you can read in books and it's all there, everything you need to know. But you guys never quite put words on what's the most important part, you just talk around it."

He was silent and thoughtful for a minute as we dropped down into the valley of the Nespelem River, the dark hulks of mountains closing in around us.

"The only difference is your people talk like they the ones in charge on earth. Just some lie they been tellin' themself for so long, their want to act like they know everything there is to know about the world. But how can you know what is greater than you? Who give you your life? What little you can know, you learn like the child learn from the grandparent.

"What I know, I have to train for in life. Can't be just say it, and read it in some book. No way how to tell what I know. Just a path I walk, and when you on that path, you know. What can be said, one person to the other, just maybe how to walk that path. What you find goin' down that trail only for you alone. But now, you can tell when somebody know. You hear how they sing the song, like maybe they sing to the river, to the mountains. You feel in your heart what they feel, that they just like the earth, the river, the mountain—or like you, the wind. But the only way to know is if somebody train for it. Once they start to train for it, they get on that trail, and they walk that trail from then on, all the way till the time come to leave this life. And not just pow! you got it. Somethin' more and more to know as you walk along.

"I guess maybe to say, you maybe know what I know if you in the power. If you feel in your heart you walkin' that path that all peoples used to know, to walk here on earth. That kinda knowin' is a feeling you have in your heart. Not somethin' can just say, but somethin' so old, so deep, so . . . well, only maybe you can sing. Maybe just sing how it feel, and there it is.

"Like my elder before me, pass on to me how to train for the power, how to walk that trail in life." He laughed, remembering something about the old man who had meant so much to him. How old Baptiste declined a White missionary's invitation to come and worship at his new chapel. "He tell 'em he worship in the oldest religion—he wander around in the mountains amazed!

"See, for him, only mountains. He from way up north, and he have the gift of the mountains in his heart. To talk to the mountains and feel in his heart what they want him to know. And he sing how that feel, to walk that path, to be on that path."

Clayton paused and his head nodded to the slow beat of a song he brought out faintly, like he was trying to remember how it went. Once he sang it through, he sang louder, repeating the same lines over and over to a tune that caught the emotional feel of what he was saying exactly.

> *Ch'maistíselux inkulwit'lwís i t'temxúúlaux.*
> *Ilí la'ḳín xwístselux ischuchoxwán, wai*
> *Ixí ilí stim ch'maistís i ispu'ús.*
> *Uhl en'ḳxám wai inchoxenmínt*
> *Atlí ya'yát ḳa'ḳín ḳ'n tla'ús ixí*
> *Muḳ'máḳw uhl nish,*
> *Muḳ'máḳw uhl nish.*

> *(The earth knows my steps.*
> *There where my feet walk,*
> *There my heart knows something.*
> *And going along, I'm on a good trail*
> *Because everywhere I look,*
> *Mountains as far as you can see,*
> *Mountains as far as you can see.)*

From that time on, I knew my town job wouldn't last. On those rare occasions when I was off in the hills, I'd come alive so forcefully to who I really was, the ache of it would linger for days. Back at work, during lunchtime I'd go off by myself and sit staring up at the timbered mountains brooding out of reach. Then one day I'd had enough. Without a second thought I gave my notice. On the way home at the end of the day, I stopped to run into the co-op and buy some spark plugs for my car.

"Heyyyy, Hippie!" I heard from the next aisle over, and around the corner came the familiar clump of cowboy boots. It was Stuart Bolster, my old boss, the foreman at one of the ranches I used to work for. Cowboy hat stained with sweat, denim jeans and western shirt soiled from a hard day's work, he reeked of cow manure and the smoke of a hand-rolled cigarette dangling from a corner of his mouth.

"Hey, Redneck, how's it going?"

We shook hands, his so rough and callused compared to mine that had lost the feel of shovels and wire pliers.

"Came in to order a part for the International tractor. You do any work today?" He looked me over appraisingly.

"Of course. All day."

He sniffed. "Must not be much to your job, then, eh?"

Before I could answer how my job burned out my brain instead of my muscles, he was called up to the counter. The counterman said he needed the number stamped on the old part to order the right one, so Stuart closed his eyes and rattled off, "R6J300589 dash 0407." The counterman wrote it all down and read it back to him, already used to Stuart's phenomenal memory, which Stuart proudly attributed to never really having learned to read. He turned back to me.

"I guess I just don't know what to make of a man who's clean after a day's work!"

"Well, you won't have to wonder for long," I said. "I decided today that I'm out of here. Had enough of town life. Won't be long I'll be looking for something to do out your way."

"Huh. I'll ask around. Might even have some work for you at the ranch, but you can't have your old trailer back. My oldest son moved in. Come and see me when the dust settles."

The night after my last day of work was close to the full moon—so bright it penetrated into my bedroom like daylight. It was hard to sleep deeply, and after waking up fitfully several times, I awoke from a dream that made me sit up and brood in the predawn darkness. The dream was short, simple, and vivid. I was out in the mountains, in the timber. I found myself face to face with a big deer—a buck—and as he turned away, I grabbed him by the antlers. Because we were in dense lodgepole pine forest with leaning and downed trees all around us, as long as I held on to him, he couldn't really get away. But with both my fists clenched around the wide-apart tines of his antlers, there wasn't much more I could do but hang on. I yelled for my two friends, two men who were somewhere nearby. When they came running down a logging road to help me, I woke up, sweaty and full of adrenaline.

I wondered who the two friends were, since they didn't seem like actual people I knew. Yet they seemed familiar, like intimate friends whose loyalty and willingness were unquestioned, like they were my older brothers, or maybe uncles. One was bigger than the other, more a hunter type, strong and swift and leading the way as they came to help me. He was the one whose help I really counted on. The other friend was willing, too, but I didn't expect much from him.

Like anybody who has a compelling dream, I was too close to the vivid experience of it to see anything beyond the doing of it. But I knew it was something important, so I got up and made a pot of tea in the tiny, dimly lit kitchen. I dressed and carried pot and cup outside to sit on the woodpile and brood some more. It was cold in the irrigated autumn dampness where the sleeping town ended and a peach orchard stretched away toward brushy hills. The harvest moon was low, pale, about to set, and the eastern sky glowed dimly with the false light of first dawn. Drinking scalding hot tea, I hashed the dream over and over. Whatever this dream was about, it was energizing me like nothing had in a long time. I'd been given something valuable, but it was a puzzle just exactly what. Certainly it had to do with hunting and getting a deer. I'd been around Clayton and other Indians long enough to know that if this was a message from my *shumíx,* then it had to have some practical benefit in this waking world. But how?

True dawn arrived, filling the world with gray shapes becoming solid trees and houses, and on the very horizon the morning star appeared from behind the mountains. It was easily the brightest star in the sky, an unlikely, glimmering something against the eastern radiance. I instinctively spoke to it, and to the dawn—to the awesome awakening of light we take so for granted in our routine lives we rarely notice the miracle of it. And thanked them for this moment, for this gift of daylight, brightening so rapidly that the morning star fades and disappears altogether.

Full daylight and it's the tamed, unnatural world where I lived, the houses and streets, the peach trees in precise rows, the sounds of cars going by on the highway. On this first day of who knows what, I want nothing more than to head off into the hills and be who I really am. Loading my old Falcon station wagon with everything I can possibly need, I drive out of town, west and north, toward the mountain borderlands, my old stomping grounds. Out there where I first put down roots—the lake and the bend in the river under Chopaka Mountain. Maybe Clayton would be at the nearby Woods place, and I could ask him about my dream.

7

"YOU KNOW MAYBE WHERE that happen?" Clayton asked after I finished telling him the details of my dream. We were outside the Woods family doublewide, leaning against cars in late morning sunshine, picking our teeth after breakfast. It was good to be back where the mountains were so tall and near that the steep slopes were right in your face. The marshy smell of the river, the stink of rabbitbrush in full bloom lying in deep, broomlike thickets, a scattering of timber up steep mountainsides tawny with autumn-faded grass. And cattail fluff blowing in the wind high up into a deep blue sky, with huge puffball clouds like freighters easing off the the summit of Chopaka, so close and so high we have to look almost straight up to see it.

"Where?" I had to close my eyes and think about the lodgepole pine forest where I'd grabbed the deer's antlers in my dream.

"Yah, that thick timber, all crossed around with dead logs, all one kinda tree. The pole-wood, taste good to pry off the bark and eat in the spring. Go up like one thickness, not taper off like them other pine trees. I know that kinda timber. But where you see that?"

It was just like Clayton, like any Native steeped in the old language's focus on exact locational knowledge, to seek for where my dream had taken place. First things first. Where had my dream-soul wandered off to? It hadn't occurred to me to wonder where I was when I was brooding about it afterward. Now I did, and I realized I knew the general area.

"Up in the headwaters of Toats Coulee, there below Thunder Mountain, back where the logging road comes around the ridge from the upper meadow. Somewhere in there, by that road."

"Aaaa," he said, nodding. We gazed idly around at the cold dirt dooryard steaming in the sun after a frost overnight. The years had been rough on the mobile home—the paint flaking off aluminum corners and a piece of plywood nailed over the door to replace the flimsy porch roof broken off by heavy snows. The cottonwoods along the river were turning gold, and a blue heron lazily flapped along over the water behind them.

"So, well, what time of day? Or maybe at night, eh?"

"Light comin' at me, right through the trees, level," I said, remembering the reddish glow, the sense of waning light. "I was facing into it, west. So I guess sunset."

"Nik'hnaaaa, awhá nakwá tul tanmúsh ki xwíchehlts i sisiyúsch! (Goodness, it's sure not for nothing someone gave you his power!)" he exclaimed in a sardonic voice, his head shaking. ("You remember every little thing just like it happens to you!")

I thought he was scolding me, suggesting that I was embellishing my dream with details I couldn't be sure of.

"Loot inmálxa (I not lie)," I said.

("No question of that, nephew. It might be that the White people don't feel in their hearts the lies they tell. But someone made-a-relative knows we can't be going off *far away* into the mountains on a guess. Things are true, or they aren't. Those powers, they help the ones who pay close attention.")

He seemed to be suggesting a trip to where the dream took place, and had stressed the word for "far away," *lekuuut,* as if we would have to walk the thirty miles to Thunder Mountain.

("We go maybe by car,") I said in my lame Salish.

Clayton laughed and shook his head like I just wasn't getting it. He switched back to English.

"My words to say, we tell the truth, not fool ourself. Bad enough, a hunter in the old days, he lie about where he dream the deer to be. People die, starve to death when somebody do that. But now, this dream for you—just yours. Maybe that power test you, see what you do. Very serious business. See if you do what you shown to do in that dream."

A smile crinkled his wide cheeks as he lapsed back into the Native language: ("Anyway, I wasn't with you in your dream, was I?")

("No, my two friends, only, whoever they were.")

("Well, right there, there it is. . . .") he said, making some kind of cryptic point, but looking away as if reluctant to delve any deeper. He watched the way the vultures roosting on high cottonwood limbs held their wings open to the warming rays of the sun. A line of horses belonging to Jim stood with heads over the corral fence, all facing in the direction of the travel trailer where Jim now lived, waiting patiently for him to emerge and throw them some hay. I decided Clayton was just making the point that I should go to the place of my dream without him.

("Of course, without you will go I.") Just as I had learned to decipher his use of English without reaction to his sometimes strange constructions, he ignored my broken Salish.

"*Wai, ixí asláxt,* them two friends of yours, two buddies. They be all you need, ain't it? Maybe you tell me about 'em?"

I couldn't think of anything to say about them. Usually I appreciated how indirect Clayton could be with things that were personal for me. That way when I grasped things, the insights were truly mine, unclouded by his own interpretations. But I was really stumped this time. Where was he going with the two men in my dream? Some guys I might run into up in the mountains? His interest in them seemed unfathomable.

"Well," he finally said. "You gonna be the White man or the Native?"

Despite his smile, his words stung me, drove me back deep into the memory of the two men. Don't try to figure it out before you figure it out. Keep it direct and simple. Blurt out what I saw and felt: "It was the older, stronger one I really wanted help from. The other guy was not good for . . . like in a fight or something like that. Just a mouthy, troublemaker kind of guy. Somebody who would say anything. He was along to help, but the big guy—quick and strong—he knew all about hunting and I knew I could depend on him. But like, the two of them hung out together, you know?"

"No, nephew. This the first I hear about it," Clayton said, his wry smile growing wider. "I only know you got the one."

It dawns on me that he's taking the two men in my dream for *shumíx,* spirit partners. Suddenly the dream looks different, feels even more amazing, and the sense of something important about it when I woke up returns with a vengeance. Something familiar about the bigger, older man clicks in my mind, and my feeling for him resonates all the way back to the childhood memory of him grabbing a robin out of the air as it flew by.

"So . . . I guess I know who the older man is, the hunter, the one I figured would really help me with the deer," I say with conviction. "But who's this other guy?"

Clayton shrugged. "Maybe some other *shumíx* helpin' you."

I stood there letting it all sink in. The day had taken on a whole new look. When I'd arrived to find Clayton here, there was a pickup load of firewood, chain-sawed into lengths that would fit Grandma's woodstove, piled in a heap where Jim had unloaded it days before. When I went inside, Clayton and Grandma and Charlene, Jim's mother, were just sitting down to breakfast with other adults and children. In the traditional hospitality of Native manners, Charlene automatically set another place for me to eat with them. Whoever showed up was always treated like family, but Charlene's eyes were always watching for willingness to reciprocate in those she shared with so generously, especially Whites who often took advantage of it. Grateful for a lavish homemade breakfast and missing the feel of mindless physical work, I had casually announced I would split and stack the firewood piled outside. Afterward, when Clayton and I were drifting outside to talk privately about my dream, I'd heard Charlene mention that the beef we'd eaten that morning was "the last of the meat."

Now I see how the power moves, how things fit together neatly— the dream, driving out here to find Clayton, the revelation of who the two dream-friends were. I can split and stack the wood like I said I would and still have time to drive up to Thunder Mountain to hunt, to be there at sunset, the time I dreamed of being there. And if this dream is what it seems to be, I might bring back a deer for Charlene, to help out with the Woods family food stocks.

Clayton and I have been leaning against cars in the sunshine, lost in our own thoughts, saying nothing for a long time. As usual, it's not uncomfortable simply to be together without saying anything. Over the years I'd fallen into the Indian way of being as content to say nothing as talk in social situations. Sometimes I'd be with Clayton or Jim for hours without saying ten words, just sitting around being together. It was so unlike my own people who felt uncomfortable when conversation lapsed, who became uneasy in long silences, who felt obligated to fill the void with small talk. The Indians I knew spoke or remained silent, came and went, as they pleased—without the pressure of expectation that Whites imposed on each other. One of the benefits was that real understanding could take place when nobody was compulsively keeping the talk going. In the long silence between me and Clayton, I sensed he had more to say. That he wasn't quite done. So I waited.

"This, what we been doin', to talk about that dream you have," he finally said in a quiet voice. "We call that *en'shmix'chútin,* power talk, to tell about what come to us. How the spirit move, show us things, tell us what we gotta do. And I been thinkin' about what you tell me, from way back. How that one you remember give you the gift, he the one catch birds in his bare hand. When you just a boy. How you tell about that when you come back from bein' sent on a mission. So I see that in your dream. The bare hands grab the deer antlers. I been wonderin', maybe that somethin' you notice, too?"

"Huh. Yeah, I see that now."

"We look for what they tell us, what they show us. How to call on the power, how to bring that power out. *Sen'ch'ch'wístem,* that how we say it. Somethin' somebody know to say over, say to hisself. Maybe the words, maybe the song, maybe the move of the hands, the body. Maybe somethin' else. Different for different person.

"Show you somethin' in this dream, somethin' more, like added to what you got before. The hands grabbin'. He grab the bird flyin' by, you grab the deer horns. Somethin' there, somethin' for you to figure. Just you. I see maybe just the least little bit, how this power do with you in life. You the one livin' with what you got.

"Maybe you find out who that other man is, too. See who else helpin' you. Maybe show hisself, the animal, the bird, the mountain, the cloud. Any kinda thing out there. Who knows? Maybe he not one you like to have. Badmouthin', not much help, maybe just trouble. Have to see what come of it, eh?"

"*Aaaa,*" I said. We were both watching Jim throw hay to the horses, the sleepy, docile comrades standing side by side suddenly transformed into snapping, kicking enemies until the pecking order was established. I rummaged in the back of the station wagon for my old splitting axe. Still leaning against my car, Clayton said, "You sure you wanna park your car here?" He had a funny look on his face, like he was concerned about something. I'd parked at the end of a row of broken-down cars, all Jim's, and all left to rust away nosed into the knapweed and rabbit-brush along one corral fence. Johnny Stemilt laughingly called it Jim's Used Car Lot. It looked as if I'd added my Ford Falcon to the junkyard row. Jim came walking toward us with a grin of having overheard his uncle's question.

"Me, I be worried what his cars got is contagious!" Clayton said.

We all laughed, but after they went inside, I noticed for the first time that even Jim's yellow Barracuda was in the lineup, dead with the engine missing. I started my car and moved it away from the others. Just in case.

Up in the mountains again, but it's different driving the forest roads in my old rattletrap Falcon, dodging rocks, fishtailing through mudholes, trying to keep the tires on the high sides of ruts gouged deep by logging trucks. I miss my old pickup truck. Having to go so much slower to avoid high-centering and damaging something vital under the car, it's a long way to go and taking a lot longer than I thought it would. My shoulders, arms, and hands are stiff and sore from splitting and stacking a cord of wood.

It had been such mindless, repetitive, satisfying labor, unlike the interviews and paperwork of my desk job. Productive in a way I could see with my own eyes—how the stack of firewood grew higher. Sweating away in autumn sunshine, feeling my body getting back into the remembered rhythm of swinging an axe. Setting each round on the block, studying the growth rings to see how best to make the first split, lining up with faint cracks radiating out from the center, aiming and bringing the axe down with an overhead swing, twisting my wrists at the moment of impact so the two halves sprang apart. Smelling the Christmas-tree smell of Douglas fir sap as I carried armloads of wood to the stack rising over my head along the trailer wall under a corrugated tin roof.

Once I knew I was going hunting, going off to see how this power worked in my life, I knew better than to eat any more. So I was hungry and thirsty and reeked of fir sap and sweat. Up above the dense forested country of pine and fir and tamarack, things opened up with grassy balds, the rich, high-altitude sagebrush grasslands used by ranchers as summer pastures. I drove slowly through a tightly packed throng of hundreds of sheep being driven down to the lowlands by dogs and men on horseback who didn't even look at me. Out in the open on Skull and Crossbones Ridge, I spotted alpine fir trees and stopped to chop boughs and rub myself down with the balsamy needles. Then I rubbed my rifle with it, and my bullets and hunting gear, remembering how this tree with its corky white bark mottled with blisters of medicinal sap was called *merrílhp* in Salish, "medicine tree."

Thanking the tree, I drove on, up into the high country, spruce and alpine fir and lodgepole pine forest closing in. Up where the season was more advanced, where aspens were flaming yellow blind spots shimmering in dark, wet woods, or thinned by loss of leaves to bare white trunks standing on golden carpets. Pure stands of fireweed stood faded and bedraggled with fluffy seed spikes so thick, when a gust of wind hit them, it was like a fog wreathing away through the trees.

I was thinking I probably should have bathed in the river before I came up, or even had a quick "wipe-off" in the sweatlodge. But then I dropped down into the pure lodgepole pine forest under Thunder

Mountain just as the sun went behind it, and realized I wouldn't have made it up here in time if I had. The light was fading into evening softness as I drove even worse roads through recently logged stumplands and the dense pole forests left standing between them. I was trying to find a pile of rotting logs I remembered from being here years before— "yum" logs that were left behind as unsuitable for making lumber, and stacked to one side along the road that figured in my dream. But everything looked different with new areas clearcut and freshly bulldozed roads where none had been before. I gave up trying to find my way and drove along turning onto any fork that felt right. Then it came to me that I was past the area I was looking for, that I'd never find the log pile. Automatically, I turned around and started driving back, feeling somehow relieved. Oh well, it had been worth a try. I drove back the same way I'd come, the station wagon bumping along slowly in the last light of day.

Around a curve, movement ahead, and I brake to a stop, my eyes locked on a doe deer crossing the road. She bounds uphill into the timber and two yearlings emerge from below the road, stand frozen with ears erect, staring at my car for a moment, then turn and follow their mother. Then a buck steps out, big muscled body, wide rack of antlers, but he ambles across the road without even a glance toward me, his nose down, hot on the scent of the doe in this time of rut. In an instant he's gone uphill after the others.

I'm sitting there, still and alert through it all, locked on every movement until they disappear. Completely shifted into hunter mode, all thoughts narrowed to considerations of how to hunt the buck. A lifetime of deer hunting kicks in. The doe is startled and moving the whole bunch of them uphill, away from me. They have four legs, I only have two—no good to try and stalk them from below. Not much time before dark. But that means they just came uphill from the creek below— they've had their drink of water and are heading up to feed for the evening. Won't go far. Farther down this road there's a spur road that cuts uphill. I saw it when I passed this way earlier. Does it go above them?

I drive on, come to a road angling uphill, but it doesn't look like what I remember. I hesitate, then hear the *kwash! kwash! kwash!* of a bluejay, and see the black-headed blue form flying up the spur road, following the open avenue between trees. Bluejays have always led me to game, so I don't even have to think about it. Drive slowly up the new road until I top the ridge. Park and get out, load my rifle. Light fading fast. Too bad it's so cloudy to the west—thick overcast coming from the coast. Getting hard to see far back in the trees. I walk silently, slowly down along the more open ridge. No thoughts, total alert, eyes scanning. If they came up this far, they'd probably come out about here. I stop, listen, sweep the darkening world around me. It's probably too late, too dark, too unlikely. I'm about to give up and go back when I hear a noise behind me, hooves running, the deer crossing the ridgetop back the way I came. Well, that's it—they must have gotten by me. But I'm still alert, still scanning for sound. A fainter sound. Walking. The buck lagging behind the others. Comes into view and stops, backlighted against the sky. Antlers turned so I know he's looking at me raising my rifle. "Thank you, brother," I breathe, aiming. He doesn't move. Bang, and he goes down on his front knees. It's fatal, but he's up and disappears quickly downhill the way he came.

I follow the sound of him crashing through the brush, my heart pounding, lungs working hard in the thin air. I stay far back but close enough to keep him within earshot. I don't dare stop and let him die undisturbed—I'd lose him in the coming darkness. He angles uphill and I have to run to keep up, lungs burning now and leg muscles cramping. Out into the open and across the road my car is parked on. Then I hear him stumbling into heavy lodgepole timber, thrashing around because there's so many down trees crisscrossed and tangled together.

I come upon the buck just as a sudden reddish glow of light blinds me—the last seconds of distant sunset penetrating the timber. Laying down my rifle, I dive in and grab the buck by the antlers. He goes down with the force of my weight, but there's still some struggle left in him. I've grabbed the most dangerous part of him, and when he comes alive for one last fight at the moment of death, my unthinking leap and grab seem suddenly foolhardy. I can't let go to reach for my knife. His hooves dig in and his massive neck muscles yank his antlers around, slamming me against tree trunks, the bloody froth from his mouth drenching me. But my adrenaline-locked fists don't let go. He's so big I realize that if he hadn't been shot in the chest and lost so much blood, he would have easily overcome me, gored me. He weakens and sags, panting out bloody bubbles. Each breath becomes a frothy, rattling struggle. I don't let go. The kill trance is passing and I'm overwhelmed once again, as I always am, with regret at taking another's life.

Not letting go of his antlers, I speak to him, voice full of the emotion I feel. Tell him in these last moments of his life how grateful I am he's dying for me. How I'll treat his body good. How we'll eat his flesh and be strong and remember this gift of himself so we can live. He draws his last, long, sighing breath and goes still. We're both covered in blood and reeking of the deer-rut smell permeating his body hair. My hands go limp on his antlers and I feel like I have no strength left, but it's almost dark so I have to keep moving. Stand up and start to drag his deadweight by the antlers, back toward the road. So heavy. So hard over and around logs, under leaning snags. Inching along, jammed and then freed, his body heavier than I am, dragging and then resting to pant for a few seconds. So grateful it's not uphill, but still feels like my arms are being pulled out of their sockets. Wish somebody was along to help me . . .

I stopped still, the feel of my hands holding the buck's antlers just like in the dream sending a chill down my spine. I had forgotten all about it. When I first saw the deer crossing the road, all memory had disappeared. From then on I had acted only on what was in front of me to do. Now it all floods back. I'm stunned at how so much has happened like the dream. How even though I couldn't find the pile of logs, it happened anyway, and there I was, grabbing a buck's antlers. Facing the sunset. In the pole forest with down trees blocking things all around. And then wishing I had someone to help me. How I had been thinking there was no use going on, but this deer was practically handed to me anyway.

I slump down, overcome with wonder. Hands still holding the

antlers, I look around at the dark forest I'm in, at the darkening world becoming vague and remote.

"Thank you, thank you," I blurt out, straight from the heart, feeling the presence of that man so long ago in childhood who said it was easy to catch birds flying by. Then the other man in my dream and the blue-jay that led me up the road connect in my mind. "And you, too, Bluejay. If that's who you are . . ."

But there's no time to linger. It's almost pitch dark. I get up and drag the buck onward until I come out at a wide place on the road, what looks like an old landing, a place bulldozed flat where logs were loaded onto trucks. I leave the dead buck at the top of a cutbank and trudge back for my rifle. Then go a different way through the woods, stumbling and snagging myself on invisible limbs, until I come out on the road again near my car. Exhausted and drained, I get in, start the engine, turn on the lights, and drive to the landing. Everything flat and mechanical now, I get out, lower the tailgate, and back up to the cutbank so I won't have to lift the deer up. He weighs over 200 pounds, so it seems impossible. But it's easy to drag the body downhill onto the tailgate and into the back of my station wagon, onto a canvas tarp. When I have the back slammed shut I lean against the fender, relieved. In the glare of the headlights, I see some kind of horizontal structure behind a screen of young trees shooting up at the far side of the landing. Curious, I walk over for a closer look.

My god, it's the pile of rotting logs I was looking for . . .

With nothing more to do but drive back, I linger. Muddled thoughts drift by. The doe and yearlings out there in the darkness somewhere, no longer followed everywhere by the buck. The buck's spirit hovering somewhere nearby, aware, watching me. I move to the back of my car, crank down the rear window, sprinkle loose tobacco on his body, say "Thank you," my voice breaking the silence. It's getting really cold now, and spreading overcast is blotting out the first stars overhead.

Then the long, winding miles back the way I came, down to the valley below, musing on how simple life was, how good and sweet and true when I followed my heart and acted on things like this dream that had come true. Along the way, I remembered to stop and chop Douglas fir boughs, and piled them on top of the deer in back.

Early night in the lowlands, electric lights locating each homestead. Driving the paved road in a daze. Finally I turned up the river road and pulled in at the Woods place. No outside lights—just brightly lit windows. I stopped and sat there, wondering what to do next. I'd helped Jim and Clayton butcher deer and mountain goats on a little grassy rise by the corral, so I turned around and backed up to it, dimly visible in the brake lights.

Clayton and Jim came out to see who it was, followed by Jim's nephew, four-year-old Brandon. I was shivering in the damp, river-bottom cold as I opened the tailgate and dumped out all the fir boughs, making a bed on the ground for the deer.

"Huh, somebody come back with you," Clayton said with studied casualness. But both of them were leaning over the tailgate, looking the deer over by the dim glow of the dome light, barely restraining their interest.

Then Jim: "Hey, nobody took the guts out and cooled 'em off." Nothing more than a statement of fact, but there was an accusation in his words. If a large animal isn't opened and cooled soon enough, the meat can spoil from the lingering body heat. This was no way to treat such a gift. I knew better—hadn't I promised to do right by him when he died for me?

"Too tired," I said lamely.

"Have to work quick, then."

"I brought him here for Charlene," I added, unable to remember the formula way of saying it in Salish.

"*Aaaa, wai i hwi* (So be it)," he said.

"She's in the kitchen," Jim said, smiling, always the big eater of venison. "Hot coffee on the stove." They both knew I was the one who'd have to take the consequences of mistreating a deer I'd killed.

As they grabbed hooves and antlers and dragged the limp body over the tailgate, I went up the porch steps and inside, suddenly aware of how grubby and bloody I was in the bright lights of their clean house. My hunting eyes were still reading the significance of everything I looked at. The three girls of other mothers that Charlene was raising had grown into gangly teenagers doing homework around the big table. Charlene looked grayer but more dynamic than I had noticed before. More authoritative and more an elder now that Grandma was fading into her late eighties and lapsing into long silences and seemingly unaware of much that went on around her as she sat in her favorite dining room chair. I stood in the kitchen doorway smelling of deer musk and blood and fir sap, waiting for Charlene to finish what she was doing and acknowledge my presence. I heard someone sniffing and turned to find Grandma next to me, looking up at me with shining eyes and a devilish smile, as if the good, old-time smell of me had awakened her to the vivid present.

Charlene glanced at me with a hardness that came of her conviction that she had to hold strong to the ways of her upbringing for the sake of others. Moments like this, turns in the road of life—a White man accepted into her family bringing her a stick with blood on it, a token of the larger gift outside—she typically used to drive home her messages of how to live like a real person, a Native, a *Skélux*. I said nothing but offered her the stick, and she took it, her lips pursing for the words I knew were coming.

"*Liiiimtenun'tum,* make me feel glad. Be given the gift, this make my heart feel good. To eat good because somethin' helpin' you in life. Make me feel glad that you maybe see it don't come to you, for you alone. The power be easier to handle when you do like this, give away what good he bring. Like to feed that *shumíx,* tame him, when you benefit others."

Back outside with a mug of steaming *lecaapi* in hand, the hot black medicine warming my flat, empty insides, I see the buck on his side on the bed of fir boughs. Only Brandon is there in the dark, shivering with no coat in the cold stillness. There's no stars—the cloudiness that I saw coming from the west at sunset has spread over the whole sky, a dense overcast muffling and silencing the world. Jim comes back from his travel trailer swinging an old kerosene lantern, and as he lights it, Clayton shows up again to sit on the tailgate, sharpening some knives on a hand-held stone. Jim sets the lamp on the ground and Brandon bends over, hands propped on knees, studying the deer's face, the sightless dark eyes, the bloody tongue hanging out one side of the mouth. He listens to his uncle and great-uncle speaking in soft voices to the buck, thanking him and saying see, we laid you on the fir bed, just like how you want to be butchered. He listens to them promising to treat the deer's body how he wants, how the first deer at the time of the coming of human people said he wanted to be treated, in return for giving his body as food to the new people. Saying more than they usually do at times like this—indirectly making a point I don't miss.

Brandon straightens up and says unself-consciously: "You can't get up, deer. You can't run any more. Tom shot you with his rifle. Now we're going to eat you." Then he turns and runs back into the house.

Smiles all around at the mature sound of his words. I'm sitting on the tailgate, exhausted and weak, sipping my coffee with a hand barely strong enough to lift the cup. It's been a long, hard day. Jim and Clayton go to work without me, moving slowly and expertly by the dim lamplight flickering in the gloom. They turn the buck onto his back and straddle him at chest and hindquarters, propping his now stiffly extended legs upward and apart with their own legs. Then Clayton slits open the skin of the belly with one smooth stroke of his knife blade held between two fingers of his other hand. They fist the hide back and Clayton opens the gut and spills the steaming entrails off to one side. Their movements are confident and efficient from a lifetime of butchering animals. They work together with few words, Jim doing the heaviest parts, Clayton commenting on what he finds: the healthy condition of the buck, the thickness of the fat, the large size of the liver, the bullet hole through one side of the heart.

They pause to eat slices of liver, and a bloody hunk is placed in my hand. The familiar salty, quivery, raw-meat taste of deer liver—and as I eat more and more, a fire begins to burn inside me. It always amazes me how fast raw liver and blood races through my body, energizing me and bringing me back to life. I killed a deer, and with this simple ritual that non-hunters never seem to understand, I suddenly feel his death giving me new life. Nothing else I've ever eaten has this immediate effect, this rush of energy and renewed strength.

It's so still, so hushed, so oppressively musty and muffled by the invisible roof of clouds that I can't even hear the nearby river. The mountains are so socked in around us that the circle of feeble light cast by the lantern illuminates the two of them butchering the deer as if inside a cave. The sounds and grunted words are flat, cut short, unnaturally muted. But then I hear the rustle of leaves—the distinct sound of a breath of wind blowing through the tall cottonwoods along the riverbank. Clayton and Jim stop abruptly, straighten up, and listen as I do. The sound comes and goes, rises and falls. Yet there's no wind where we are, not even a breeze. And no sound anywhere else but from the nearby cottonwoods.

Clayton cocks his head and I see him by lantern light, eyes closed, listening intently, his hands hanging at his sides, shiny with blood. As we listen, it's clear there's no wind whatever, just the same utterly calm, gloomy stillness, yet every once in a while, faintly, the leaves of nearby *múl'xilhp,* cottonwood trees, rustle as if moved by wind. I stare into the darkness where I hear the sound coming from, expecting at any moment to feel the wind hit me, to hear it move around us, move in the bushes and other trees. But it doesn't. There's no sense of wind anywhere—just the soft soughing of invisible cottonwood leaves.

Jim lifts the lantern by its wire bail and takes a few steps toward the sound, holding the light high, at arm's length. We can dimly see the individual fluttering of hundreds of drying leaves. Only the cottonwoods are moving. The leaves of other trees—willow and birch and alder—are perfectly still beside the cottonwoods.

"That's the sign, ain't it?" Jim said.

"Yah, that's it all right," Clayton responded. Then he turned to me.

"*Múl'xilhp* tell us somethin', if we have the ears to hear. They do like that, shake around when no wind is blowin', tell us a big storm is comin'."

8

THE NEXT MORNING, winds of an approaching storm blew hard from the west, and the sky in that direction was an ominous slate black. The wind would drop for brief rain showers, then turn into blinding, wind-driven snow squalls. Back and forth, rain mixed with snow alternated with damp cyclonic winds that tore through the valley, stripping leaves from trees. The western peaks began to disappear in an oncoming blurry vagueness, and I knew we were in for a big one, just as Clayton had interpreted the sign the night before.

He and I were out in it, of course, on foot heading east, dressed for the worst, no food or weapons or packs impeding a footloose wander in the hills. Letting the wind push us along from behind. Following the horse trail up Little Brother Mountain, and then once through the flimsy gate, we turned steeply uphill, scattering a flock of magpies gathered at something that smelled dead back in the brush. I was exulting in the blow, grinning like a fool at how alive storm winds always made me feel, and marveling how the route Clayton picked out going up the slope always kept the wind huffing at our backs, making the climb easy. Fueled and warmed by Charlene's breakfast of venison, bitterroots, serviceberry pudding, and other Native delicacies brought out of storage on the occasion of fresh deer meat, we ascended the steepest part without stopping and came out on top.

But Clayton didn't pause or look back, just kept striding along in his mile-eating pace ahead of me, and I knew I was in for a long day's hike. I should have known what was up when he'd suggested early that morning that we "go for a stroll" *(ḳwu taḳu'út),* the same thing he always said when a forced march was what he had in mind. Not that it mattered. It was such a relief to be done with the indoor nine-to-five, to be a hunter, a wanderer, reading it all, taking it all in, off with Clayton again to who knew where.

Up on Little Brother's rolling, open plateau, the wind was fierce and shooed us along like unwilling children—all we had to do was move our feet and keep our balance as it pushed us from behind faster than we ordinarily walked. Streamers of cloud racing by sometimes closed in on us as fog, as icy breath blotting out anything but the ground before our feet. It was so much fun I laughed for the sheer joy of it just like the ravens croaking past sideways on the wind, whose acrobatic antics in the midst of such a ferocious wind couldn't be anything other than play. We followed a long ridge that led gently downward into heavy timber, miles of pine and fir trees creaking and swaying in the wind, limbs lashed and tossing in sudden gusts.

A familiar dulling of my mind settles in. Memories float by. I remember the time Old Willie's grandson, Roger Antoine, and I killed an elk on top of a mountain in deep snow right at sunset. We'd been tracking them all day and were desperate for meat during a long, hard winter. Even though we were exhausted, we were elated by our success and worked fast to skin and gut and quarter the huge body of the animal. Unfortunately we had no pack frames with us, so we each shouldered a massive hind leg and staggered the long downhill miles in the dark, back to where his car was parked. We found a rope in his trunk and hiked back up. By tying the rest of the meat up in two halves of the skin and rigging loops for our shoulders, we managed to pack down the rest of the elk, each of us stumbling along in deep snow bent under hundred-pound loads of dripping meat. The pain of ropes biting into our shoulders made us stop every few yards and shift the load. Light-headed, dizzy, so utterly exhausted we could hardly get back up to go on, we laughed at each other every time one of us fell floundering in the snow. Halfway down, the moon came up and we stopped to rest in the snow, leaning back against our hairy packs, both of us gazing around at the stark wintry world lit up by moonlight. It was bitterly cold, the wee-hour stillness so vast in the desolation of mountains, the open sky, the endless white to every horizon. We were suffering, frost-bitten, beyond any normal limit of endurance, and there were still many miles to go, yet were both moved by how beautiful the world was. Far away we could see the faint lights of a town.

"Nobody but fools like us would be up here killin' ourselves like this, in the cold, in the night," I said. "But I'll tell you what—I'd rather be up here than down there in a warm bed, or starin' at television!"

I remember Roger sighed in agreement and said, "Yeah, this is what a man was made for, eh?"

Clayton turned abruptly left, bringing me out of my reverie. I followed him picking his way down a steep ravine along a game trail that rounded a bluff. We were shielded from the worst of the wind and sleet, and the trail widened and became a well-worn cowpath leading to a spring on steep slopes facing north. We stopped to lift handfuls of sweet, organic-tasting water to our mouths, then sat and rested, for the first time in hours not battered by wind.

The high black roof of cloud was closer, nearly overhead, and the hills to the north were only faintly visible through the horizontal racing of rain and snow. Around us the first snow of the year was filtering down and whitening the wet ground in patches. Gusts found their way into our protected hollow behind the bluff, stirring the Scouler willows and brush maples standing in mud, freeing the autumn leaves to flutter down like bright yellow and red litter scattered under the dripping forest trees. The hissing, muffled silence of the world being transformed by snow, the last circles of green grass around the trunks of trees, the patches of lichens peeking through the thin skin of white in luminous shades of lime, orange, and yellow. And both of us in a daze of fatigue, drinking it all in, shivery lips and watery eyes, our soggy boots and wet gloves and wool layers steaming from the inner fire of bodies at rest after hours of exertion in the storm.

Clayton began humming softly to himself, breaking the long silence between us with a tune I vaguely remembered. It sounded like a sweat-lodge song, rhythmic and monotonous, following a melodic line that slid quavering from note to note, and repeated the same pattern at different tones. Minutes passed before he finally caught the emotional power of the song and sang out loud with unusual passion, his body swaying back and forth, his eyes staring blindly downward.

I began to hum along, and soon I was singing with him the way I used to learn sweatlodge songs from him—lagging slightly behind, concentrating on matching every sound, putting my heart into it until I could feel the power of it myself. It was some kind of song to the weather and felt very old with oddly constructed phrases about the color of the sky. When I had the song memorized, anticipating every change so our voices were synchronized and rising above the distant roar of wind, his voice faded away and abruptly stopped.

"*Aaaa,* there, you can sing that song, I give that to you," he said. "Sing to know the weather."

"*Limlempt* (Thank you)."

"*Wai, ta'lí anhamínk i skesásket, i sniwt, ixí asisyústin* (You sure like the stormy weather, the wind, that's your power)."

"*Wai, wuníux* (That's true)," I said. "Have to have somethin' extra to keep up with you!"

He laughed.

"My want to show you somethin'," he said, fingering the loose ends of a black bandana tied around his wrist. "That why I come this way. Place I know, not far. Good place for the spirit, *en'x'xá'em,* like I show you some others. But this one good place to talk about what I got. This one weather power, my want to pass on to you how this gift come to me and I know the weather. Like my elder, long ago, take the time to tell me how to know the weathers. So now, I pass on the gift."

"*Aaaa.*"

"We look in life for the ones who respect our feelings, who have that *xast pu'ús,* that good heart. Not many have that want to live, that want to know how the power move in the world. Even my nephew Jim, he not care for the hard trails. We look for the one who have other eyes. Who don't suffer in the bush. Who have that respect for someone's feelings. Go off like the power show in a dream, grab the deer by the antlers. Bring 'em home and give away, the keepsake, the gift passed on to others. Make me feel glad, so in this way, we devote ourself to each other in life. Share what good come to us."

We got up and drank from the spring again, then backtracked, rounding the bluff into the teeth of the storm. The way he was heading—striking off south into lower country along a chain of hills—put into mind a hidden alkaline lake I'd once seen years before, when I was a ranch hand working for Stuart Bolster, walking out range fences to repair winter damage. Clayton was heading in that direction, and the lake was definitely *en'x'xá'em,* a power spot, a sacred place, literally "where something is powerful or dangerous." Even the local Whites called it a spooky place. And Stuart, who'd ridden the range with Indian cowboys all his life, called it "Naháhum" Lake, the Anglicized version, which he said meant "haunted."

It took another hour of steady hiking, much harder with the wind driving against us from the side, before it became obvious that's where he was going. The country was more bare and open, mostly brush and grass with timber only on the north-facing slopes. Clayton kept to the east side of the rolling hills, walking ahead of me, picking a route that I could see wasn't the easiest way to the lake. But it afforded us some protection from the wind and wet, and kept us well away from the dirt roads and barbed wire fences that followed the easier way through this heavily grazed cattle country. He led the way down a deep draw that approached the lake from the north, then before reaching the bottom at the water's edge, he sidehilled around the base of a cliff where we picked our way carefully over loose slides of boulders to a rock overhang.

It was a natural shelter from the storm, a dry, musty-smelling recess under dull, olive-gray rock that curved up out of sight above us. A place big enough for many people to crowd into and camp, as the fire-blackened roof gave sign of happening in times past. A huge pack rat nest cluttered up one side with tangled sticks and cactus pads, showing that few people ever came here anymore. We sat down and made ourselves comfortable on the other side. Below, the water washed noisily at the base of a steep talus slope.

Really not much more than a big pond, a pothole left by glaciers, Naháhum Lake spread out below us in a bowl of steep-sided hills. In the misty grayness of the storm, the water revealed nothing of the blue-green color that such alkaline lakes loaded with minerals usually have. Unlike the other side of the bowl where grass and individual pine trees grew, our side of the lake was steep and rocky, almost inaccessibly brushy with tangled sumac, chokecherry, poison ivy, mock orange, and wild rose. Where the bare dirt of the rock shelter fell away into the broken, angular rocks of the slide, there was a thick stand of gromwell, bushy plants that typically grow in pure stands a few feet tall on warm, south-facing slopes. This late in the season the plants were faded, gone to seed, bedraggled, moving in the wind on stiff stems with a dry, autumnal, hissing, clickering sound that was somehow soothing. The soft clicking came from hundreds of white, hard, glossy seeds touching in the sway of wind, and looked like big white trade beads loosely strung through the thicket at our feet. The seeds stood out brightly against the wet drabness of withered plants and dark rock.

After a long rest out of the wind and wet, Clayton finally spoke.

"You maybe know this plant?" he asked, gesturing at the gromwell.

"Yeah," I replied. They were distinctive plants, very noticeable to anyone in summertime with their creamy lemon flowers massed in huge clumps, always found in warm, protected pockets of the land like this. I knew Old Willie dug the roots to make a tea that tasted terrible but stopped a person from spitting blood or passing a bloody stool or getting bloody noses. He'd told me it was the best medicine for any kind of internal bleeding, but I'd just filed it away and never used the plant. Now I listened to Clayton telling me how these plants "knew" the weather better than any other plant, and that's why they grew in protected places like this, facing the sun, never bothered by even the worst of storms. Always the first to emerge from the snow, or living in places that were bare of snow even in winter. Even though there was no sign of the sun, sitting in the protection of the rock overhang I was warm and comfortable for the first time that day, so I could easily understand what he was saying about gromwell's preferences.

"We come here to this place good to talk about weather power," he said. "First, to know this powerful person who show hisself as the little plant, what we see, live together only in the warm place like this. Lotta old timers, they won't touch this here plant, don't walk in it, don't let it brush against 'em. A real mystery what this one can do, and maybe they respect that. Call 'em 'hailstone plant' and leave 'em alone."

I looked closely at the shiny white seeds waving before us, how the ones that had fallen looked like hailstones scattered and drifted into piles on the rocks. And how each seed, I now noticed, had a prominent ridge across the top, a tiny linear deformity that looked like a raised point, the way the arrowhead shapes pointed outward on the edges of painted figures in old pictographs that signified having spiritual power. Clayton opened his coat, unbuttoned his flannel shirt and showed me he was wearing a necklace of strung gromwell seeds against his skin.

"But now, for the man who want to know the weather, this the one who give the gift," he said with a smile, his eyes shining, letting his words sink in. "With this one, I talk to the weathers. To the storm, the rain, the snow. To the thunders, the dry wind, the drizzle. To whatever, sing their song, and they have to come, or go. And this one, he know 'em all. Just like my elder tell me, come to a place like this, all alone, suffer for the gift, maybe this one take pity and instruct about the weather.

"Like I tell you before, any power man have that thing to say over, *sen'ch'ch'wístem,* whatever the power instruct 'em to say or do to call on the power. Now the one other thing. Maybe show you somethin' to have, to hold in the hand, for you to call on the power. What we call *shiyá'ut,* maybe like to say, some little thing that have the power. Some kinda thing, like this here necklace, strong to make you feel what you got. Some little thing, you touch it, you hold it, make you shake, tremble all over, feel that what you got comin' to you right from it. Only what they show you to have, to keep, and then bring out when you have need. Some little part of themself, how they show themself in the world to the ordinary way of lookin', but sent just for you, and have that power you can feel."

Immediately, I thought of the falcon tail feathers that inexplicably washed up at my feet from the ocean years before when I was watching the sunset. I'd carefully kept the feathers with me for years and preserved them in a fan hanging from my wall at home, to honor the many times falcons had appeared at critical moments in my life to help me, teach me, warn me, or show me something to do.

"*Aaaa,* I hear you," I said, letting him know I understood that he was doing more than just revealing his weather power, he was also using it as an example to teach me more widely about the lore of having power.

"So this here one we call 'hailstone,' he the one we go to if we want to gain that power, that knowledge. He the first. But now, not anybody can be the one who know the weather. Only the one the power choose to be that. See, to have the story handed down, to live what I learn from my elder, many years pass and I do what he show me, then I have it, but not quite. Good enough to see how the weather move, to move with the weather, to know what the weather gonna do. But not to have the weather do what I ask. Have to suffer on my own in a place like this for that gift, like my elder do, and his elder before him.

"But then, to know what to suffer for, where to look, eh? That the second part, the number two thing I pass on—how the weather move."

He scooted forward and gestured for me to join him, both of us sitting more out in the wet, our knees pressed into the bushy gromwell right at the drop-off, leaning forward so we could gaze down at the expanse of lake below. The roar of wind seemed distant in this protected hollow, and the showers of sleet and rain slanted from right to left in gusty blasts out in the open. He had me study the water below, take in how it showed itself to us, using *wik'wst,* the Salish eye-training that hunters used to scan the surroundings (usually translated as "seeing what's hidden"). He said to stay with it until I was sure what color the lake was showing. "All one color," as he put it, and there were only four possibilities—red, blue, yellow, or black. Then we were quiet for a long time. Clayton faintly hummed the tune of the song he'd given me back at the spring, while I sank deep into the task of observing the water of the lake.

At first it's hard to see any color at all—the whole world is gray and dim and misty, a watercolor vagueness that seems to be mirrored in the shadowy shifting of churning waves trending so relentlessly from right to left. There's the usual effect of steady movement to the left that pulls my eyes along, staying with the wind-driven lines of waves until they wash up on the eastern shore. I finally stop thinking about how that's just water flowing by down there and really lock onto the entire field of exactly what my eyes are seeing. I'm so weary from hours of walking in blasting wind that it's easy to let go into the single-minded glossing of what is coming to my eyes. I'm no longer looking at where my eyes are focused but am studying the blurry outer edges of my field of vision, which holds my eyes locked in one place. When I feel the familiar tingle behind my eyes that comes when everything freezes, there's a rich, vivid blackness to the water that is unmistakable. My attention is so narrowed, I forget what I'm doing and simply lose myself in the undulating, glossy surface of the lake water, marveling at the spumes of frothy white that blow out from the tops of cresting waves, and wondering vaguely how I never consciously noticed before that lake water was always this glassy obsidian during a storm.

"So, we gonna sit out here all day?" Clayton said quietly at my side, breaking the spell. "There not much to it. . . . What color?"

"Uh, black," I said.

"Aaaa," he responded, holding up his wrist with the black bandana I'd noticed before tied around his wrist. It was the typical kind of cotton cowboy bandana for sale in feed stores, the same kind we all used in outdoor work to catch sweat around our neck or head, wrap up cuts or wounds, or any of a number of uses.

"This not the same as the *shiyá'ut,* not somethin' to feel the power and call it up. This the badge of *sen'ḵwúlchinum,* like to say in English, 'weather.' This now how I tellin' you why I wear this piece of black this day, how we know the weather, and so we have the way in to the power. See, the weather paint the sky, fix the one color, and right there on the lake is where you see it. On the river, whatever. The open water. You lookin' at the water to see how the weather is fixed for the day. Just to look at the sky, you don't see so well, but now, you look down into the water, then you see it. See, you lookin' *down* into the sky. So that's what happen, you stare like that, *wik'wst,* not to any one place but around the edges, and what you see shiver a little, feel your eyes, take you to that other lake way up above. You see what they see, the lake spread out below, all one color, whatever color the weather paint. See, what up there, that's what down here, and what down here, that's what up there.

"Maybe the red, and that's good, that the best power kinda weather for just to be alive. Real hot, kinda burn you up. Full of life so much it weigh you down, push you down to just sit and breathe. Best for how this plant like to live," he said, brushing his hand through the gromwell.

"Just the four colors, like the wind blow, four directions. Come from the south, the east, the north, the west. Blow from there, from that direction, and each one the person. But they not choose which one to blow. They take the turns, whatever color paint the sky. The day is fixed for 'em and they switch. Like the blue, now, it have a paint like blue, and that's the cool, the north, clear-like, or maybe it's winter and you just lookin' at where the river is open, where it don't freeze, no ice, and it's blue. That the coldest then, that *iyoh'músh* so hard, north wind make it hard to live.

"Then maybe you see the yellow. You lookin' down deep into the sky and you see the yellow, and you know the Chinook is comin', he's here. That east wind come and thaw the world, or maybe at the other season, blow the fresh and clear. Whenever, always bring the relief. Switch places.

"Or like the black, what we see this day, the weather paint the sky, and everything down deep look like just dirtied-up, dark, nothin' but black. And that one from the west come with the storm, bringin' the stormy weather, the wet, the snow. Maybe many days, weeks—all like one day to 'em. One turn. Then change, another power, another wind. And even when they still, don't seem like no air move, you the good hunter who know where the scent go, you know which way it move." (He meant like on still days when hunting, licking your finger and holding it up high to feel which side gets coolest, or letting fine dust pour out of your hand and seeing which way it moved to the side.)

"But like my elder say, they don't choose. The one choose, she the real shiny one, live in that big water in the sky. She make the color, say what we have down here. Show herself as the light that shine out between the clouds. All how the water down here just hers, and so we see her, show herself the bright light between the clouds, and we look in the water at that, look down and see that, same as in the sky. Both places the same, like I said. And the water, that her power, so we look down in the water at that light shine out from the clouds, and we see like more, we see her show herself the woman, so shiny she blind us.

"Not like some say, she live in the ocean. Up there," Clayton said, lifting his chin, eyes looking upward. "Maybe like the ocean, all water, but not what over on the coast. Well, that's hers, too. But she up there. Up above.

"She a great woman who do that. She set the day, fix it, and so we have the red day, the yellow day, the blue day, the black day. All a different wind, a different weather power to live by. And the man who know that, he can get on the right trail for that day, the good trail like we follow today, the black day, the west wind, storm blow so hard to blow us along. Follow that trail away from the water's edge to whatever he have to do. Whatever the power of that day good for. What color that is. And they used to do that, the ones who want to know the weather, make a piece of somethin', four of 'em, and paint each one the different color. Only now with the colored cloth. Like when you set out to travel, to go on the mission or to go a long ways, maybe to hunt. But every day, no matter what you gonna do, to look in the open water and see what the weather fix the day for, and you put that color out, like to wear that, like tied around the wrist. Call to that shiny woman, wherever she may show herself the light between the clouds, say look, I wearin' your color today. Draw her with you away from the water, to help you where you goin', what you doin'.

"Her want to be with the man or woman who do like that, live in her mood like that. And you doin' that, you learn what that power is like. You live it, you see what move, how things go. What work and what don't. The different way the weathers make things happen.

"And like how your own power work in the different weathers, the different wind. How one feel good, another one just so, and maybe another one don't like much at all. Can't hardly call up nothin', maybe, because don't care for that weather. But then the one feel best of all, that one feel like the power just oozin' out of everything, call it up in a snap.

Or maybe just one part of that weather, like when it first come on, or when it fade away.

"Like today, to be painted the black weather in the sky. But now it come on the big one, the storm wind, and I know that, but that not quite the part for me, what feel the best for me. Maybe for you the favorite time, the power of the wind easy for you to call on the power, eh? But for me, I lookin' for the change to the steady fall of wet. And when that man I know, the one I got, he doin' the work, pourin' out the steady wet, the rain or snow, that when I feel the best. How the power fill me up in the rain fallin', the snow fallin' just endless. Maybe you notice that?"

I nodded. I'd noticed it for years. Once the wind that brought a storm faded into serious rain or snow, became what for me was just wet, dreary weather, Clayton came alive more than at any other time.

"But now, we here for you, the White man who maybe want to know the weather. Blowin' like this, I see you at your best. So I know you hear good what I have to say. This one way to keep the power close, keep you ready for when the power come on you. Puttin' the color on you to live in the weather. That way, no matter what, you paying atten- tion, you thinkin' about power, you always watchin', lookin' around at how the power move in the world. But also, you do this in life, you get good at it, train for it many years, you find you know somethin'. Know the sign and feel what comin'. Like now, for me, the old man who maybe know little bit about the weather, to know what comin'. You watch, keep comin' on like this to just before the light fade. Then the heavy rain, all rain, no snow this time. And rain all night. Come the new day, still rainin' till about late morning. Fade away and stop before noon. Then sun come out. You see if that don't happen how I say. This kinda knowin' come to anybody who follow how this go, live it, train with the colors. Well, maybe not anybody, but like the weather man on TV, have that want to know, train for it the years of education, learn to see the sign, what to look for. The most nowadays, even the Indian, don't have the desire. Maybe just *xwupt,* not up to it. Sorta like big kids, and don't care how the world work. Don't pay attention, ain't it?

"No, we look for the ones tryin' to wake up. Those the ones we pass the power on to. Like my elder, he see me like that, *ḳilht,* when I just wakin' up the grown man. I just cryin' about how I see that light between the clouds, that shiny woman, and so he take me as his nephew, he take the time to pass on to me what he have. And that how it go, *ḳ'empla enchútments* (he or she claims you as a relative). So I just pass it on, pass it on, what been passed on to me.

"And no good but you do it yourself. Not like the priest make the sign of the cross and that's it, you got it. No, first it like a story. You hear it, so you walk that trail. You get on the good trail, the trail that story tell about, the trail that have power. You face into the trail that just yours to go on, and you learn somethin' as you walk that way. And all that story tell about, you live it, you see it. No story anymore. Then someday, you have that, you know how the power move, and you live by that. Maybe the time come you tell the story, you pass it on. And you know what I tell you this day, same as I know now about my elder tellin' me so long ago, to not fool ourself about power. Power can be the biggest liar if we foolin' ourself, if we just foolin' around. But now, you can tell when you listen, how the man tell it, whether he livin' the story he tell."

9

CLAYTON TALKED ON FOR something like an hour, telling me specific things that gave sign of weather changes, most of which were things I'd perceived but not seen how they were connected to weather. Some I'd never even heard of, like how a certain little fish in the Okanogan River, a tiny sculpin, if bothered could bring on prolonged periods of rain, or how slight differences in the way snow smelled could predict how soon it would stop falling. Then he shifted to telling me more about the shiny woman and how everything you learned about the weather led back to how the light looked shining between the clouds. If I learned something, recognized some sign, saw a prediction come true, I should stop and look at how the light looked coming between the clouds in the sky at that moment, preferably by looking down in water at it if there was a body of water close enough, but in the sky if that was all that was possible. That way I'd begin to see how she showed herself differently at those specific turns in the weather, and eventually I would get to the point where all I had to do was "cloud-gaze" in water to know what the weather was going to do. Even in clear weather there were usually some clouds somewhere in the sky, where she was hiding. And in those times when there weren't, usually the red days of midsummer heat, but sometimes in the blue days, especially in winter when the north wind brought the coldest temperatures, he said these were the times to look at the gromwell plants. Particularly in the long dry days of summer, I should learn to see how these clumps of gromwell presented themselves, because such times "belonged" to this plant. And even though where you found them was in the hottest, sunniest, most uncomfortable places in such weather, you could learn to glance at them and know instantly what weather was coming.

Finally he told me more about his own particular weather gift, something I never expected from an old Okanogan, most of whom go to the grave without ever spelling out the particulars of what they "have" in life. He told me he was doing it because ever since the Whites had come and changed the world, it was harder for anybody to "grab onto" the power. He related anecdotes of how he received messages or warnings from his spirit partner, and how, as a grown man with other power from his childhood, he was quicker in taming this one, in learning how to call on him and in knowing when his power was trying to "come on him." He said that most of the time his power just "gave him a picture" of what was coming or what to do, and he used that to arrange his preparations or take action in life, or to "look into" things for others. Only rarely did he call on his *shumíx* to actually change the weather, and then only at times of great need, like the time Johnny Stemilt's nephew, Kootch, was stranded in the mountains by a big snowstorm.

It was a story I knew well—how Kootch had stayed up there too long on horseback searching for a cow and calf that had evaded being brought down with the rest of Old Man Rutherford's herd for winter. How he'd made a shelter in trees with his rain slicker to wait out the heavy fall of snow, and how his piebald mare got away and made it home without him the next day. How the snow came down without stopping for two days, prompting Johnny and Clayton to fire up a sweat and go in to see what they could do to find Kootch.

Johnny got a picture of where his nephew was, stranded in deep snow and suffering without a fire or any real protection from the cold. Clayton said the snow wasn't going to stop falling for another day, so he remained behind in the sweatlodge alone, calling on the storm to "take a breather" while Johnny went and borrowed Stuart Bolster's snowmobile, and started up the mountain in blinding snow. When the going got so tough that Johnny could hardly find his way, the snow suddenly stopped falling and the sun peeked out. He was able to make good time to the place where Kootch was shivering and delirious, and put him on the snow machine, no small task considering the younger man's immense girth and weight. Johnny raced back as fast as he could because the sky darkened and he knew it was going to start snowing hard again, which it did about the time he got to the unplowed forestry road. By then it was only a few miles to get where Stuart waited in his four-wheel-drive pickup, heater blasting and hot coffee in a thermos. The funny thing was, it never stopped snowing in the valley—it only cleared up where Johnny was in the mountains.

Johnny felt so grateful for what Clayton had done that he bought him the car that Clayton had been driving ever since I met him. Clayton told me in detail what he did with his necklace in the sweat-lodge that time, and how such times were the only time the necklace touched the ground. "Because then they listen to me, they know I doin' what I showed to do by the power, to let 'em know I not foolin' around, that the need is great." It didn't matter if he revealed what he did, he said, because a person did whatever they were shown by their partner to do. If somebody else tried to do what he did, followed the same steps, sang the same song, nothing would happen.

Then he was quiet for a while. Both of us were leaned back against the rear wall inside the overhang, looking out on the windy world framed by rock. In the relative dryness and calm, my clothes started to dry out and I was beginning to feel sleepy. I was on overload from absorbing the vast extent of all he'd told me, and humbled by his willingness to share such things with me. But as I pondered how I might act on what I'd learned, there seemed to be something missing.

"I wish I knew how to call on what I have," I finally mused aloud. "But I don't remember being shown how."

"Yah, hard to call it up, hard to grab onto it," he said softly. "Every little bit you remember of what he say, he do, he look like, everything like that, that how he showin' you."

I tried to call back the memory, to look at every detail that remained after all the years since my childhood, but it was so long ago and buried for so long unexamined in my memory that it seemed like a dream—

vague, blurry, uncertain. A strangely significant encounter with a man who called me over where he was standing in grass, in an opening between trees far from my home, backlit by the rising sun. How he seemed to know me and had been waiting for me. How he wanted to show me something. How he simply reached out his hand and caught a robin flying by and held it up for me to see, as if showing me a magic trick that was easy to perform. He'd said that it was easy, nothing to it, that it would be easy for me to do the same. And the sense that there was more, that he shared with me a secret that I grasped at the time, but that eluded me now whenever I tried to recall it. This secret had to be what Clayton was referring to as "grabbing onto" the power.

"You said it was harder nowadays to grab onto the power," I said to Clayton. "I wonder what made it any easier before my people came?"

"Somethin' anybody have to have, to know the powers, to feel 'em when they come," he mused, yawning, looking as sleepy as I was. "I think maybe you got it. How you know what you know, how you do what you do. Hard to find the words. Maybe you could say like a religious feeling. Somethin' like that. Feel touched, feel humbled by the world we come alive to be in. Feel it right here," and he pressed his left hand flat over his heart. "And that what we reach out to 'em with," he added, extending his right arm out and up, hand open, gesturing to the world beyond the rock shelter.

It was the last thing I expected him to say. I didn't think I had a religious bone in my body. I had a deep aversion to anything that smacked of the forced pose of devotion that passed for religious training in my childhood. But I had to admit my feeling for nature—for the wild, windy world we were looking at—was the closest thing to devotion I had in my life. And unlike the head-bowed, hands-clasped-together posture of submission that my own people adopted at "religious" moments, Clayton's hand gestures and awed look—the same as elders I'd seen praying in the longhouses—was head-held-high, direct, and a heartfelt reaching out to what was there around us. It was similar enough to how I remembered the *shumíx* man in my childhood reaching out for a robin flying by that I felt a bump, an unnamed recognition in Clayton's gesture.

"Maybe I've got some feeling like that," I said. "But I don't know that it does any good in trying to figure out what to do."

"Not many come around like you, *Skélux,*" he said, using one of his nicknames for me, the word for "person" or "Indian." I knew he was pulling it out now to reassure me. "Not the Indian or the White, either one. Why you think we talk to you how we do? What I sayin' to you not ever tell just anybody. We look at who come, look into the person. See what they know about, what they do, what they have interest in. What they have the gift for in life. Like Kenneth, now. He what he say, the biologist, and his want to know how the Indian know the animal. So we tell him what he can understand. Because we know what he thinkin'—that what we know beyond the muscle and the bone, what we have passed down the generation, just some song and dance. Some way we used to live so we could eat good, get enough to live on. Like we didn't know no better, but now with the White world, we oughta forget all that playin' around. But you see different."

"I suppose I do. . . . But I still don't get what it is we're supposed to grab onto."

Clayton made no sign that he'd heard me. I didn't really expect him to be any more specific than he'd already been—I knew that going at power with direct talk was useless. Then he sighed.

"Well . . . we see if you understand or not. This how they tell it:

"*Ks'aaaa'pi,* long, long ago, they go back into the mountains to hunt deer, pick berries. Some families, they go to that lake, the one you and me huntin' around that time the grouse was drummin'. Where those two blue mountains look at each other over the water of the lake. Just the two beautiful mountains, and so pretty you say you glad they save it, make it the state park. You remember that lake?"

I nodded.

"Well, used to be, they went up there and they camp on that lake. Two camps—some families they camp on the east side, some camp on the west. With the tent and the sticks put up to dry things, you know, what they catch to eat in winter. And each camp to be under one of those beautiful blue mountains.

"So, the one time, there's this boy who take the canoe like they used to make, and he go across the lake to the east side, to play with his friends. He do that every day, get up and paddle across, the sun hot, shinin' on his forehead. Then he play the most day with his buddies, you know. Sun go overhead, and pretty soon afternoon come, he feel that sun on his head gettin' lower, goin' down. So he paddle across home, that sun hot on his forehead again, that he facin' into the other way.

"See, that little boy, he's blind. He can't see nothin' but he can feel with his head where the sun is, and use that to guide 'em across. Well, so one day, he havin' so much fun playin', you know, havin' the good time with his friends, his cousins. And he forget about what he feel on his head. Just like anyone, he not think about what he have to do in life, he just let go and enjoy hisself. Till maybe he just remember, and it's late. Already low in the sky, the sun, and kinda weak. Just about to go down behind the mountain. So he quick, find that canoe, and he paddle fast as he can across that lake. He keep that feeble warm on his forehead, to know which way to go, to get across to home. But then, maybe in the middle of that lake, the sun drop behind the mountain. He can't feel no warm heat on his forehead, and he have to stop paddlin' because he don't know which way to go now. Maybe just go in circles.

"So that blind boy, he's *en'haitl, en'ḳopíls* (scared, lonely), and he just sit there wonderin' what to do. He can't do what he always used to doin', what heat up his head, what he come to rely on in life. He feel he have to reach out to what he don't know about. So then he do like that, he get up, stand up in the canoe, and he cup the hands and call out, '*La'ḳín?* (Where?)' Turn a little, call out '*La'ḳín?*' See, he go around and call in every direction, send the voice far with the hands cup around his mouth. 'Where? . . . Where? . . . Where? . . .'

"Just then, that boy's father, he comin' back from huntin' in the timber. He come down the mountain to camp, and he hear his son out there, callin' in that loud voice that is so scared. He see what happen, and he know what to do. He go down to the shore, cup his hands, and call out, '*Aḳelá!* (Over here!) . . . *Aḳelá!* . . . *Aḳelá!* . . .' And he keep that up so his blind son can paddle toward the sound of his father's voice. The voice he know, that he hear all his life since he growin' up. Maybe he get to the one side, and maybe to the other, and he have to turn a little when he hear his father call out. But he get closer and closer, that voice louder and louder, and then he make it to shore."

After a short pause, Clayton said, *"Wai i hwi,"* abruptly ending the story. He tilted his head back against the rock and closed his eyes.

It was a story I'd heard many times before, from other elders, and he was aware I knew the story because I'd asked him when we were hunting that time if that was the lake in the story. I'd never thought of it as a particularly interesting story, and wondered why elders seemed so into telling it. I once asked Johnny what he got out of the story, and he replied brusquely, "To have pride in my Indian heritage!" When I said I didn't understand what he meant, he said, "This story handed down, tell by mouth Indian to Indian, and to hear it and take it to heart, to have pride that we are the Indian and we know what to do."

After sharing with Clayton what Johnny had told me, I said I'd wondered afterward if the story was some expression of the Native way to handle blind or disabled children. Giving them the freedom to make their own way in the world, unlike the overprotective controls put on them in the White world, and relying on some ancient intuitive sense to be there for them when they faced unexpected danger, like the father in the story.

Clayton laughed with his eyes closed. Tears formed, and he shook his head, incredulous.

"That what you think now?"

"Well . . . no. I guess there has to be something else." Something was boiling under the surface of the story elements for me, but I couldn't dredge it up.

"Yah, what Johnny say is right. To hear the story, we know what to do. That story what you call the real deal. That the story how it is for us in the world, if you can catch it, eh?"

He was looking at me out of the corner of his eye.

"How it is for all of us come-alive people . . ."

"What? . . . Oh!" It went through me like an electric current, like a light suddenly going on inside me. We were all of us blind like that boy. . . . What I had considered a simpleminded story in my too-literal mind suddenly became a sophisticated parable about the nature of reality, about human relationship with nature spirits, about our limited

perception of the world, and a vivid set of instructions for how to proceed based on that picture. Every turn in the contrived plot described
the experience of anyone living an ordinary life who at some point had
to call on a higher power to go on. And yes, it was a very Indian sort of
story, a gem of insight hidden inside the clothing of everyday events
told in everyday words.

Clayton sat silently as I went back through the details of the story in
my mind, ruefully aware that I was at the same point as the blind boy
when the sun went down. That I couldn't do what I was always used to
doing, what "heated up my head," what I'd come to rely on in life. My
thoughts, my moves in the world based on my limited ability to perceive, were of no avail. I saw myself as the boy in the story—having to
call out blindly, call to someone invisible, someone who cared about me
like a father. Someone I had come to know as real by the effects of his
actions in the world I *could* see, which, to tell the truth, was pretty
flimsy evidence in a world where explanations of cause and effect were
king. Especially compared to the usual daily evidence of his absence.
Would he stand on a distant shore and call back, "Over here"?

More than anything else, I wanted to call on him, the man who
grabbed a robin out of the air, but my memory of him was so ineffable,
there was nothing clear to visualize about him. I began to sink into my
feeling for him like a longing, an indefinable emotional shifting downward that by degrees shut off my awareness of anything but a narrow
range of what was immediate in my surroundings. The natural world
in front of me seemed richer, brighter, more holy, as if something I
knew but couldn't remember was hidden in what I saw, waiting for me
to find it. The presence of Clayton beside me, the sense of being inside
a rock overhang, the line of thought and conversation that had led me
to this moment—it all faded in a thoughtless, pinpoint awareness of the
intricate detail the world presented to my eyes. And I let go into it with
the unlikely certainty of having done it before.

Showers swept over the lake in a blurring of nearby brush, a slapping of tiny drops on rock, a rustling of ironwood shrubs. The ironwood hung with wispy sprays like dried foam, what had brushed off as
hairy seed-dust on my coat sleeves. The wilted scarlet of sumac held up
cone-like clusters of seeds that showed sign of birds feeding on them.

The last stiff raisins of serviceberries clung to faded branches tossing in the wind. The untouched thickets of coyoteberry farther down were loaded with waxy red fruits so overripe they were dropping into mildewed masses underneath. The wind-driven wet so fierce from the west made the trunks of pines dark on the side facing into it . . .

And I vaguely remembered that this was what I was doing when I almost froze to death, when I heard my mother's voice calling me— that I was oblivious to myself and lost in a rudimentary examination of whatever presented itself to me. And then another, deeper memory— that this was what I was doing when I was a young boy that summer sunrise, drifting along watching robins stalking alertly in wet grass, and looked up to see a man.

Nothing has prepared me for how obvious it is. The way in for me is the way I wander around alone in the bush, taking in whatever's there in a transfixed reverie, like a child studying the wonder of what he hasn't learned yet to recognize. But as an adult, the analysis of what I'm seeing is slow to fade. I'm still somewhere above a bowl of lake, under a low, racing roof of cloud. The wind drops and there's a profound still-ness. How sadly beautiful the world is. Time stands still and I know a sweetness that's unbearable—that I have to leave this, that I'm only here for a short time, here in a world that is so immediate and familiar. How is it I forget what I've always known until I'm here like this?

There's movement at the periphery but it seems unimportant. An old man lighting sage and waving smoke over me. The acrid smell, stinky-sweet and commanding, makes me aware of an intense nausea I wasn't paying attention to. But I hear the old man say something like, "Here, breathe in what smell they like," and each breath is like slowly opening flowers, dulling the sick feeling. I no longer care about any-thing, and the pressure of the old man's hand on the back of my neck, fingers and thumb squeezed on the throbbing places below my ears, seems to dissolve any lingering distraction.

Someone is coming. I can almost hear him, and then I do, but it's like the scraping and jarring of something immense just out of sight. Everything fuses on the one point of something dark coming across the sky toward me. I'm suddenly intensely afraid, but the feeling descends into an emotionally distraught incomprehension, a grief that sobs out of me. My ears hurt, and then it's as if a bullet has shot through my ears, leaving a burning opening on a roar of sound. The sound produces waves of images, the sense of uninspected events unfolding nearby.

Then the house lights come up, a blinding blurriness of white light that quickly fades away. I have a fleeting moment of sobriety, aware that Clayton has dropped his hand, that he wants me to stay awake. He's singing the weather song, but it sounds faint, as if I have earplugs on. Individual bits of hail are falling here and there, and all I can hold on to is the click-click-click of hail hitting rock. A jet-black squall line is sweeping over, and there's a hissing roar coming from the west, enveloping the hills to the right in a wall of white. My grieving for whoever that force of nature is who showed himself to me as a man seems to be relieved by what is arriving—a roaring fall of hail, a thousand pebbles thrown into the lake at once, everything swept away in a furious blur. Millions of tiny hailstones ricochet around in the rock shelter, striking every part of me, stinging my face and hands as I squint into something, like seeing a waterfall from behind.

But then there's that voice I remember, saying things I can't make out, speaking to me from behind a roaring so loud it's as if there's no sound at all. At the same time I'm following a feeling of humble despair into the presence of someone terrifyingly powerful who is ripping open the fabric of the world, another part of me is watching how what my eyes are seeing is blurring out. It's just like when I was a child outside playing on the ground and sensed an adult looming over me—someone large coming to take charge, and then nothing.

I came to, out of what seemed like a complete blackout, snorting and choking on the pungent smoke of *xas'xas* root. Clayton's face peered down at me with a drawn, dull-eyed concern, and I realized I was lying on my side on the rough, wet floor of the rock shelter. I thought he was saying things to me in Salish, so I kept murmuring the one phrase most used in my Native-language night class, "*Loot kin t'enshúxna* (I don't understand)."

His face spread into an amused grin. "I not sayin' anything."

Turning my nose away from the smoke, I sat up. Clayton continued to "smoke" me with *xas'xas,* the root of the lovage plant we dug in the high mountains, waving the embered, smoking end around me, then handed it to me to hold. I'd seen elders use it in the winter dances to bring back spirit dancers who passed out, but never imagined I'd be coughing in a cloud of it myself.

It was already getting dark and a heavy rain fell steadily in the gloom beyond the overhang. The only sign of hail left were skiffs of shiny white clumped with gromwell seeds on the rocks outside. I felt drained and weak, but refreshed. And vaguely indifferent, as if the pounding hailstorm had given me amnesia, a memory of a passage of time that was empty. I was morbidly hungry, too, made worse by remembering we'd brought nothing to eat.

"Somebody . . . was coming," I said, every word impossibly complex to come up with and string together. "And then . . . I guess I passed out."

"*Aaaa,*" Clayton said, trying not to laugh. He crossed his arms over his chest, becoming dim and indistinct in the failing light.

"Somebody was . . . telling me things. But . . . not you?"

"*Km'a' inchá* (It wasn't me). What you got come on you. Run over you like a semi. Sometimes happen that way, like at first, because you not know each other, been so long. To use the power, gotta stay hard, stay awake. That what you train for, ain't it? But this a good thing. He come on you anytime now, eh? You on a good trail now, and when the power come over you again, you know the sign, you be more ready."

But the memory of somebody talking to me nagged at me. I could almost remember what was said. The words ". . . because she's old" surfaced in my mind, and it was like waking up in the morning knowing I've had an important dream while I was asleep. Triggered by the words, the memory of what I experienced flooded back.

I'm in the woods with someone who's showing me something. It's the twilight at dawn and a car comes along a logging road I know, driving slowly, a man sitting on the hood with a rifle held at the ready to shoot. I know they're poachers, road-hunting deer. I recognize the car as a blue Chevrolet I've seen around the area. Then we're looking at rows of picker's shacks, the prefab log cabins at Big Check Orchard that face the road out of Loomis.

Then as if we're continuing down the road from Loomis, but it's night, we see Jim Woods stopped at a rollover car wreck that's just happened on the shoulder. Whoever's with me says, "She wants to live with him."

Then I'm coming out of it, the feeling of waking up and Clayton nearby muttering something. I wonder what his dead brother told Willie to tell him that time in the sweatlodge. It's only an idle thought, but I hear whoever was with me answer as if over their shoulder as they walk away. I hear, "Well, just something about Grandma because she's so old."

When I told Clayton what I just remembered, he nodded his head slowly, listening, and when I finished said, "*Aaaa,* maybe what you got show you some things. Just for you, I guess, and to scratch my head about the most of it. All but the end there, and that's right, the dead tell about his wife's mother, somethin' to know, to prepare, because she so old. Maybe we talk about that another time.

"This how it go when you don't have no thing to hold in your heart, why you callin' on the power. Maybe just want to know 'em, and have nothin' to concentrate on. No need for somethin' that you askin' for, that you want to use your power for. Then they just look into things, show you things, and maybe later you know why. The next time, to have the need of somethin', like that time we want to help Kootch, to find Kootch and help 'em, eh?"

Unimaginably exhausted, I could hardly listen to what he said, being somehow more engaged with the stippled pattern of falling rain and the oddness of his voice coming from somewhere near in complete darkness. When he'd pause, I'd instantly gloss the import of his words after the fact. He told me there was another *en'x'xá'em* connected with the lake, not far, about a mile or two away, that he was posing as a problem for me to find. He said it was a "doorway" you could see from the top of the cliff above us if it was daytime, a notch you could see through in the saddle of a long ridge, to the very top of Chopaka Mountain beyond. A "line of sight" that Indian doctors once used in training new doctors, he said, and the kind of place I should be able to find easily since the wind was always blowing hard through it.

I stood up when I heard him getting up, and got ready to feel my way out into the rain and onto the narrow trail at the top of the talus slope, wondering how I could find anything in the pitch dark. Clayton laughed and said it was hard enough to find your way at all in this kind of utter darkness under complete overcast and heavy rain, much less find your way to some place you've never been to before. The only way was to call on what you had, your power, who knew where everything was in the world. He said maybe this time I wouldn't pass out if I was walking and held just the one thing in my mind, the place he wanted me to lead him to. He hinted that it was a test to see if I was ready to be sent on the long wander *(k'ulsht i t'taku'út i lekuuut),* but even more important for "an old cripple" like him, it was a shortcut back to the Woods place.

Even though I couldn't see him, for some reason I could see his neck-lace glimmering as if gromwell seeds were phosphorescent. I stared at the faintly glowing string of white blurs as he moved it with his fingers and switched completely to the Native language, speaking to me in a dry, slow singsong.

"*Wai, ch'mai mut ku kl'a'kl'ám i sxi'míux k'elhk'láux* (Now, maybe you'll look for some place specific out of sight)."

I made a dubious sound but he went on, almost chanting some instructions and interjections, repeated over and over in different ways, yet saying the same thing:

"*Wai uyá'* (Listen) . . . *loot stu'tíwastemen* (I'm not going to baby you along) . . . *kwen'ta'líls* (come back to yourself) . . . *kwk'ehlmaipenúmt* (figure it out for yourself) . . . *kla'ús* (look around) . . . *ka'kíchem ixí sxi'míux* (find that place)."

It wasn't much to go on, but I led the way out and felt my way along with feet and hands until we emerged onto the soft ground of the ravine. I already loved wandering thoughtlessly around in the hills in the dark, and fell easily into a mute awareness of the vague area of ground directly in front of me. Using *wik'wst* to discern obstacles looming up out of the periphery, I made my way around unknown things more felt than seen. Stumbling and slopping around in the endless rain with the sound of Clayton following behind, I kept the place he wanted me to find as the only thing drawing me on, concentrating on it in a moody single-mindedness that bordered on indifference. I simply felt ahead for where I wanted to go, sensing when I was straying to one side like a blind boy paddling toward his father's voice, correcting back to what felt just right. A sensation of floating that was like groping through dark, blind passages toward a distant pinpoint of light.

After crossing three barbed wire fences, two rutted roads, and a deep mucky draw, we climbed up into dense forest where I followed whatever game trails I could feel my way along that felt like they went toward what I was seeking. I became aware that everything was suffused with a white illumination coming vaguely from above, and realized the moon was up. The land began to level off and we emerged into what seemed like a grassy meadow. There were no more trees or bushes or rocks, and the increasing wind drove fiercely into my face. Nothing was visible but wispy shreds of something racing by, as if we were walking inside moonlit fog. Then I felt suddenly tired and worn out. My jeans were sopping wet to the hips and rainwater ran down my neck inside my clothes. I simply stopped.

Clayton came quietly up to my side, but said nothing. I knew I'd found the place, but the sense that I was standing in a low meadow was hard to shake. The wind gusted in sheets of icy rain, and I began to think, to wonder where we were in the familiar countryside I knew so well. I knew I'd never be able to retrace my steps by the light of day.

There was a glimmer of bright light ahead, and the fog lifted for a moment, making me realize I was looking at the undersides of clouds reflecting a blurry line of electric lights far below. Startled to see the ground fall steeply downhill a few yards ahead, I stared in complete incomprehension at what appeared to be a deep valley with a little town strung out that I never knew existed in this country before. And seen through abrupt walls of bare rock I didn't realize flanked us on both sides. Then as if yanked around mentally to face a different direction, I suddenly recognized the familiar lights of orchard buildings and summer homes scattered along the east shore of Palmer Lake where I used to live years before.

Clayton was already walking away downhill ahead of me, so I leaned into the rain and followed him.

10

A S AUTUMN GAVE WAY to winter and leaden skies lay heavily on snow-white peaks, there was one last drive-out in my car loaded down with household goods for me to be officially moved back. One last tour along the ribbon of winding pavement west from Tonasket past the "hoodoos" on Whitestone Mountain—ghostly spires of chalky rock almost hidden in the timber. Hugging the two long and narrow trout lakes, through irrigated orchards soggy with fallen leaves, under sagebrush grassland hillsides where cattle and horses had waxed fat for generations. Up the side road to the right was a mile of barbed wire fence I once built. Over to the left I once found a back way through the Cayuse Hills when I was delivering two horses to town, riding one and leading the other. Up that cutbank track was where we used to drive cattle onto Horse Springs Coulee in the spring. I'd followed behind in a stock truck, getting out every time a cowboy roped a bawling calf that was falling too far behind, to muscle the struggling critter into the back with the other slowpokes.

Then at the low pass before dropping down into Loomis, there's the sudden view of dark hardrock mountains ahead, and the same old feeling comes over me. I've come home. There's just something about it— what little civilization has made it out this far comes to an abrupt end and hundreds of miles of mountains stretch away beyond, like passing through a gateway into unknown realms. Peeking up above and beyond ridge after ridge of heavy forest, the sharp point of Windy Peak stands bare white in the remoteness of the Pasayten Wilderness. Every time I see the mountain's familiar shape, I'm reminded of the time Clayton sent me on a mission and I saw it from the other side at sunrise. Dazed by fasting and wandering for days, recognizing Windy Peak was how I figured out where I was and how to get back.

The backcountry does that to you: the mountains, the distinctive features of the landscape witness the events of life lived in their shadows. The air carries a smoky forested thickness that veils the present like layers of memories. Like the time Stuart Bolster stopped his pickup one day to gaze at an old pine snag that marked a crossroads in the high country, and told me how he'd once tied a horse to it when he was a boy of four or five, so he could mount up for the first time by himself. And the Indians had a name and story for everything that stood out in this country—Coyote Rock, Where the Ghosts Stand Watching, Skunk's Cliff, Horse Springs, Pinched (the narrows where Coyote got stuck), Medicine Lake. So that every time you looked around, where you were felt known and loaded with particular memories.

Back into this I went, hungry for more of what I thought I'd left behind. Keeping a little money coming in by doing after-harvest cleanup in orchards, I made handshake deals with orchardists to prune their trees later in winter, and with Stuart to repair fences. My landlady who'd rented to me in town also had an old, broken-down cabin on some isolated family land in the mountains, and offered it to me in exchange for just fixing it up and keeping an eye on the place for her. A few days of hammering and sawing was all it took to set up for winter in a one-room plank-and-shake-shingle shack next to where a creek went over a low falls under towering spruce and tamarack trees. There was no electricity or plumbing; just a woodstove and a kerosene lamp and a sleeping bag on the floor and water hauled from the creek in a bucket. Not much more than a bush camp at the end of a miles-long rutted track through pine forest, but it suited me fine. Just the place for me to savor the solitary silences, to hunt and wander and sweathouse and train in the power way.

Curious about what I'd been shown in my blackout at Naháhum Lake, I drove into Big Check Orchard one day and got out to nose around the seasonal workers' cabins when everybody was away working. The same blue Chevrolet with Arizona plates was parked there, but since I didn't have a clue what I was looking for, I idly walked up and down the rows of housing. Nothing was out of the ordinary— empty apple crates stacked high and aluminum ladders leaned on the eaves of uniformly brown-shingled roofs. Laundry hung on lines and garbage spilled out of old oil drums used for burning trash. The typical stuff at the low end of North American working life.

I stood in the muddy snow at a loss, wondering what I was doing there, momentarily comparing what I was seeing to the memory in my mind's eye of how I'd been shown these prefab log structures in rows. Then I felt a shiver and my eyes came to rest on one of the cabins. It was the only one with all the curtains closed inside the windows, as if to keep anyone from looking in.

A stout padlock on the door made it look like a storeroom, but it didn't feel right. Around back was a high window under the eaves that had no curtains. Using one of the ladders, I climbed up and looked in, appalled to see numberless deer carcasses hanging from the rafters and piles of antlers, bones, hooves, hides, and heads heaped against the inside walls. From what I could see, there were the remains of at least twelve deer, obviously an illegal deer-meat operation run on the side by someone working at the orchard, most likely the two men I'd seen who came up from Arizona in the Chevy.

Stupefied by the magnitude of surreptitious deer slaughter going on behind everyone's back, I climbed down and replaced the ladder where I found it. Poaching the occasional deer out of season to feed your family was one thing, but this was obviously being done on a large scale for money. Once back in my car and down the road, it came to me that the deer in the mountains I roamed wanted me to know what was happening to them. That's why I'd been shown things to lead me to Big Check Orchard—so I'd discover the secret butcher shop and do something about it. It only took one call from the pay phone at Sully's Store and a successful bust by Fish and Game officers followed that afternoon.

When I wasn't stocking the pit cellar with home-canned foods and stacking firewood high for the deeper snows to come, I was down in the valley, working in the orchards or hanging out at the Woods place, where I'd spend nights in Jim's vacated travel trailer. His former bachelor quarters was connected to the doublewide by a series of extension cords strung along the corral fence to bring electricity to the bushy grove of alders where he'd been pursuing his womanizing in privacy. Jim had left behind his rodeo photo album and his more inflammatory pants and shirts still hanging in the closet, the ones he used to wear dancing at the Peerless Hotel in Oroville or the disco in Penticton. He was finally monogamous and settled into a life of dutiful husband and son-in-law so far up in British Columbia we seldom saw him.

What happened to alter his self-proclaimed destiny as the most permanently available single man on the lower Similkameen began late one night when he was driving home alone and came upon a car that had rolled off the road to Loomis. I saw the crumpled Toyota the next day, upside down against a scraped-bare trunk of ponderosa pine, roof missing and resting on flung-open doors, the untouched grille nosed upward. The skid marks and trail of beer cans where the car had rolled through brush told a tale of going too fast to make the curve.

Jim had been the first on the scene—smoke still rising, the headlights of his most recent horse trade, a '69 Camaro, illuminating the form of someone not moving inside. He parked and jumped out to see what he could do. No stranger to encountering beer- and gasoline-smelling rollovers on rural roads, Jim nonetheless spoke with horror of finding a White woman with arms and legs at rest in unnatural positions, of the dry stare of her eyes and the butchered-animal look of her intestines bulging from her clothing. Coming upon her dead was made bizarre by the sound of her car radio still blaring out a popular rock 'n' roll dance tune, he said, one that he always liked. Then he recognized the woman's face—he knew her, he'd gone to school with her, he'd gone out with her. He'd even danced with her to that same song now mocking his feeling for her with its message of eternal youth and endless partying.

Jim told me he started to shiver uncontrollably because he felt the woman's presence somewhere in the darkness beyond the headlights' glare, looking at him, wondering why he was there after they'd stopped seeing each other so long ago. He went back to his car just as a pickup

pulled over, the driver already calling in the wreck on his CB radio.
When Jim drove on home, he couldn't shake the feeling that she was
riding with him, like she didn't know she was dead and was going
somewhere with him.

"She never could take things fast," he said in the whispery, listless
voice he spoke with in the days that followed. "We used to drive out to
the Overlook after football games, and like, park. Any other girl and
we'd just do it, ya know? But she'd talk, just talk, with that lisp of hers,
and that rowdy sorta voice. Took a lot of times before she got interested.
Like, slow to figure things out, eh?"

He sat in his trailer in the alders not eating, not going anywhere,
barely responding to his mother and sister and me. What he'd experienced was so uncannily like what I'd been shown in my blackout memories, I wondered if I should tell him about it. But too uncertain how it
might affect him, I kept quiet until Clayton showed up. When he heard
what was going on, he turned to me in Charlene's kitchen and said,
"Her want to live with him, eh?"

I shrugged.

"Tell 'em what you tell me, what you see that time," he said, and I
briefly explained to Charlene and Grandma about seeing Jim stop and
get out at a rollover wreck before it happened, and whoever was showing it to me said, "She wants to live with him." They both looked
alarmed.

Jim refused their request that he move into the family home, so
Charlene filled his overheated little space with wild rose branches and
piled a bunch on his doorstep, which we all had to step over to go in or
out. Grandma kept a pot of water bubbling with rose petals and hips
and leaves on his one-burner propane stove, and got him to drink sips
of it from time to time. After long Salish consultations in the kitchen
and on the phone, it was decided that he shouldn't be left alone. We all
took turns hanging out with him in his trailer, but at night it was his
sister, Lucy, who stayed with him, sitting up all night in a kitchen chair
doing beadwork, relieved once in a while by Charlene to go and nurse
her new baby girl. She said he moaned and tossed in his sleep. Clayton
took me aside and told me that what my power had said had convinced

them the woman would try to take Jim with her when she finally figured out she was dead.

Days later, when I returned from the burial service in Omak and told Jim she was in the ground, he seemed relieved and ate a big meal and even switched on his tiny black-and-white television to smile at the antics of the Brady Bunch. When Lucy came to sit with him, I left and ate some dinner in the doublewide. Lucy came back later saying Jim had told her he was all right now and wanted to be alone. Charlene looked nervous at this, and after fidgeting around, abruptly went out to check on him.

He told me later how he'd been watching TV alone after Lucy left when somebody knocked on the door. Since only non-Indians would knock, he felt a chill and ignored it, keeping his eyes on the TV but listening for sounds outside. Even with everything closed up tight, he said, he felt a faint breeze, and then felt the trailer rock to one side, like someone had stepped onto the doorstep. He yanked the door open in a desperate move, but nobody was there, and the bunch of wild rose had fallen off to one side. He couldn't remember anything else after that. Charlene found him in bed, shivering and sweaty and delirious under a Pendleton blanket pulled over his head. The left side of his face sagged, his left eye barely opened, and the left side of his mouth hung slack and numb. His paralysis extended downward to a tingling in his left hand and foot.

"*Kuk'wíkst,*" Grandma pronounced. "Ghosted. Now we call 'em in, the doctor."

She insisted on sending for Matilda Bruyere, a well-known ghost doctor who lived up in the Chilcotin region of British Columbia. Charlene suffered misgivings about relying on someone unrelated, and while she didn't openly oppose her mother's decision, she continued to talk about having Old Willie come and doctor Jim.

"Jim always have the fright of Willie," Grandma said, referring to how the old man's powers had accidently scarred him in childhood and left Jim wary and timid in his presence. "Besides, a woman maybe better at this kind of doctoring."

Charlene sighed, nodding her assent.

Unwilling to drive Jim's "contaminated" Camaro, Charlene set out the next morning in my car to drive the almost 400 kilometers to present Grandma's heirloom greenstone pipe filled with Bull Durham tobacco to Matilda at her home on the Chilcotin River. Requests for help had to be made the way a doctor said their powers required, and since Indian doctors traveled around to various winter spirit dances, Matilda's requirement that an old family pipe be presented was well known. If she lit and smoked the pipe, it meant she was accepting the request to go doctor somebody, even before she heard who needed her help or what the problem was. When she smoked Grandma's pipe immediately, Charlene said she felt instantly relieved. Matilda told her she knew what was wrong and would ride back with Charlene as soon as her daughter came home from work as a nurse at a clinic nearby.

While Charlene was gone, I worked a few days alongside Larry Dubois, another Native friend, doing wage work in an orchard. Since all we had to do was drive a tractor up and down the rows of trees, pulling a flatbed trailer that we loaded with wooden props, we passed the time catching up. Larry had always been a fiery little guy with aspirations of starting his own rock 'n' roll band, and rarely made reference to his Indian heritage, even though his family dragged him along to Native gatherings, and his wife, Elaine, was related to Margaret and Old Willie.

But now Larry seemed more subdued and mature, and talked at great length about how he'd joined a drum group and had spent the summer singing at powwows. I knew he had a beautiful singing voice, so I asked him for a song, and he broke out with one he'd learned, a war dance song that was rousing and unforgettable, beating time with a stick on the deck of the trailer. This was answered by a plaintive love song from the Mexicans working in the next orchard over, a tear-soaked lament about a girl left back home in Chihuahua in the style of *musica ranchera,* which made us laugh. Then it was my turn, so I sang a popular country-western tune, exaggerating the nasal twang until Larry covered his ears with his hands for me to stop, gasping with how hard he was laughing.

I knew Larry didn't get along very well with Jim Woods, but I figured with his changed attitude about his heritage, he might be interested to hear about Jim's face and the diagnosis of ghost sickness. He listened but said nothing until I was done. Then he told me in a self-consciously somber voice how the spirits had come over him the winter before, when he was attending a spirit dance in one of the Colville longhouses. And how one of his uncles, a longtime dancer, had taken him into seclusion for nearly a month of training with little to eat and constant sweathousing and dives in freezing water. He said he'd just started singing a song that came out of nowhere, and was surprised to find out later that the old people recognized it as one sung by his own grandfather, who died before he was born.

"We can do that, you know. Not like the Whites. It gets handed down, even if you don't know nothin' about it. Jim better watch out. He don't have any protection."

"You don't think he has something?"

Larry smirked and answered, "Who ever heard him sing?" Meaning, come out with a power song from a *shumíx* in the winter spirit dances as he had. It was a phrase I'd heard when somebody was putting someone down. Saying they were pretending to have power when they'd never gone public with it at the dances, and never demonstrated the kind of practical results beyond the normal range of human capabilities that came with having power.

Then he said, "*Loot stim ḳs'meis tul naḳ'wá t'uuul ḳtl ḳ'laux!* (Nothing's for sure because there's dangerous things you can't see in the dark!)" It was an old saying, something elders said to children to warn them about ghosts when they went outside at night. Larry had told me in years past that he knew nothing of the Native language, so I'd never talked Okanogan with him as I was learning. But him quoting this adage made me think he was learning the language now, too. Before he could translate it into English for me, I said, just to be funny, "*Loot swit ḳs'meis ixí náḳ'wem ḳ'im i Jim Woods!* (Nobody knows that better than Jim Woods!)"

Larry looked startled and uncomprehending, then turned back to work with a pained expression darkening into a sullen anger. He hadn't understood what I said, and it came to me that he'd probably just learned a few common phrases. I'd inadvertently shamed him without knowing, a White man speaking his own language better than he did. Not knowing what I could do about his hurt feelings, and already familiar with how my knowledge of things Indian provoked deep resentment in other young acculturated Okanogans—who considered such things to be exclusively theirs by ethnic identity—I said nothing more.

We worked out the rest of the day together, but Larry was changed, distant, uncomfortably silent around me. After we got our pay from the orchardist, I didn't bother to ask Larry for a ride to the Woods place. He was going the other way and it was only a few miles to walk. When I got there in the dark with a flutter of snowflakes beginning to fall, my car was parked out front so covered with mud it looked like Charlene had just returned from driving the Alcan Highway.

Later that night the big living room of the Woods' mobile home filled up with relatives and friends arriving to help Matilda doctor Jim. I knew almost everybody present but my experience with Larry Dubois kept me quiet and unobtrusively in the background as people sat talking in low voices and greeted each other with even more joking than usual. Jim was still refusing to leave his trailer so there was a lively discussion among the oldest present about what to do since Matilda insisted he be treated in the living room where everybody could join in and add strength to her songs. She was a short, burly woman in her fifties with a large bosom straining the limits of her Cowichan sweater. As she conferred with Grandma and Charlene, the idle part of my mind wondered what she was like as a woman to a man, but the sudden severity of her look singling me out in the crowd stilled my speculations. Her daughter sat close in a white nurse's uniform, a younger and slimmer version of her mother, a pinned plastic nametag announcing her as Celeste Bruyere. Her voice was more musical and she was more fluent in English as she translated her mother's occasional phrases in the *Tsilhqot'in* language.

Easing away down the hall, I absented myself from what was going on by hanging out in one of the bedrooms where all the children played with toys or chatted together under the bored watch of a teenage boy flashing a flashlight's beam on the ceiling. Jim's nephew Brandon had climbed up onto my lap and fallen asleep when Matilda came in with a look of wanting to talk with me. She sat down on one of the beds with a sigh, and Brandon's little sister, Lucy's new baby, turned from where she sat in her crib and stared with solemn eyes at the new arrival, smiling with pudgy cheeks at Matilda's motherly resemblance.

"Somebody thinkin' to have the White friend have words with the sick one," she said, glaring at me. After a few moments of silence, I realized she meant for me to go and try to talk Jim into coming into the living room. I wondered what good it would do for me to talk to him. What he told me on the drive up to Old Willie's house came back to mind—that he wanted to kill somebody after his father died, when he ran off to Wounded Knee, went militant.

"He's angry," I said with quiet conviction.

"Of course he angry!" Matilda snorted. "Why you think the ghost come after 'em? But he never show that anger to anybody, now do he?"

"No, he never does." I had a theory which I didn't share with Matilda, that the Indian history of losing wars and being coerced into an alien way of life had produced the kind of personality Jim had—extreme control over his anger and unwillingness to express his sense of loss. Like a lot of Indians in his generation, he'd joined in the passionate militancy of Red Power activism for a while, but ultimately returned to the strong traditional roots that so many others—raised in cities—lacked. Unfortunately his participation in the non-Indian world made him wary of full participation in traditional ways, so he was trapped, one of the "two heads" *(asíl chásyakin)* as the elders put it, and his rage hidden under an easygoing, humorous veneer. Others like him drank and partied, or ate themselves into diabetic stupors, but Jim had buried himself in endless sexual escapades with women.

"This what happen when you see a ghost," Matilda went on, as if instructing the White man in esoteric matters beyond his understanding. "The face show what is bad in the heart. The anger that paralyze you, even if you don't want nobody to know. This why we say the ghost sickness can be the good thing, not to be afraid of it, eh? But another way, maybe don't want to be doctored, and just give in to that ghost, that dead person who want you to go with 'em. Some choose that, waste away to the shadow and die."

Matilda looked up at her daughter who had come to stand in the doorway and listen. "But only the Indian. Not the White. Well, the one or two, I treat 'em. But the most of the Whites, no. The White doctor don't treat for the ghost. Just for the face go bad. What they call that, the face sag on one side?" she asked her daughter. "What the sick have in White man?"

"Bell's palsy," Celeste answered. Matilda turned back to me even more severely.

"Yah, that's it. But they don't even do no doctorin' on 'em, do they?"

"No," Celeste sighed. "Maybe give the patient aspirin. They say it's only temporary, eh? It goes away in a few days."

"Hah! That what they think to say! They don't see how the ghost come after the one who don't show the anger he have. But we have the way to doctor 'em, Indian way. Take away that bad in the heart. Start over, want to live again. You maybe want to see that come for the sick friend?"

Some of the older girls sitting on the bed behind Matilda had been listening raptly, and one of them, who lived in the Woods household as an adopted daughter, spontaneously answered, "Yes." But I knew Matilda's question was aimed at me. I looked up at Celeste's face and considered her pleasant looks, her youthful attractiveness in nurse's uniform, her self-confident firmness of manner.

"You'd have more luck with him than I would," I said to her, and she smiled at what my suggestion implied, revealing an unsettling beauty probably not often exposed with her overly serious manner. She looked at her mother, who met her eyes and shrugged.

It was after midnight. Jim came in the front door wrapped in a bright red and green Pendleton blanket, Celeste leading the way, the half of his face not sagging showing a sheepish smile, a spark of something that wasn't there before. They sat together on the couch talking quietly while the older people moved around making preparations the way they knew Matilda required for doctoring, turning off all the food cooking, pulling curtains tightly closed on windows, filling the wood-stove with cedar boards brought for the purpose. I wondered where Matilda had disappeared to, and went into the kitchen for a drink of water. Grandma stood at the window, listening with her eyes closed, a slight smile creasing her wrinkled face. I heard what she was listening to, faint singing from someone out back by the river, and realized it was Matilda, singing to her power, calling her helpers in for what she was about to do. After a candle had been lit and placed on a dish on the floor by the woodstove, everybody who was still awake found a place to sit around the living room, some on folded blankets on the floor. Clayton followed Matilda's instructions to turn off everything electrical by unplugging the telephone and throwing the main electrical breaker switch. The house became still and dark, illuminated only by the flame of one candle. Someone coughed, and the only other sound was the crackling of the cedar wood burning furiously in the woodstove, raising the temperature dramatically in the room.

The sound of Matilda singing moved around to the front outside. There was a stolid vagueness in most eyes around me, as if in a moment of such expectancy they were even less inclined to acknowledge anything out of the ordinary going on. Celeste got up and opened the woodstove door for a minute, letting out wafts of cedar-scented smoke until the room was thickly smudged, then opened her mother's soft basketry bags, selecting certain items. She moved the candle to the middle of the floor and strewed wild rose leaves and petals, beckoning Jim to come and sit on them between the woodstove and the candle, facing the front door. She sat to one side of the candle on the floor with Jim, and we all waited as the singing grew louder and closer.

Then the door opened with a cold gust of blowing snowflakes, and Matilda came in singing. Her sweater and long, loose hair were covered with snow as she came forward, moving with big-hipped restraint and tiny, shuffling dance steps to the steady rhythm of her song. Someone closed the door and she paused, swaying to the move of her feet in place, the fingers of one hand clasping a leather pouch at her neck, her other hand holding up a fan of almost pure white Arctic owl feathers attached to a beaded handle. The snowflakes on her instantly melted away in the overheated room, her severe expression was gone, and she looked transformed into the role of Indian doctor, her eyes staring somewhat cross-eyed across the room at Jim. Her lips barely moved in a trancelike concentration as she sang in endless repetition, and the song itself was like nothing I'd heard before. Seven syllables of unknown meaning repeated over and over, with one set rising in pitch at the end, and the next falling. And sung with a driving rhythm and emotional intensity, and such an uncertainty as to where one note ended and another began that it exerted an arresting influence on me.

In response to a gesture from Matilda's fan of white feathers, Jim's closest relatives got up and closed in around her, shoulder to shoulder in a loose group, Grandma and Charlene flanking her, Clayton and Lucy behind. Adding their voices to her song, they took up the same swaying dance in place, all five of them gazing across the flickering candlelight at Jim, who was hunched over and visibly trembling. Hands at their sides and looking no different than usual in their every-day clothes, they moved to Matilda's rhythmic song with ease and casual restraint. Johnny Stemilt stood by the door with a plain hide drum and began beating time, slightly before the beat of the song, giving it the even more driving feel of Native dance songs. His drumming was gentle at first but slowly grew in volume as their voices rose in emotion, and when they were swept up in the singular power of Matilda's song, to a thunderous, rhythmic booming as the room was flooded with a singing in unison that was awesome to witness. Then with Matilda in the lead, they all started moving forward in the same side-to-side shuffling steps, inching slowly across the ten feet of floor toward Jim in one great wave.

It was suddenly impossibly moving as the rest of us joined in singing. There's nothing like the power of human beings joined singing and dancing in unison to sweep clean the mind and open it to the body's awareness of the invisible. Grandma with otherworldly eyes moving only imperceptibly to the beat, Charlene biting her lip in the fierce moves of mother love, Lucy swaying with the practiced ease of a fancy dancer, Clayton with chest out and only his knees and feet moving—all joined in voiced, danced solidarity with the Indian doctor. Their advance across the floor was so slow, so restrained, so united as one, the outpouring of sung emotion in the room seemed to coalesce and become embodied in their approach. Something grew more potent and commanding the closer they got to the candle, and there was such care and compassion in their eyes for poor, stricken Jim that he crumpled sobbing to the floor.

At that, Matilda turned aside with something like a shriek, and her body bent forward, never missing a beat as she danced more expressively back and forth in front of the candle. Jim's relatives stopped where they were, dancing in place, looking on. The drum and song continued, all of us caught up in the flood of rhythmic power we were creating, raptly watching Matilda dance swiftly around the small area. She moved as if possessed in furtive, stylized moves suggestive of a wild animal hunting prey—her eyes glinting and vague—gesturing with her feather fan in graceful, swinging strokes, as if drawing in things unseen around the room, and then all at once threw them with a flap of the fan at Jim. The woodstove behind him burst forth with loud pops and crackles, and she moved beyond the candle, no longer dancing, slowly brushing the air around Jim's form on the floor. From head to toe she brushed and stroked without touching him, then Celeste helped him lie flat on his back. Her mother lightly brushed the sagging side of his face, snapping the fan toward the woodstove after every stroke.

Our singing hadn't faltered, and when Matilda finished, she swayed in time back to face Jim over the candle and ended the song with a long descending "Hoooooo. . . ." Lowering herself heavily to sit, she started another song with a flourish of her fan. Immediately the relatives who'd danced with her sat down behind her and we all pressed forward, packed tightly around in a circle, but not touching Jim, Celeste, or her mother. Celeste had Jim sit up as Matilda sang, gesturing with the fan in different directions. Little by little we picked up the new song, and when all voices were joined in confident singing, she blew out the candle. Instantly there was the electrifying intensity of thirty voices singing in pitch darkness.

Matilda is no longer singing, but she can be heard sighing and moaning. We sing for a long time, maybe ten minutes without her, then a cold breeze sweeps through the room. It's so hot and stuffy, it feels good. There's a sudden pop in the woodstove, Matilda growls, slaps her hands together, and everybody stops singing. She's talking as if her head is down, a drowsy, droning voice talking in *Tsilhqot'in,* so much more vowelly than Salish, with nasals and the kind of unpredictable up-and-down intonation of tonal languages. My ears are ringing in the expectant silence of everyone listening to Celeste's low voice, translating into English what her mother is saying. Struggling to keep up, her phrases are short and choppy, and she mimics how her mother switches from one kind of voice to another.

"Where you been? What take so long?"

"Oh, oh, long way to find you. All the way to here, so far. From Ice Mountain. You gone a long way, mother. What you want?"

"This man name Jim Woods. This man in a bad way. Go find out what happen to him."

"He look fine to me. He look the handsome man. Always the different woman fall all over him. Now just one. She take 'em with her. Let him die like that. I go home, back to Ice Mountain."

"No, don't talk like that! He's a good boy. You told me you always help. Help me when I call on you. See, I feed you cedar. I want to help this boy. His people are afraid for him. His mom is cryin' for him. His grandma. His sister. His uncle. All the people come here, want me to help him." (Murmurs of *"Aaaa. Aaaa. Wai i hwi."*) "Go and find out. Find out what happen to him."

"Okay, mother. I'm going. That's right. I just want to know. Maybe if somebody care about him. That's right, so his people care about him, pity him. So I going now."

"Go now! Find out!"

There's a dead silence. A match is lit and Celeste relights the candle. Matilda is slumped over as if asleep, her fan flat across her extended legs. Once in a while she trembles, she jerks with spasms. She moans, she sighs, then she's humming. Her head rises and she's singing in a low voice, her eyes staring blindly ahead. It's a different kind of song, more relaxed and loping, like a round-dance song, with a heartbeat time to it. A walking song, a traveling song—and when we all join in, Matilda's voice fades away as her head drops again. It goes on so long, maybe half an hour, some voices turn hoarse and fade out, too. By the end, I'm struggling to keep singing like most of the others, but the oldest, like Grandma and Clayton, seem animated by an incomprehensible energy and endurance, as though they could sing easily until dawn.

There's a sudden breeze again, like a breath of fresh air, and the candle flame goes out to the sound of gasps in the darkness. After a few heartbeats, over the sound of singing, there's a sudden startling boom on the outside wall, like someone outside slapping their hand hard on the aluminum siding. And then a howling and rattling on the roof like small animals running from one end of the trailer to the other, making my hair stand on end. The things that happen when Indian doctors are doing their thing, always blowing my skeptical mind.

Matilda starts talking in the dark with a breathless excitement, and Celeste translates again.

"Mother! Mother! I'm back. Well, here I am."

"You come back. Good. What you find out?"

"Have to go far. Way to the other side. And find that girl have his breath. She hold on to it and wait for this man. To join her. But another man, two men. This man's dad, and his dad's dad. They talk to me." (Clayton's voice saying *"Aaaa."*) "Tell me not this man's time to come over. Love him and watch over him." (Other murmured *aaaa*'s. Charlene is sobbing.) "Tell me where to go. Where she keep his breath. Have to go over to the coast. They tell me, look in the school. Where they learn how to draw pictures. In the little box, in a hat. Where they keep their things. And I found it. In a hat. Red hat, with a bird face." (Sudden gasp from Jim.)

"What you got there? You bring back something?"

"Yes. I found it. That man's breath. Bring it back for him." (There's a faint glimmer of bluish light and the sound of Matilda's fan shaking. Gasps all around.) "There. Bring it back for him. Now he'll be all right. Release that woman and live. Now I'm going home. I'm going. I'm done."

Matilda's voice segues into another song, a joyous, rousing, lilting one that even without knowing what the words mean feels like singing of going home. Again, we all join in the unfamiliar song with passion, and when we've caught the vibrating force of this one, Celeste lights the candle and there's her mother already standing up, dancing slightly in place, snowy owl feathers pressed to her chest, gazing off in the distance transfixed. We sing for a long time again, moved by the release of pent-up emotions, the faces all around me radiating a kind of transformed otherness. In ones and twos people stand up and move in place to the power of the song rocking the trailer, until we're all standing, all moving in time to the tune, except Jim, who's bent over his crossed legs in a kind of daze, the blanket fallen in folds around his waist.

Then with a "Hooooo . . ." that takes the life out of the song, Matilda signals us to stop. She looks severely at Jim and all eyes quietly fall on him. In the flickering light of one candle on the floor, it's a pregnant moment. Jim squirms and sways like something's at war inside him.

"Maybe you have something to say," Matilda intones in a hoarse, strained voice. "Maybe share something with all who care about you, to gather and help me sing over you. All gather and work so hard to give you life, eh?"

Jim says something in a tiny, inaudible voice. Celeste kneels and leans close. They whisper back and forth. Celeste seems to be repeating back to him what he's saying until she gets it right. He nods, and Celeste straightens up.

"He says he knows what they were talking about. Years ago when the dead one went off to art school in Seattle, he gave her a hat. A Cardinals baseball cap, red, with a bird's face on it. That's the only thing of his he ever gave her, eh?"

Jim nods again. A murmuring of approval flickers through those crowded around me by this confirmation of Matilda's doctoring powers. Matilda shudders and sways as if holding something to her chest with the feather fan. Celeste confers with Jim in whispers again.

"Yes," Jim says, clearing his throat, trying to speak up in his usual voice. "Yes, I let go . . . I let go of her. I . . . I saw my dad. He waved to me . . . waved me back. Yes, I want to live. I want to live."

Amid the murmur of *aaaa*'s, Matilda trembles and begins to sing yet another song. Once we've all joined in, her voice fades away and she moves forward around the candle where she leans over Jim's bowed head. Looking oddly like she's about to vomit, her bulky body spasms several times, and then with great force, she flaps the feathers downward toward his head and blows a blast of her breath. It's so loud over the singing, it sounds like the snort of a horse. Jim shudders and moans as she brushes lightly around his head, smoothing something in, then pats his head with the feathers, her lips moving with unheard words.

As she backs away brushing the air around him, Jim looks up. I'm amazed to see only a slight sagging remains on the side of his face. He gets up with surprising agility, letting the blanket fall, and begins to sing and dance with us. It's a touching moment having Jim back, moving with his casual, big-bodied ease and smiling at the faces of people gathered for his sake. Whooping cries punctuate the song as some men express their feelings. Only Matilda seems unmoved as she sways, so exhausted and drained she is hardly able to stay on her feet. The song goes on and on in a long outpouring of joy and release, then one last "Hoooooo . . ." and it's over.

Sometimes I think the best part of doctoring ceremonies or spirit dances or sweats is right after they're over. That's when you come back to ordinary things so altered it's like seeing life on earth for the first time. You've done everything you could possibly do about what's pressing at the moment, and you're left with a sense of having delved into and participated in the way the world really is. And there's a special, unspoken bond with those who sang and danced and experienced it with you. A shared knowing that is only dispelled slowly with the passage of time. It's no wonder Native ways are clung to so fiercely. Everyone who sang at Jim's doctoring was healed in some way, fortified in their convictions and commitment to each other, and returned to everyday life stronger in the power way.

As the lights were turned on, food was heated on the stove, and water from a sacred spring was passed around in a jug from thirsty mouth to thirsty mouth. Some shook hands and talked quietly, some went outside to smoke. Jim and Charlene were instructed by Matilda slumped wearily in a chair, prescribing the things he'd have to do in the coming days to cement the treatment into his daily life. After an offering of food to the spirits was thrown into the woodstove, a meal was served on paper plates just as the first glimmering light of dawn showed through open curtains. After most had eaten their fill, blankets and presents and money were given to Matilda. Other gifts were given to those who helped by singing—Charlene presented me with a beautiful pair of deerskin gloves she'd made from the brain-tanned hide of the deer I'd given her. It had been a long night and Grandma fell asleep in her chair with her plate still on her lap. Only in the full light of day did some people leave for home and others, like Matilda, go find someplace to sleep.

Jim came up to me outside with Celeste at his side, obviously smitten with this very different kind of woman. She seemed to be enjoying getting to know him, but was definitely her own person, firmly unresponsive to his habitual charm. We spoke in the elation of exhaustion about the songs, and Celeste told a little about what they said in her language. She spoke of how they came to her mother in long fasts in an ice cave under a glacier in the Coast Range of British Columbia. Looking at the fresh snow on everything, at the open hills and the tall mountains towering above them, she said it was beautiful here, so different from the rolling forested country where she lived, where the mountains were so far away. Jim said he'd like to see the Chilcotin country, and offered to be the one to drive her and her mother back home.

"Yeah, well, talk to my mum, eh?"

"You pretty tired, aren't you?" Jim asked.

"Mmm," she nodded.

"Hey, you want to sleep with me?" He gestured toward his little travel trailer.

"No," she said simply.

"Okay, well, you want to ride my horses?"

"Sure."

They started to walk away toward the corral, then Jim turned back.

"Hey, I don't know what I was thinking, eh? I don't even want to go inside that trailer again! You want it, Tom? I'll give it to you."

"Yeah, sure," I said.

"Okay, it's yours." He waved as they walked away.

Jim didn't come back from the Chilcotin country for weeks, and then only to get his things. When we saw him again, he referred to Matilda as "my mother-in-law."

11

WINTER IN THE BACKCOUNTRY. The time of year we rarely see anybody we don't know, and when we do, we recognize the bright, unnatural colors they wear, the showroom look of outsiders from the city. Those of us who live and work outdoors wear the oldest, used-up things we have, and even new coats and gloves get quickly grimy and ragged, worn to the faded tones of everything exposed to the weather and hard use. And probably make us all look like homeless people to city eyes.

We saw them coming down the mountain road in a shiny new Blazer four-by-four, two men passing us in the colorful, catalog-new attire of roughing it for the weekend, but something didn't seem right. A furtive look in their eyes when they waved at me and Clayton, like trying too hard to seem as if they belonged. What were dudes doing up on Aeneas Mountain anyway?

Clayton hadn't told me why he wanted me to drive him up there either. I'd had a vague dream about driving around and seeing bighorn sheep, and had told him about it. How I woke up the night before in Jim's (now mine, but ever after called "Jim's") travel trailer, sensing a change in the weather. Instantly I knew I'd be wearing a yellow bandana, even before I looked out the window and recognized the slow dissipation of clouds before a fresh east wind. Which probably drove out the details of the dream as I marveled at the vault of stars so close overhead, outlining the dark shapes of mountains, and listened to a distant cow mooing forlornly. Since it turned into a rare mild day, the snow melting under dazzling sunshine, he'd said we could probably make it up the Aeneas Mountain road in my car. I'd been around him long enough to know how his mind worked—the closest bighorn sheep in that country was a herd that roamed the open, rounded ridges of Aeneas Mountain.

There were so many scattered, diverse locations in the Okanogan country named Aeneas—mountains, valleys, creeks, passes, flats—that I asked Clayton if he knew why. He said his father talked about it once, how it came from the Salish word for "something to trade with," *en'íyus,* which was changed by early settlers as so many Indian words were, to the current "EY-ni-us." He said the name became applied to Indians who bartered with the Whites, and then to the places where such bartering often took place.

We made it all the way up on top where an ocean of snowy mountains stretched away in every direction except the south, which was blocked from view by the heavy timber marching down from Lemanasky Fire Lookout. We drove in the tracks of only one other vehicle, probably made by the Blazer that passed us on the road up. When the other tracks veered off across country, I kept on the main road through untouched snow until it got too deep for good traction. I parked and we got out, both of us tying yellow bandanas over our faces and pulling hat brims low to protect from the blinding white of noonday sun on a world of snow. Dark bandanas would've been more effective but we were having too much fun secretly trying to outdo each other in the display of weather colors.

Our boots dragging in wet snow, we studied the tracks and droppings of the wild sheep. Not hunting, not talking, not in a hurry, we wandered west, examining the world on a lazy, balmy day. The only relief from the endless rolling glitter of snow were groves of fir and individual pine trees whose shadows were so dark by contrast they seemed like pits of unreadable blackness.

Soon the land sloped downward and we came to a drop-off where bare rock on the south faces showed wet and steaming in the sun. From there we could see the whole western slope of the mountain to the bottom of the Sinlahekin Valley, the usual haunt of the bighorn herd.

Well-trod trails showed where they angled up and down the mountainside, and groupings of oval depressions in snow where they bedded down at night. But after a long and careful study, no bighorns were seen.

Clayton gave me a significant look, just the glimmer of his eyes between bandana and old felt hat that made him look like an outlaw of the old west.

"What you think, power man?" he murmured. "Maybe somethin' spook 'em, make 'em hide somewhere, eh?"

"It does seem odd, a day like this."

I laughed. We sounded muffled in our bandanas, like outlaws discussing a holdup. The Yellow Bandana Gang, sniffing around for loot.

"Well, maybe somethin' for you," he said, pulling his down, revealing a questioning smile. "Maybe a dream don't mean nothin'. Then again, maybe it does. Who knows? But a power man have to look into it, eh?"

"You mean like seein' if I can find 'em?"

His smile faded. Reluctant to spell it out any clearer, he said, "Somethin' like that. Find out what there is to find, anyway. What else there to do up here for a power man?"

Taking off my soggy bandana and gloves, I must have looked dubious because he made a sudden gesture of exasperation and sat down in the snow. With a sigh, he studied the sky thoughtfully. The reinforced seat of his snowmobile suit protected his backside from the wet snow, but I only wore jeans, so I squatted on my heels.

"You tell me, your want to be on the earth's side," he said, choosing his words carefully. "I can't be tell you what to do all the time. I give you what I know, and you be the one to take the action. No good but you do how your power show you. Anytime we off in the hills, we lookin' for how the power move. All I can do is maybe talk the words around it. Say what they been sayin' for the way back, to the beginning."

Abashed at how easily he could read me, I said nothing. He repeated things he'd already said to me many times, and it wasn't due to his Salish love of repetition for repetition's sake. Probably the oldest mnemonic device and critical to passing on tried-and-true ways for a people who wrote nothing down, saying the same things over and over had lodged big chunks of lore in my mind where it was always ready to surface, guide, be tested, and confirmed in my own experience. It was sometimes astonishing how exactly he'd repeat something, rarely trying to find another way to say it, so that what I remembered was never some abstract concept, but his actual words—even his voice and inflections and tone and the look on his face.

Sometimes to highlight and make memorable what he was saying, he'd add some new bit of lore he felt I was ready for. Or add some new twist to how he understood things, especially designed for how he saw me struggling as a White man with the baggage of modern categories of thought and action. He did just that when he saw I wasn't going to say anything more—that his reminder to call up what I already knew had quickly taken effect. I could see it coming a mile away in the tilt of his head and how he prefaced his thoughts with, "In another way . . ."

"In another way . . . we wonder about all those religions, those great religions that heat up our great minds. All over the world, and to wonder: how do they help us know the earth, who is our mother? Because only one religion rank the earth first, ahead of the human person, ain't it? The oldest religion of all, what the few Natives keep alive and pass on. From the beginning to right now, right here, on Trader's Mountain.

"Like that First Hunter, he also the first power man. So we know how this to be, what we have to do to be on the earth's side. The person with power, he always pay attention, think about what he see, what he hear, what he smell, what he dream about. Always lookin' for somethin', some sign, and learn to read it all like a book. Not spend his time thinkin' about somethin' else than what show around him. Because he lookin' for some sign from the power. See how the power move in just anything, if he pay attention. *X'it i tlakwílux,* the real power person, he know somethin' show up in the littlest thing, be just maybe the tiny sign. And so he thinkin' about the power move all the time, eh?"

Then he was quiet. I thought about how he'd had me find our way in the dark and rain to the gap in the mountain ridge. This time, I realized, he wasn't going to set anything up. He probably had no more idea than I did what my dream of seeing bighorn sheep was about. I was on my own. If there was something for me up here on Aeneas Mountain, I'd have to open myself up to whatever it was.

As I instinctively began letting go of any further deliberation, I awakened to the vast flood of the world around me in the brilliant silence of the high drop-off. Clayton turned away and began to hum. I recognized the tune of an old Salish hunting song, and knew he was trying to help me concentrate on where I could be aware of power, a place devoid of conscious thought and reflection, kindled by the ancient language that came before everyday speech—song. When he began softly singing the words to the snowy vastness around us, words only remotely recognizable as current Salish words and put together in the odd syntax that made a regular beat (and therefore gave unexpected force to the single point of the song), I joined in.

> *(All around the country*
> *That's what I see*
> *All around the country*
> *That's what I see*
> *Good things to eat.)*

Our voices seemed small and lost in the emptiness, but the old, hand-me-down power song worked to fuse me in a singleness of seeking for something in everything that was coming to my senses. A breeze sprang up from behind us, blowing snow off the trees in soft plops. By the time our voices faded out after the usual five repetitions, I was silent inside and gazing at a lone bird flying against the breeze. It was so far away the only way I could identify it as a bluejay was by its distinctive flight, a series of dipping arcs. When the jay disappeared over the horizon, I abruptly stood up and made my way over the snow in that direction. I was only peripherally aware of what I was doing—that I was shut off from normal thoughts and simply acting on impulse, on a sudden certainty—that the bluejay was a sign to follow.

It's a timeless, expectant wander over snowy hills in a familiar reverie. Trudging blindly along for miles wherever the bluejay leads from tree to widely separated tree, registering the sound of Clayton following distantly behind, strange unspoken certainties begin to float by. Heightened convictions that I receive somewhere else than in my mind and seem to lodge in parts of my body—that are only accessible when I'm moving over the land like this—and that only later am I able to put into words, feebly, laughably. That come off as arbitrary commands or insightful asides. Scribbled later in a dog-eared spiral notebook to read years after like notes taken after a class: "You have to be a physical body off in nature. One of the animals. Letting go for your body to do what it already knows to do." And, "How ironic that the way into experiencing the hidden trueness of nature is a concentration on the surface of things." And even, "Craving the wilds, the feel of untouched nature, is craving that unused part of me denied in modern life."

Out there like a child of the earth with all senses engaged, receiving the flow of incoming world, wind blowing in my face, limbs of trees tossing, smell of melting snow, feel of steps in slushy wet, blur of horizon and everything slowly coming at me. So much attention focused for so long on whatever's there, the anomalies begin to show. The things I stopped acknowledging in childhood when I realized the older, wiser people around me laughed at what only I saw, so that I hid from ridicule in the comfort of what everybody would agree was really there. An arm where a branch should be. A woman's voice in the wind. The unlikely (in winter) arrival of a darting, hovering hummingbird nosing around my bandana as if to a giant yellow flower. The glimpse out of the corner of the eye of a tiny, human-like figure motioning to me, that turns into a clump of snow animated by my own moving shadow when I look right at it.

The ripple in the guts at each new anomalous thing until I hear a male voice talking nearby and abruptly stop to listen. From right over there, where the bluejay landed in a grove of fir trees. So unexpected, I wonder who could be out here and what they're doing. I can't tell what's being said, just snatches in the wind, but definitely English, local, like a rancher greeting somebody else and maybe "something good to eat." The loudest voice is very familiar, like a man I know from the Loomis area, so I go on, heading toward the dense fir grove to see who's over there and what they're doing.

As I wade through deepening snow at the edge of trees, there's a sudden explosion of frantic movement and I freeze, startled by dark flapping forms rising up from the shadows. Ravens, magpies, and blue-jays fly up, cawing and scolding in alarm, some of the ravens flying around in tight circles overhead, reluctant to leave while others disappeared in every direction. It's such a shock, I'm thrust back into the everyday world where the realization that no people are in the fir grove seems impossible. But I can see through and out the other side. Besides, all those birds wouldn't have been gathered if people were present talking. There has to be something dead, an animal they're all feeding on, for the scavenger birds to have gathered here like they were.

Clayton came up beside me.

"Did you hear people talking?" I asked. "From here in the trees?"

He pulled down his bandana and shook his head no. When he went ahead, I followed him into the shadows of the fir trees and we stopped, letting our eyes adjust and looking around. It was all there to read at a glance. The two outsiders in the Blazer had been headhunting poachers. Here were their tire tracks coming in and going out. Here the remains of their campfire, here where they cleared away the snow and pitched their tent. Two gut piles stood out, bloody and bare and decimated by feeding birds, surrounded by bird tracks in the snow. Why the dudes had removed the guts was not clear, because off to one side lay two bighorn sheep carcasses, both large rams, both unskinned and only the heads and hind legs missing. They'd hacked off the heads for trophies and the hind parts for the hams, which were the biggest, easiest chunks of meat to get off. The gray, disfigured bodies with white rumps seemed otherwise untouched lying still in the bloodstained snow.

A few ravens and magpies settled in the trees above, waiting for us to leave. A bluejay called stridently behind me, *kwash! kwash! kwash!* and I turned to see it hopping from limb to limb, black crest wagging, white eye lines standing out sharply on the black of its face as it peered at me. I shivered, the realization washing over me of who the loud male voice had been. I'd been following him across country, from tree to tree, to join sociably with others where something was good to eat.

"*Aaaa,* thank you, Bluejay," I said with a sudden rush of feeling.

"Yah, they still good, still fresh," Clayton said, straightening up from where he was inspecting the rams' condition. "Shot 'em yesterday, last night maybe. They even gut 'em for us!" He laughed. "Their heads are really gone away!" This was a pun on the Salish name for bighorn sheep, which translated as "head going away," the usual way of glimpsing such canny, hard-to-get-close-to animals. Then he sighed at the waste typical of so many White hunters. "*Lekwíluhkin* (bighorn sheep)," he said, switching to Okanogan. ("This day to take pity on how they left you, and accept this gift of your bodies. So be it.")

All he said about what I'd done was, "This how the power man, have that kinda power, how he feed the people." As usual, he had little interest in the particularities of how a power of the world worked through me, only in the results. A bluejay had led me to food, one of the ways my power did things, and that was all there was to it. The details were my business. End of story.

There was no way I could drive my car to where the headhunters had four-wheeled it into the fir grove. It took the rest of the afternoon with Clayton skinning and butchering and me carrying loads of unboned meat about a mile in snow before we had everything usable loaded into the back of my station wagon. That night there were feasts of fresh bighorn sheep in homesteads all along the lower Similkameen, and plenty of jokes about the Yellow Bandana Gang having sniffed out somebody else's abandoned loot.

Something about Clayton's use of the English word "pray" always seemed to stick in my craw. All I could think of were old formulas of biblical beseeching to a high god which seemed at variance with what he actually said when he was praying. It wasn't that I wanted to know the Okanogan or "Indian" way of praying—Clayton happened to be Okanogan, happened to speak Okanogan Salish as his first language, and framed things he said in commonly understood Okanogan ways. But that wasn't to say he represented some uniformly Okanogan way. He was the only Indian I knew who spoke out loud to animals, for example. The elders were all so unique, even often eccentric, and every family had its own versions of the old stories and what they meant.

I only wanted to know Clayton Tommy's way, so I asked him why he used the word "pray" when he spoke to the powers of the world, since he didn't look or sound like what I'd learned in Christian churches. He thought my question was funny.

"We hear how the White people don't go to church anymore. The churches maybe dry up and blow away if the Indians don't take pity and fill up the pews every Sunday, eh?"

He said that Indians always knew how to pray more realistically and that was why they became more dependable churchgoers, as long as White church leaders didn't try to coerce them into following exclusive dogmas. When they did that, they offended the Indians' deep sense that such things should be left to individual understanding. "See, when the *Suyápi* pray, he not talkin' to the world here. He talkin' to somethin' he never see sign of. Have to have all those rules and rituals. Indian pray, why, he talkin' to who he can see, for what he know they can give."

I said it made sense how the Okanogan word *k'wówim* had been translated as "to pray" since they both meant to ask for something wanted with strong feeling, but the English word was more like pleading or begging and was usually used to address God as someone beyond anyone's understanding. Was I sensing something fundamentally different in the usage of the word *k'wówim?*

"Yah, well, maybe that *k'wówim,* better to say in English like, my want to hire you for somethin',", he said. "Offer this tobacco or this blanket or this knife or somethin' valuable, that you give me what I ask for. And what they give in return, like maybe the recovery from sick, the food, the husband, the job—we call that *schk'wówim,* like somethin' paid for."

We were up in the deep snows of one of the Ashnola creek valleys on the Canadian side of the line, engaged in what Clayton called "gravel fishing" for trout. It snowed the whole time we were there, two nights, and I was so used to working in the endless hours of falling snow that I hardly noticed it. We were the Black Bandana Gang now, mine tied around my upper arm, uncomfortable and always reminding me— keeping me aware of what the weather was doing. Clayton's around his neck was virtually hidden, only an afterthought for him. His brisk, infectious enthusiasm for the continuous drifting down of snowflakes through forest trees was all I really needed to know it was going to keep on snowing. He wore his deer-head hat that made him look half-animal with the snout pointing out low over his eyes, the sewed-up ears peeking out of mounded snow, the neck ruff hanging down onto his back. He dried and smoked it over a smudge every night to keep it waterproof. Unfortunately it was becoming a little bare of hair after all his years of wearing it in the bush when it rained and snowed. So naturally it was the butt of recurring jokes, each a variation on his preference for hunting unique deer—the "bald" ones, or the "mangy" ones, or the deer that were undergoing chemotherapy treatments. Otherwise the muffled silence and solitude of the mountains in falling snow encouraged a quiet, meditative concentration, broken by his occasional terse instructions, and short exchanges around the campfire at night, like talking about the word "pray."

We'd snowshoed into knee-deep snow because his sister, Annie, had been craving the taste of fresh trout and for some reason none of the old-timers who still snuck around fishing the open spots on the Similkameen were finding any trout. Most of what they caught anyway were "planters," hatchery fish released for each summer's onslaught of city folks fishing for sport, and Annie wondered if her "little brother" could go up the Ashnola River and find some native trout that were so rare now. She was too old and sick to go with us, even though she wished she could keep a bush camp in snow for us the way she used to. About all she could do outdoors was her daily chore of feeding the horses she didn't ride anymore—that stood shaggy with winter coats on trodden, green-stained snow at the fence corner where she threw them hay.

So we'd gone up with an axe and a shovel and almost-empty backpacks, and been working the heads of beaver ponds for two days. Clayton said there were so many trout "sleeping" in the creek, he wanted to gather enough to smoke and feed people at winter dances that were about to start. What we did was clear the snow off the places where the creek widened into the beginnings of beaver ponds, broke up the ice with the axe, and then Clayton showed me how to feel around in the silty gravel under icy water for the trout that burrowed in for a winter's sleep. Near each spot he chose, I built a fire of dead branches on top of green boughs laid on snow, kindled with brushy twigs of dried bitterbrush we all carried in winter because it was so hot and fast starting a fire with wet wood. We'd take turns feeling through the murky creek bed for the long, slippery shapes of trout that would come out limp and motionless and throw them into the snowbanks. Working at it until our bare hands and arms lost all feeling, we'd dry out and warm up at the fire. The ice was a foot thick in places and sometimes we'd turn over a chunk of ice with so much gravel frozen in on the underside, the backs of sleeping trout could be seen exposed and the fish easily pulled out without having to feel around.

Clayton always stopped short of taking all we found, and sometimes put back the smaller ones. None of the fish were very big. But there were so many of them—anywhere from two to a dozen from each location we chopped open—Clayton cheerfully kept saying, "Oh, this won't take long" when it seemed like my skin was going to come off if I struck my hand in the frigid water one more time. We'd gut the ones we kept before they froze, and store them in the backpacks. Then we'd strap on our snowshoes and move on to another place he chose as likely for finding more.

For two nights we camped in a *takalímxu,* an old campsite he knew hidden under the spreading branches of a circle of enormous spruces and firs. It was so protected from the direct fall of snow we hardly needed the wagon tarp we strung between the tree trunks to shelter our bough beds and sleeping bags. The first night I slept like the dead, but the second night I dozed fitfully, my hands and arms burning and tingling so much they kept waking me up.

At one point in the wee hours, I was aware that some change had occurred, but not able to put my finger on what it was. There was the sound of Clayton's steady breathing, the faint pattery hiss of falling snow, and . . . what else? Something was missing. Oh—the sound of the creek. From the place nearby where we'd chopped open the ice. I was not aware of the bubbling rush of open water all night until it was missing. It had finally frozen over and gone silent.

I went back to sleep thinking about how the cold and snow worked to cover over the land, how it changed the appearance of everything.

I thought about how I'd been in that creek valley once years before, though I hardly recognized it as the same place. We'd camped on the mountain above, gathering *xas'xas* and other plants, and had been searching for a stray horse that broke his hobble. At a spring overlooking the beaver dams strung along the creek, I found the troublesome Appaloosa gelding mixed in with some other horses somebody had left up there for summer pasture. The bubbling spring had been such a beautiful spot, a hidden bowl of lush aspens and alders and marshy grasses and wildflowers on an otherwise sun-baked, south-facing slope of brush and scattered ponderosas. When I woke up in the morning, I realized I'd dreamed about the spring, but it was under snow, as if I'd hiked up to it from our camp, and there were deer all over, browsing the bitterbrush hillsides and bedding down in the trees above the spring.

I mentioned my dream to Clayton when we were about to set off for more creek work, and he laughed.

"My, what you got sure makin' the lots of food. Up to you if your want to go and see, but I gonna keep after the trouts. And you don't have no gun. What you gonna do, rassle 'em down and kill 'em with a knife?"

I laughed. "No, I'll stay with you and rassle trout—they're smaller and they don't fight back." We grinned at each other.

"Well, maybe that's right. You didn't hunt 'em in the dream, did you? Maybe just to know they there. Wait and see if anything come of it."

The second day our hands were so raw and chapped we spent as much time warming them at the fires as working the creek gravels. The first day we'd worked upstream from our camp, but the second day we broke camp and worked downstream carrying everything with us as we went. About mid-afternoon we gave up, our packs so heavy with trout that snowshoeing through the falling snow was too brutal to continue. The whole time we were up there we'd been eating nothing but trout roasted on coals and drinking ice water from the creek, so I was daydreaming about hot coffee and anything but fish as we climbed out of the creek bottom. Clayton led the way up onto the open, south-facing slopes where the snow wasn't so deep and we could stagger along game trails without snowshoes.

We still had about two miles to go to make it all the way down to the Ashnola River when we smelled and saw the smoke of a campfire ahead. For the first time it occurred to me that what we'd been doing "gravel fishing" for trout was probably illegal according to B.C. Provincial law. But as usual, Clayton showed no concern and turned, heading straight for whoever it was, even with our clothes stained with bloody, glittery slime, and our packs reeking of fish. Like the time we hauled away what was left of the two bighorns, he always said the earth wasn't going to give us something just to have us get busted for it. The power would take care of us, would warn us if there were some threat. And that's the way it always happened.

I didn't know either of the two Indian men out deer hunting that we found by a fire under a shallow rock overhang. Clayton seemed to know them both, but they'd obviously never seen him in his wild-looking headgear. They stared at it openly when we appeared trudging out of the snowfall to set down our packs and warm our hands, but neither said a word about it. One of the two sounded depressed as he spoke politely about the falling snow. The other was slumped back in the garrulous, advanced stages of a drunk, his hands cradling an open bottle of Canadian Liquor Board rye whiskey. (Half full? Or half empty?)

"Ahh, shomebody to drink with me," he declaimed, offering the bottle to Clayton.

"Not likely, eh, wino?" Clayton said, stunning me with his open disdain. But it kept the drinker mumbling and out of the conversation.

They were both young, in their twenties, wearing ragged coats and boots too thin for the weather. They had only one rifle between them, an aged British Enfield combat monster that weighed a ton and had the scars of having knocked around Europe during World War II.

"His dad's. From the war," the short, thin, sober one said, gesturing toward his buddy. He had nothing to offer us but a candy bar, which Clayton promptly ate up without sharing. I figured it was payback time for all the hairless deer jokes. When the guy shrugged apologetically at me, Clayton assumed an innocent look and lied, saying, "He's diabetic." I couldn't help breaking up. Then Clayton opened his pack and gave the guy fish, one after another until he blushed and became flustered and said, "Oh, that's enough—more than enough, eh?" Immediately spreading out the coals on one side of his fire, he put some fish on to sizzle and sniffed the searing smell like he was starving.

They talked and laughed about mutual acquaintances and discovered they were distantly related. Out of their talk came the young man's story of being out of work and having no money with a wife and children at home. Wino had been the one with a rifle and bullets. They'd thought the snow would stop and they could find a deer in the easy tracking that would follow, but it hadn't let up. I got the impression he didn't know much about deer behavior by the kinds of places he said he'd been looking, and felt sorry for him still hoping to get meat for his family even with his partner having given up. He persisted with indirect questions about whether the snow would stop before it got dark and they'd have to go back, showing he knew Clayton's reputation with the weather. Clayton confirmed my own feeling about it by shaking his head dismissively, then added, "You be better to ask this *Suyápi* if he know anything. The deer just give theirself away to him."

The young guy had been pretty much ignoring me the whole time, but now he looked at me in curiosity, and asked dubiously, "You hunt, eh?"

Not wanting to go through some kind of trial by questioning to convince an inexperienced hunter I knew what I was talking about, and knowing exactly what Clayton was hinting at, I said brusquely, "Yeah . . . so you know this country around here?"

He nodded. I asked him if he knew the big spring uphill from the beaver ponds, describing in detail where it was from where we were. He said he knew it from when he ran his dad's horses up the creek valley in summer, because they'd hang out up there to get away from the clouds of mosquitoes in the pond-filled valley bottom.

"Well," I said. "There's a lot of deer feedin' in that brush up there, and they bed down in the trees above the spring."

His eyes lit up. When we finally lifted our packs and went on, he was cooking more fish for his buddy, hoping to soften him up for what he wanted to do—borrow the Enfield and go alone to the spring before it got dark.

Having forgotten all about it in the weeks that followed, I was pumping gas into my car at the Chevron station in Keremeos one cold and windy afternoon when the young guy pulled up in a battered green Nissan pickup, the tiny cab filled with wife and kids. He got out and went inside the convenience store. When he came out, I waved to him. He recognized me and came over, shaking my hand and laughingly asking about my sidekick, the deer-man of the Ashnola. Then he unbuckled and pulled off his belt from under the same raggedy coat he wore in the mountains. Presenting the belt to me as a gift in his shy, off-hand way, he said the deer had been right where I'd told him they'd be, and he shot two of them. The gift was a beautiful hand-tooled leather belt with a silver concho buckle inlaid with turquoise and other stones, a prize he won in bronc riding at the Calgary Stampede.

"No, no, it's yours, eh?" he said when I protested that it was such a valuable heirloom. "We got through the worst of it okay. We ate good, and now I got some work." He beamed.

"Well, thanks." I took off my own belt and put on his. It was so excessively ornate and priceless, I felt humbled and proud at the same time. Before I could think of anything more to say, or even ask his name, he turned and walked away.

12

THE SHORT, GLOOMY DAYS of late winter snowed in at my cabin in the mountains were hard but unexpectedly eye-opening. The expanse of forest around the clearing where the plank shack sat by the creek became lined with radiating, well-trod foot trails from my passage out and back from the hub of a hushed and isolated existence. I hardly remembered what the place was like with bare ground to walk on—everything outside was done on deep snow. Only the short paths to my woodpile, outhouse, and the hole in creek ice where I drew water were packed down enough to provide much of a hard surface underfoot. Beyond the fringe of bare poplars that on rare, blue-sky days let through low and feeble sunlight to brighten my dooryard, there was the somber, sloping forest of conifers, a twilight world of boughs and bark buried under snow. Where the footprint evidence of wild animals showed they moved about the world quieter than I ever could. Some I never saw, like the marten who left tracks up the lean of a snow-banked log, scaling a tree hunting the squirrels who announced each coming of daylight with long, chattering calls to business that sounded like old-fashioned alarm clocks.

I'd walk the trails until they faded out into knee-deep struggles in powder, then strap on bear-paw snowshoes and go on wherever I pleased. The main trail followed where an old truck track had been cleared through trees, winding along the creek downstream and then contouring around ridges to join an old logging road, my way in and out. Another trail led beyond the outhouse, through a dense thicket of red-barked osier dogwood and spiny raspberry canes to an open ridge leading south into climax Douglas fir forest so heavily logged, the vast openings and slash piles were home to a population boom of snowshoe hares.

Right by the hole in creek ice was the tiny sweatlodge I had built, half-buried in the snow I kept shoveled off so the weight wouldn't collapse the flimsy, curved-willow framework covered with blankets and an old cloth tarp. Beyond the fire pit, another trail forked, one way following the open pathway of the frozen creek upstream to where I cut down dead tamarack trees to skid home in short log lengths for firewood, and ultimately miles farther to lodgepole pine flats, even-aged pole forest coming up after a forest fire where porcupines sat eating bark on high limbs. The other fork crossed the creek and climbed a steep mountainside until it reached a maze of deer trails on brushy, south-facing slopes. That was my favorite way to go, where the high-mountain deer had drifted down and congregated in such numbers for so many winters their main browse, bitterbrush, was pruned into fantastic shapes, from masses of low, twiggy bonsai to stiff, twisted trunks eaten bare as high as the deer could reach. And where the sun-weathered bark of solitary ponderosa pines stood out in cinnamon-yellow contrast to the bleached smoky dark of fir trunks. Above it all, the uppermost granite crags stood free of snow, glaring out with a creamy ocher smoothness left by ancient glaciers and showing veins of black mica and rose quartz. Hidden in the deep recesses of rock were faded flecks of red pigment lingering from pictures painted of power gained on quests in the old days, too weathered to recognize anything, and hidden behind bare-branch screens of ironwood with their peeling, coffee-colored bark.

I hunted the snowshoe hares with a .22 and gathered the stringy brown Coyote's hair lichen hanging from tree limbs with a long pole, combining them in a feast of pot-roasted *ananík* and *skwálip,* the native black pudding. I pounded dried serviceberries and mixed them with powdered deer jerky and melted deer fat, coming up with a granola-like pemmican so sweet and fueling that even on long snowshoe treks in blinding blizzards, I burned with a fire from within. The windows of the cabin were merely two layers of clear plastic, so at night I could hear everything going on outside as if I was camped in a tent. During nights of polar outbreak when subzero cold made the air as empty as outer space and the snow as hard as powdered ice, I would listen to the crumping tread of coyotes sniffing around for a way in to the stored food of the cabin, or to the hoots of a great horned owl that could have been a mile away but came to my ear with such rasping detail it sounded like right outside. Once, the bloodcurdling scream of a mountain lion woke me with such a start I expected to find it standing over me. The lion's tracks by daylight, unmistakably large, wide prints without claw marks, showed the lion had nosed its way inside the sweat-lodge.

The time I spent alone in the mountains was a time of retreat and self-training. Almost every day I was there, I built a fire to heat rocks and sweated alone in the dark, mildew-smelling hut. My hoard of lava rocks dwindled as time went on, shattering from repeated use, and the initial shock of pouring a bucket of creek water over my head when I came out naked and steaming gradually became second nature. As the uninterrupted flow of time passed in meditative solitude, I began to observe one of the things Clayton Tommy said would come of training for power—a heightened ability to concentrate and discern subtle differences in how I perceived things.

Like in how I dreamed: There was definitely a different feel when it was "just a dream" *(kays)* than when it was what he called "be given a dream" *(kultkáysent)*. An ordinary dream, no matter how vivid or unusual or compelling, felt only like it was something I experienced. A dream "given to me" had an added quality, a sense of watching things unfold that I had no control over, like watching myself on video doing unfamiliar things. It was the added distance—the being there and doing and yet simultaneously being a passive observer of myself in the experience that lingered when I woke up, that made me sit up and take notice of what was being given to me. Dreams like that seldom contained the outlandishly impossible features of ordinary dreams, but usually included me grabbing something with my hands, like my dream of grabbing the deer's antlers.

There was a third kind of dreaming that Clayton said people with power did, what he called *asxa'xá i ks'káysem,* "your power dreamin'," or "be given the dream you ask your power for." This he described as calling on your power but asking for it in a dream. It was done at times of great need at first, something important you wanted help with because it took sacrifice and concentration, and your power had to be focused by invincible feeling to give you the dream you asked for. He said it was dangerous, not to be done lightly, because it "made things happen in the world just like you dream 'em." If your attention wavered, if you let other things intrude, if you harbored resentments against other people—any of these things could "point what you got in a different direction," do harm to others, and "come back to haunt you." Power dreaming was how some people became attracted to and infatuated with *tlaxx,* witchcraft, he said, and was not something to train for if you didn't have a generous heart, if you didn't have the conviction of a man "who know the power gonna give him all what he need in life, and don't have envy for what others have."

How Clayton decided I was ready to try power dreaming came one bitter, clear morning when he walked out of the woods while I was splitting firewood in front of the cabin. He seemed to enjoy my surprise—he'd been away for a month to winter dances and I had no way of knowing he'd returned. Never having been up to visit before, his eyes shone with curiosity as he looked around, his breath rising in clouds of steam from walking without snowshoes for miles on the trail in. With typical aplomb, he minimized the difficulty of his early morning "stroll," saying it was nothing compared to spirit dancing all night, and besides, the trail in was like a Forest Service trail, "a freeway through the timber, eh?" He said jokingly he'd hoped I wasn't home because he was "like a bear come out starving in the spring," planning to raid the stores of fresh meat from all the game I was presumably hunting and hoarding for myself. Tied to his coat's buttonhole was a turquoise blue ribbon, and he nodded approvingly at the matching blue bandana tied around my wrist, both of them flapping in the brisk wind from the north.

He walked up accompanied by a big dog, which was strange since he never kept dogs. He often said, usually with a look of resignation, "What I got don't like dogs." Once I looked closely at the dog, a powerfully muscled black male hound with crazed-looking eyes, I recognized him as one of a pack of lion-hunting dogs belonging to a cattle rancher near Loomis. Clayton said the dog had come running up to him in the deep powder of bottomland timber along the creek just below my cabin, and assumed the dog was mine. When I told him he wasn't, Clayton's eyes narrowed in thought. When he heard who owned the dog and that he was an accomplished trailer and treer of mountain lions, he said, "*Aaaa,* an omen!"

I said the dog probably got loose somehow and was out speculating for lions on his own.

"There's one hanging around here," I added. "Lots for 'em to eat— lots of snowshoe rabbits, deer." I told him about hearing a lion scream and finding its tracks leading in and out of the sweatlodge doorflap. "That's what probably brought him up here."

"Well, sure, sometimes a dog is just a dog," Clayton said. "But what he doin' comin' up to us if he such a great hunter out huntin'? And look how he takin' to you!"

It was eerie having this particular dog nose up to me, tail wagging, licking my gloves. I knew him as a vicious, menacing dog with no regard for anyone but his master. The other times I'd seen him he'd been chained up or kenneled in the back of a pickup truck. He'd always growled and lunged at me. Yet here he was, sitting attentively in the snow beside my chopping block, eyes glazed at the feel of me petting his enormous head and floppy ears.

"Maybe he's lost," I said.

"Maybe. Or maybe he a sign about you. Not likely that a huntin' dog who roam the mountains get lost so close to home. This dog is tame, like a puppy for you now, eh? This what you call a very good sign. *Xast awhá ksch'ewxítems.*"

"Huh. I wonder what about?"

"This the great lion hunter that come tame to your hand, ain't it? That we see the power ready to come and be like your dog, ready for whatever you ask."

"Huh."

"And now we get the message, I wonder what that dog gonna do?"

I stopped petting the dog and stood watching with Clayton. Nosing around the dooryard for a moment, sniffing the smells and leaving his yellow mark, he soon lost any further interest in us. Trotting away nose down through the snow, he disappeared into the trees.

Clayton beamed. "Maybe no better sign than that. Here and gone. Sometimes the power give you somethin' like that, eh? A power man watch for it, ponder on whatever happenin' might mean. And not just the dog, but the lion—come in the night and go in where we warm ourself for the power. And my want to know, why the sign come for you? Maybe some trouble, maybe you have somethin' botherin' you, that you want to look into. *Stim aspu'ús awhá sin'ḳa'íls?* (What is in your heart about this matter?)"

"*Uch ḳu'íluxt? Mi ḳwu'xóoy ḳul chítux uhl chem ḳwu'ítlen* (Are you hungry? Let's go in the house and we can eat)," I said.

We went inside to thaw out at the woodstove. Talking over hot cups of coffee while I warmed up some food, I told him he was right—I'd been bothered by the disappearance of an old friend, Sid Loughren, a military buddy who'd also settled in the Okanogan, and who'd gotten into legal troubles because he was such a fearless environmental activist. Sid was a tall, lanky Irish-Chippewa from Minnesota who was always showing up at hot spots of confrontation, like the demonstrations against the raising of Chief Joseph Dam on the Columbia River, or against the radioactive waste seeping into the river at the Hanford nuclear plants farther downstream. I didn't see him much once he started hanging out with the traditionals on the east side of the Colville Reservation, joining with them in opposition to the tribe's development of a molybdenum mine on Mount Tolman. Then I heard a warrant was out for his arrest on federal charges of damaging machinery used to build a road and prepare the site for the mine, and that Sid had disappeared. For months I'd been wondering what had happened to him and what I could do for him.

"*K'wai* (So then), I come at just the right time, eh?" Clayton said unlacing and kicking off his boots, making himself at home. "*Ixí k'kewápa,* that dog, not just a dog. *Ixí shwá',* not just a lion. You feel you ready for it?"

"For what?"

"To show your power in the dream you ask for?"

"Yeah, I guess so. It's not like Sid to disappear like that. At least, not without some word to me. . . ."

Sipping his coffee thoughtfully, Clayton said we could build a fire and sweat later that afternoon. After that, we could stay up most of the night singing. He said he'd talk more about it in the sweatlodge, and I shouldn't eat anything and should stop drinking coffee. Maybe only have a sip of water when we sweated. Meanwhile, he was starving, he said, and got up in his stocking feet to poke around my pots for something to eat. As he rummaged around, buttering bread, pouring the last of the coffee, sitting down with the pot of leftover rabbit roast, he told me the mining company had really pulled a good one on the tribal business council. Once they got approval and desecrated Mount Tolman with their road and preliminary work on the site, they quit and pulled out because molybdenum prices were so low. The economic windfall the tribal leaders had planned on vanished overnight. But the mining company held the rights now, and could come back and mine anytime they felt like it. Clayton said "all those apples" who'd promoted the mine as imminent prosperity—as steak on the table and new cars out front for tribal members—now looked like the fools they were.

Then, "What's this?" he said, tasting the leftover *skwálip,* the black pudding made of tree moss that Charlene had taught me how to make. "*Aaaa,* now this what the real Indian like to eat!"

High, thin clouds came up in the afternoon and it wasn't so cold outside. As I built the fire and heated rocks, Clayton went off by himself following the trail south that led up to the granite crags and rock pictures. I studied the sky and felt the shift—a front was coming from the west, building clouds slowly. It would snow again tomorrow or the next day. There was a flat emptiness in my guts from not eating since the night before that gave me a familiar confidence in the moment. When Clayton returned later, I'd switched to a black bandana on my wrist and noticed his turquoise ribbon was gone, replaced by a black one. He laughed when he saw mine.

"No need to put you on the spot anymore, eh?" he said, untying his ribbon and tossing it into the flames.

After warming up at the fire, he went downstream to cut fresh fir boughs for the sweatlodge floor and came back with armfuls. The creek stepped down in a series of rapids and pools until it went over a low falls far downstream from the cabin, which Clayton said was frozen over completely like the rest of the creek. After laying the fir floor, he took up the axe again and began widening the hole in ice where I drew water. The ice was so thick it took many chops to break away a chunk, Clayton's powerful blows shooting sprays of ice shavings twenty feet away. Eventually he had a big area of floating icebergs and slush, and I went over to help him fish out the bigger chunks. I knew he was making a place for us to wade in and go under between times of sweating, and he'd opened the ice out to the deepest part where the bouldery bottom could be seen under four feet of greenish water. The current was strong and some of the ice chunks turned under and got sucked away, bumping along under the firm ice where we stood.

"When you come and jump in, don't be like that ice that dive under," he joked. "Have to try and save you, eh? But I'm too old to run down to that waterfall with no clothes on and chop you out a hole!"

Every single one of my sweatlodge rocks was glowing bright orange in the fire and Clayton shoveled half of them—an alarming number—into the pit inside the doorway. We undressed and climbed in with a bucket of water, pulled down the coverings so it was pitch dark except for the dull incandescence of clicking rocks, and as we bent over in the cramped confinement, Clayton intoned the ritualized Okanogan words that elders usually start a sweat with. Before he could finish, his voice was drowned out by him splashing huge amounts of water on the instantly roaring rocks, dimming their glow, and engulfing us in such a burning steam that I could barely stay upright. As he continued to splash on more and more water, it occurred to me that my usual way of easing slowly into gradually hotter and hotter times in the sweatlodge had not prepared me for this sudden blistering hell. I made a mental note to avoid sweating with an elder so fresh from the rigors of all-night winter dancing that he not only couldn't feel the heat, he was slapping his bare skin (which increases the burning sensation) and joking about how White men's sweathouses never got very hot.

Maybe it was just the feeling of being burnt alive, but it seemed like he was bent on humiliating me, adding that White men had such a hard time seeing "the other part of the world" because they wouldn't let go of their control, their "being in charge." They were too afraid of pain and dying, he said, and that was why their sweatlodges weren't a painful doorway into "the other side of the world," but "just bath houses." My face was finally buried in the cooler air of the fir boughs and I was struggling with the urge to bolt for the doorflap when his tone changed. He spoke in a reverent voice about the powers of the earth and sky and how they came to people suffering in the sweatlodge, offering them their help, their power to endure the heat if the people were suitably humble. Then he spoke of himself.

"They always tellin' us, the words handed down, and my elder tell me the same. When we go in the sweathouse, we humble ourself. But sometimes I forget and try to be strong. When I do that, try to be strong, those powers find a way to humble me."

His words hit me hard. I was so involved with my own suffering that it hadn't occurred to me that it had to be just as hot for him, yet he wasn't suffering from it. I thought of Sid, that I was undertaking this sacrifice so I could somehow find out about him and help him, and yet here I was sprawled on the floor, obsessed with my own misery. I knew I was only humiliating myself. Clayton's subtle reminder, conveyed in such a personal way from his own experience, sank in. I felt myself let go in the face of this sweatlodge power so much greater than my own. Something snapped and I simply sat up in the incredible burn. The other side of me, the "me" I only vaguely remember until I relinquish being in charge, took over with such hardness that I seemed to float in a sea of unfeeling nothingness. I could tell it was hotter than a body should take, yet it no longer hurt, it no longer pressed on me. "Hearing" the first words of one of my favorite sweatlodge songs—an old Bluejay power song, a "finding" song—I began to sing:

> *Pen'ḳín ta'xílem en'tliḳ'tliḳ'tálx* . . .
> *(When they cry like that,*

I fly all over the world.
Doing that, I see in the dark.

When they cry like that
I fly all over the world.
Doing that, I see what they have lost.)

Clayton joined in as soon as he recognized the song. While we sang together, I felt flooding into me such a sad joy, such a powerful emotional wonder and gratitude that my voice slid away from me, taking on the sobbing undertones of throat-singing. It perfectly expressed my overwhelming feelings, but seemed like someone else singing. Clayton continued to pour on water and it was strange—I knew it was burning hot and yet I welcomed it, hardly felt it, exulted in it, wanted more of it.

When we finished the song, Clayton began to speak to me as if to someone completely different. His words were chopped up by shallow inhales of searing air that so restricted his use of mouth and lips he barely murmured. What I was seeing inside the utter darkness of the sweatlodge made it hard for me to focus on what he was saying: A misty, tunnel-like white glow that I remembered from my earliest times of sweating; a moonlike frosty light that illuminated nothing but gave the sense of opening out into a vast expanse. Faint bluish pinpoints danced where I knew the rocks must be, and garish, incandescent masses of lit-up movement emerged into view here and there like strobe-lighted persons. They were arriving from far away at what seemed like me sitting alone on a flat, unfamiliar landscape.

Clayton's voice sounded faraway, too, but I recognized what he was talking about and suddenly wanted to hear what he was saying. Closing my eyes, feeling the salty burn, I instinctively began switching myself with a fir bough from the floor. There was nothing but the sputtering of the rocks and his voice, talking slowly and at length about the third kind of dreaming. He commended me for my seriousness in training for power and spoke of the kind of concentration that came of it, "that come of long practice, that everything is gone but just one simple thing we hold on to."

He told stories from his seemingly bottomless well of lore that detailed how men and women had power-dreamed for solutions to pressing problems, from finding game animals in time of starvation to seeking for knowledge of loved ones or enemies at a distance. Some of his stories had the vagueness of ancient retellings that included reliance on bows and arrows, and some startled me with the names of people I knew and the modern problems of keeping old cars running, or finding out about a relative who'd moved to the city. By the time he was done, I had absorbed the broad outlines of how to proceed and what to expect. He finished by saying the most important thing to do when power-dreaming was to act on whatever I dreamed—no matter how obscure—because that was the only way to learn.

Once again, I'd been instructed by an elder in the blank slate of mindless awareness that sweathousing produced in me, and what he told me became indelibly stored where my conscious thoughts could not easily call it up. Yet I knew that I knew what I needed to know, without being able to say what it was. Until I was again in the state where I needed to use it, and then it would flood out, as if he was there speaking the same words to me. The amnesia worked both ways, I realized, when Clayton asked me to open the doorflap and I was so turned around I couldn't find it. Even worse, when I bumped into his slippery body, I was startled to find him to my left, when I was sure he'd been sitting to my right. And I was dumbfounded when I got the door open and saw the snow and frozen creek—my impression from sitting on a vast plain with strange people was that it was warm summertime. I went through a series of jolting adjustments crawling out and pulling the tarp up further. Only when I reconciled myself to the reality of being in the frigid Okanogan in a wintry dusk did I recognize what my experience had been.

And I was grateful for how hot he'd made it when we tiptoed down the snowy bank and took turns wading into the creek, bracing our hands on the solid ice sides to duck under and come up spouting for oxygen like whales. I went under as many times as I could bear it, and stayed under once for about ten heartbeats—eyes open to the yellowish blurry underworld of the creek that faded into a forbidding void under the ice downstream. Then we stood dripping at the pit of glowing coals and rocks, staring trancelike at how bright and arresting it was in the faded sameness of evening. I felt so fit and poised and ready for more, when Clayton picked up the shovel, I offered to be rock-man. He climbed in as I swung the freshly incandescent rocks inside on top of the others. By the glare of their pumpkin glow, I saw him looking at me wide-eyed in mock surprise that I was shoveling all the rest of them in.

"Huh, well," I said. "I can't be havin' the Native elder feeling a chill in my sweatbath, now can I?"

After an even longer time sweating with the rest of the rocks, we emerged to complete darkness outside, only the faint glow of coals in the fire pit orienting us to find the opening in the ice and feel our way into the water. After being hot for so long, the creek felt like tepid bathwater, only adding to my numb awareness of being alive in a kind of void. One thing slowly led to another, and I began to move faster and think again only when my feet got so cold from standing barefoot in the snow that I shivered my way into the unfamiliar mechanics of putting on clothes. I heard Clayton go inside the cabin and saw the glimmering light of a kerosene lamp being lit. It was enough to illuminate the open front of the sweatlodge with clouds of steam still billowing out into the frigid air.

Inside the cabin I stoked the woodstove with logs and before I closed the metal door, Clayton brought one of the green juniper boughs I kept around, ignited it in the flames, blew it out, and walked around smudging the one-room interior with thick, resinous smoke. He usually said of smudging that it was to attract the spirits "with what smell they like," but this time he said, "Only cedar, that they like, but keep away the bad ones, the power of anybody with bad thoughts against us. So they can't mess up what we ask for this night."

After a sweat, especially a long, hot one that removes the inclination to think about ordinary things, there's a mindless just being there as if everything that was familiar before is freshly new. This sense can be dispelled by aimless talk and indulging in ordinary preoccupations, or it can be heightened by silence and concentration on a rarefied awareness of everything, including oneself, as an unspeakable wonder. So I knew what to do, and kept my attention quietly focused on the invisible, knowing power behind the stillness of appearances. What we were doing had begun with the tobacco I sprinkled on the fire to heat the rocks, and wouldn't end until daylight when I woke up and broke my fast. I sat on my bedroll on the floor and said nothing, holding the image of Sid's face in my mind's eye.

Clayton sat opposite, his back against the wall, his heavy coat like a blanket over his outstretched legs. When he blew out the lamp, the only light was the flickering of flames showing through the seams of the woodstove. I knew he'd wait until I started a song to sing with me, to help and support me in what I was doing, and between times would concentrate on what I wanted to dream about. At first I sang sweat-lodge songs to send the emotion of my appeal into the silence, but as the hours passed and weary vagueness came over me—and my mind began to wander—I sang the more esoteric power songs Clayton had passed on to me, to stay focused on Sid and the feelings I had for him. Later, in the wee hours, voice turning hoarse, I sang whatever came to mind to stay awake and remember what I was doing. Even a lilting Irish ditty I thought I'd forgotten, that I'd learned in the long ago from a woman of the Barclays who married an Indian man, that called up faraway memories of the Southwest desert of my youth. . . .

I think Clayton fell asleep at some point—he ceased to sing with me and I couldn't see him in the darkness. It got cold as the fire burned down, and I remember pulling my sleeping bag around me where I sat. I drifted in and out of consciousness, and between lapses I was reduced to a simple repetitive wordless plea that I held on to, that felt something like, "Where are you, Sid? How can I help you?" As the lapses became deeper and longer, I became even more aware that I was calling on someone to help me, someone close and familiar and always there.

Then I'm in a bright place, hunting on foot with my rifle in some lava-rock hills. It's daytime and I'm hunting deer. I'm in the open country on the north side of the Yakima River, walking out a long, flat lava plateau with steep scarps on both sides. There's only a few scattered trees and the snow is in patches here and there. I know the place because it's where I once hunted grouse.

Under a tall, spreading fir tree, I see a small cabin and go over to it.

Standing by the tree (and the cabin I don't really look at) I see coming from the other direction some people walking home to the cabin. It's a woman and her two children, teenagers, a girl and a boy. They don't see me and walk right up talking about going into their house and taking a nap. I've never seen them before, but they "feel" Native to me, even though there's nothing conspicuous about them to identify them as any different from me. They suddenly stop still when the mother sees me by the tree. At least the mother and daughter do, staring at me startled and full of dread—but the boy stumbles around aimlessly like he's retarded and oblivious, jerking in flighty spasms like he has a nervous disorder. I say something to them that makes me feel unaccountably sad for the woman. She responds, telling me to take the boy, that he's supposed to live with me now. She and her daughter watch impassively as I have to grab the boy in both hands because he's so unaware of what's happening and jerking around.

I woke up, aware that I was dreaming, that it was broad daylight in my cabin. Slumped over my lap with my head down, I lifted my eyes and took a deep breath. Clayton was asleep on his side by the wall, his coat pulled up to his cheek. Blinking and stretching more awake, I couldn't shake the dreadful sadness I felt for the woman in the dream. Without trying to figure it out, I ran through the entire experience of the dream, looking at every detail, branding everything about it in my memory while it was still fresh, so I wouldn't lose it. Only gradually did it dawn on me that the dream apparently had nothing to do with Sid. It was such a letdown, and my complicated feelings toward the woman were so gloomy and distasteful, I put the dream out of my mind and got up stiffly to stoke the fire.

Clayton stirred and sat up. I knew he wouldn't ask me anything, and he didn't. I was starving, and when I got the cabin warming up I mixed up some batter and started to cook pancakes. It was like any morning camped out in the bush with him, except that he started joking about everything—the night spent on the hard floor, the way I flipped pancakes like a restaurant chef, the weirdness of hearing me singing "bagpipe music" during the night—and didn't stop until breakfast was ready and I took an offering of the food and threw it into the fire. The ambivalence in my voice was probably noticeable as I said a short prayer of thanks for being given a dream I'd asked for.

"*Aaaa,* maybe not what you thought, eh?" Clayton said with a knowing smile as we dug into our food. "Not the dream it should be, maybe?"

We ate in silence. When we were done, he prepared to leave and saw me loading my backpack and pulling out my rifle. I told him I'd join him in the hike down the mountain because I had to drive down south to the Yakima country.

"Huh. Pretty far. Somethin' you dream about?"

"Yeah." All I could be sure about from the dream was that I'd been hunting deer on a certain lava plateau I knew. It was all I had to go on, so I was simply going to go there and hunt deer. The rest of the dream seemed unfathomable and faded from mind.

"And to hunt?" Clayton asked.

"Yeah." I told him the dream didn't have anything to do with my friend Sid.

"Maybe don't know that till you go find out, eh?"

Then after I closed down the cabin and we started down the trail on hard-packed snow, Clayton turned and said, "Or maybe just them bagpipe spirits you call for last night, sendin' you off on a wild goose hunt!"

13

IT WAS A LONG way to drive, over 200 miles south on two-lane, winding U.S. 97 through the mountains of central Washington. Back in the world of my own kind again, the paved highway and big trucks sweeping past, the orchards and towns and dirty snow and billboards that make up another kind of dream made real and palpable. After I passed Wenatchee, it started to snow lightly, then came down in blinding sheets that slowed traffic to a crawl on the climb to Blewett Pass. By the time I made it to Teanaway on the Yakima River, there were only a few stray flakes falling in the dusk and I found a wide place off the old river road to park and crash for the night. I was off the main routes, dug into my sleeping bag in the back of the station wagon, the rare passing car inordinately loud and brightly lit after the dim solitude of my time in the mountain cabin. So exhausted from lack of sleep and the grueling daylong drive on icy highways, I was about as muddled and demoralized as any man unable to see the bright side of wasting his time on a wild goose chase.

Awakened out of a deep sleep that seemed to last only a few minutes, I looked out at the darkness wondering why I no longer felt sleepy. Struggling over the seat in damp, freezing air, I fumbled for the wristwatch I kept looped around the blinker lever on the steering column. Wow, five a.m.—I had slept almost twelve hours! It would be two more hours to daylight. Car running and heater blasting, I ate my jet-fueled Indian granola and drank creek water from a jug. Itching to get off into the hills, I drove along the winding Yakima River canyon in the dark, searching for landmarks by the glare of headlights. The snow had stopped falling and it looked like very little had fallen all winter in that country.

I was sure I knew where I was when I parked and headed uphill in the dark carrying my loaded rifle and almost-empty backpack. Dawn brought me to the uppermost rolling flats that stretched for miles, the caprock of an ancient lava flow, a mesa-like plateau high and open above the timbered river shrouded in mist below. I wandered in country I vaguely remembered, the rifle in my hands awakening a habitual hunting awareness, a continuously alert, scanning, glossing, reading of everything coming to my senses that blocked out everything else. I was there to hunt deer and nothing else intruded, not even the odd details of the dream that had compelled me to be there.

It was such freedom to walk without snowshoes again—the day warming up to brief periods of sunshine, fresh snow melting, bare ground emerging. The brown soil of lava country, lichen-covered rocks, tawny bunch grass blown dry in the constant wind. No roads, no fences, no habitations of any kind, just as I remembered. Only far away, half-hidden in the wooded bottom of a canyon, some old ranch buildings glimpsed. But on top, the skyline's horizontal severity was broken by solitary, wind-shaped firs and pines alone.

There was very little deer sign. A few old tracks, some droppings. But it didn't matter. There was no point in working at it—something in the world would make whatever was going to happen happen. Meanwhile, somebody had to keep alive the oldest way of being aware—witnessing the ephemeral beauty and wonder of earth and sky around me. Gazing at clouds drifting down from the Cascade Range like ever-shifting dream barges. Feeling the race of blood when the red-tailed hawk sailed by so close overhead. Seeing the pool of clear water, the first open water that winter, snowmelt gathered in a rocky defile below a smooth and mossy lava chute. There were even a few spindly oak trees, still holding on to shriveled brown leaves from the season before, rustling in the wind with an unfamiliar sound that reminded me how far south of my usual haunts I was.

Approaching a bouldery rise, I heard the *kwash! kwash! kwash!* of a bluejay disappearing ahead. I instinctively knelt and crept to the brushy crest to peek over without being seen. Beyond, I finally saw some deer, three of them obscured in the bitterbrush thickets where they fed, showing no sign of sensing my presence. I calculated the wind direction, the lay of the land, the trend of their casual steps from bush to bush. When I backed away, I had a picture of how to hunt them.

It was a slow, time-consuming stalk. Leaving my pack behind, I crept down and around to another rise closer to the deer, in front of where they were heading. When I was finally in position, I inched up with my rifle at the ready, expecting to see them browsing slowly toward me. But no deer were to be seen. The wind was in my face and I'd made no sound . . . where could they be? Had they turned aside, gone in a different direction? Easing up higher, still no deer. Finally climbing atop a huge boulder that gave a view across the whole expanse of plateau I confirmed that they'd simply vanished.

It was unsettling, even eerie, but too much the practical hunter, I retrieved my pack and descended into the bitterbrush to look for the deers' tracks in the soft ground and patches of lingering snow. They were easy to find. Following their fresh hoofprints I could see two of the sets of tracks were smaller than the third, and the deer leaving the larger tracks was leading the way. Probably a doe and two yearlings, her previous year's fawns now nearly full-grown. The extra depth of the doe's hind tracks meant she was pregnant, probably with another set of twins on the way. Despite Clayton's influence on me that you had to hunt whatever presented itself to you, that you had no way of knowing why they offered what they did, my White man's lingering arbitrary reluctance to kill women and children came to the fore and I lost all interest in pursuing the deer. Trailing them just out of curiosity, I saw no indication that they'd been frightened away, just that they had stopped feeding and walked steadily away in a different direction. Their tracks led into a hidden fold in the land—explaining how three deer had so quickly disappeared from view—and along well-trod deer trails that kept below the skyline. Then I lost them on acres of bare lava rock.

Turning away, I hunted onward, reading the land and eventually giving in to an urge to explore the far reaches of the plateau. It was basically an elongated triangle, the long end narrowing eastward to a neck of ridge, a sinuous, flat-topped peninsula with vertical cliffs on both sides that came to an abrupt end at a sheer drop-off to the river below. The view was awesome out into the hazy vastness of the Kittitas Valley. I ate some pemmican and drank some water, noting by the position of the sun that it was mid-afternoon. The clouds were building dark and heavy overhead again. I decided to head back along the riverside edge of the plateau. Walking the rim, I began to recognize certain natural features from my time before when I hunted grouse.

Standing inland was a distinctively tall, bushy fir tree that rose from a grassy swale, a hidden pocket in the land that was the opening into a ravine that went the other way. As I looked at it, attracted by something inherently beautiful in the tree's shape and appearance, a bluejay silently flew toward it and landed in its upper branches. Drawn like a magnet, I turned and headed for the tree. As I approached, I realized I knew that particular tree—I'd shot a ruffed grouse perched in its top limbs, and then roasted the plucked bird over a fire kindled under the spreading branches sweeping so low to the ground. The tree was ancient, maybe 300, 400 years old by the thickness of the trunk, one of those already tall and old when the first of my people showed up in this country. The thick gnarls of bark showed signs of having survived repeated burnings from wildfires sweeping the plateau. Everything underneath the wide area screened by resinous, blue-green boughs was just as I remembered it: huge, exposed roots snaking away in the shallow soil, and in between were numerous deer beds, oval depressions in the thick duff from the resting bodies of countless generations of deer. Sitting down on the lee side out of the wind, I leaned against the massive trunk and rested in a reverie of contentment and rightness with the world. Fir tree and Bluejay and wind and me . . .

Soon I heard a sound behind me—the kick of a pebble—and turned to see some deer emerging slowly from the ravine and walking toward me. Easing down prone behind the cover of a tree root nearly a foot high, slowly lifting my rifle into position, I went completely still with the lead deer in my sights. There was nothing but the thoughtless concentration on a well-aimed shot as they plodded steadily toward the tree that gave me cover, three of them, oblivious to my presence, apparently heading for the deer beds where I lay in ambush. But then I saw the lead deer was a pregnant doe, the other two were young. It was a family group. I hesitated. Even though they were presenting themselves for an easy kill, something held me back. As the seconds passed it became somehow unbearable that they were walking right up to me so unsuspectingly. I became mesmerized by how they slowed down, tails and mule ears switching around in sleepy arrival at their hidden sanctuary.

Only ten feet away, so close I could see the deer's long eyelashes, the doe came to an abrupt halt and stared right at me, not knowing what to make of the motionless form of me but suspicious that something was not right. The other two deer came up alongside, the three of them side by side, unmoving, looking at me with alert curiosity. A fleeting recognition floated by—these were the same deer from before, that I'd tracked—a doe and two yearlings. I never changed the focus of my eyes, just studied them on the periphery, my years of practice with *wik'wst* kicking in automatically. The doe on the right and the yearling in the middle never wavered from their still, steady gaze, but the yearling on the left seemed unable to stay attentive to anything for long. Twitching and looking idly about, the yearling even took a few tentative steps in an oddly stumbling way. Then he—because now I could plainly see he was male and the other yearling was female—shook his head as if suffering from an earache. The two females took no notice of his odd behavior, gazing intently at me with liquid brown eyes and a still patience that was stupefying.

It was a standoff. It was up to me now. A strange feeling boiled up from within me and I blurted out: "Is there one of you who will come and live with me?"

It was something I'd done before, speak up to deer I'd stalked and give them a chance to offer themselves to me. Give me some sign that one of them was willing to die at my hands—so I'd be sure in such moments that I wasn't taking unfair advantage of them. Sometimes there'd be no sign, just deer disappearing at the sound of my voice.

Sometimes a deer would come toward me, or nod at me, or give me some other indication that felt right, that I thanked the deer for—and then fired. I'd never phrased it quite like this time, though, but I knew what my words meant: Will one of you offer your body as food to me and live on through me?

The sound of my voice only widened the deers' eyes, mystifying them, but as my words faded into the wind, the male began to spasm and jerk uncontrollably. He looked like he was having trouble staying on his feet, like he was having a seizure. Both females abruptly turned and looked at him, in pity I thought, but it was so unexpected for them to take their attention away from me at that moment, I knew it was a sign.

"Thank you for this gift," I said, feeling a twinge of pain in my heart for the doe deer that had given the male yearling life. Aiming at where I knew his heart was, I pulled the trigger and he crumpled slowly to the earth. At the loud bang, the two females started in surprise and raced away, but then stopped and looked back, seeing nothing but the male scuffing the dirt with his hooves as he went over on his side. Returning with stiff-legged steps, they edged closer to him, watching him die. It was a hard thing to see, their noses down and ears erect and forward, sniffing the blood of their brother and son as he went still. Full of remorse, and yet knowing nobody wants to die at the hands of someone not up to the magnitude of the sacrifice, I spoke to the doe.

"I'm grateful for this. I'll . . . take good care of him . . . treat him right."

They looked at where the sound of my voice came from, still not comprehending what had happened, so I rose up, a man, and stepped over the tree root toward them. As expected, the recognition of a dread human sent the two females into instant flight, the prancing, bounding gait of mule deer kicking up dirt and rocks as they fled. But then as suddenly they stopped again, turned and watched me from a short distance away. I could have easily shot them both, but they seemed to know I wouldn't. They edged closer, eyes going from the dead male to me and back to him.

I knelt and put my hand on the dead one, unable to say anything more but my feelings transparent in the release of tension from the adrenaline rush of the kill. His body was welcome food for myself and others. It was done. The two females lingered, even browsed a little as if nothing unusual had happened. They seemed unwilling to leave. Only when I turned the young buck hooves-up and started cutting him open with my knife did they slowly drift away, eventually disappearing back the way they'd come.

Alone, the intensity of my experience gave way to the mundane task and practiced ritual of gutting the deer on a bed of fir boughs. I wondered what had caused his strange and jerky behavior, but a superficial examination of his organs and insides showed a healthy, normal young animal. There weren't even any ticks on him. He was small enough to carry on my backpack without butchering or boning, so I didn't skin him, just tied his body with rope in a tightly reflexed bundle to the aluminum pack frame and tucked everything else under my poncho lashed around the bulk. Shouldering the hundred-pound load, I retrieved my rifle and set off, no more than a pack mule for the next hours it took me to thread my way down unstable rockslides from the plateau to the river bottom. It was dark when I finally made it to my car. Finally relieved of the heavy pack and drifting in the pleasant fatigue of a long day in the hills, I simply got in and started to drive home.

I'd only got a few miles up the river road when I had to pull over. Ordinary thoughts resuming had brought to mind the dream that led me so far from home. The delayed shock of recognition took all my attention as the dream images lined up with what I'd experienced. The house under the fir tree. The woman with two teenagers, a boy and a girl, coming home for a nap and finding me there. The mother telling me to take her son, who seemed flighty, retarded, suffering from uncontrollable spasms. That he was going to "live with me now." And how it made me feel bad, feel sorry for the mother. . . .

I stared out at the gloom, heater blasting, window down, smelling the smell of more snow coming. Wondering at how slow I was, how figuring things out always seemed to come later . . . yet how mysteriously loaded life felt when I did. How it filled me up and made me complete. How Clayton was right—there really was no other way to live once a man trained for power. It made life so real and purposeful, I couldn't imagine turning away from it.

Getting back over Blewett Pass as the snow came down in a whiteout was slow going. Fortunately the highway department snowplows were out in force, racing by with blades trailing sparks as they showered roadside trees with mucky snow. Because I followed one clearing the highway ahead of me over the top and down the other side, I didn't have to stop and put on tire chains. About seven o'clock I pulled into a gas station on the outskirts of the apple-packing town of Cashmere and filled up with the last of my money. That far down the Wenatchee Valley the snow was lighter, driven horizontally by the wind sweeping down from the mountains. Pumping gas, the snow glittering past sideways in the bright fluorescent lights, I felt a bump inside, a narrowing of attention. Self-conscious in the presence of strangers—the other people pumping gas, walking by to go inside and pay—I looked around at everything and everybody, wondering if I was being shown some kind of sign. Then I saw a familiar face, a familiar loping stride. It was Sid Loughren, bundled up in his faded military field coat, walking past along the road in front of my car.

"Sid!"

Turning furtively with his loose long black hair streaming out wetly from under a wool toque, he suddenly grinned in recognition. It was really him! He strode over, face tilted away from the sting of snow.

"Hey, my man, what're you doing here?" he crowed, slapping hands with me.

"Looking for you. I've got a present for you." I was grinning ear to ear, everything falling quickly into place in my mind.

"How'd you know I was living here?"

"I didn't. Lucky, I guess. What's the wanted man doing out walking the streets on a night like this?"

He winced, glancing around uneasily at how loud I'd said it.

"I don't know. Just got the urge to go for a walk."

"Well, maybe just so I could find you! C'mon, climb in. It's freezing!"

Inside the car with the heater on, the windows instantly fogged up from our wet clothes. We looked at each other with the warmth of brothers, the knowing that nothing the other could do would shake the loyalty forged so long ago in uniform. His familiar pockmarked, broken-nosed face was so ugly he seemed beautiful to me.

"God, it's good to see you again, my man!" he said.

"Same here. What a trip trying to track you down . . . the missing hundred-and-first airborne environmental avenger!"

We laughed, then he sniffed.

"What's that smell? Deer?"

"It's your present. A whole deer. Just killed it today." He looked back over the seat at the poncho-covered bundle and I added, "Tell me it's not just what you really needed?"

"No shit, Tom. Things are really tight. And I have a wife and kids now. You have really saved my ass. . . ."

"Wife . . . *and* kids? My, you really work fast!"

Sid pointed the way for me to drive him home. Seems he met his wife, Isa, a White woman with two small children from a previous marriage, at the hardware store in town where she worked.

"She's really good with power tools. Scary, sometimes. . . ."

Right up the main street into the downtown business district we went, and Sid pointed up at a lit window, an apartment on the second floor above a tavern.

"Last place they'd ever look for me, huh?" he said, directing me around the block, to the back of the row of buildings where railroad tracks and apple-storage sheds gave a dirty industrial feel to the blowing snowy night. The sickly sweet smell of the nearby candied fruit factory penetrated the closed car as I parked.

Sid seemed suddenly reluctant about bringing the deer up to his place. There was an outside stairwell, but then we'd have to carry it down a long corridor past the doors of other apartments to get to his at the far end, overlooking the main drag.

"Maybe we should go up in the hills and butcher it first," he said. "A deer out of season . . . I don't know, somebody might. . . ."

"Sid," I said with calm conviction. "This was meant to be. I haven't told you the half of it. I had a dream the other night. I woke up, got in my car, and everything that's happened to this moment has been laid out. The power doesn't give you something just to get you busted for it. . . ."

He listened, nodding. I saw the Indian in him relax.

"Is that somethin' the old guy told you?" He always referred to Clayton as "the old guy."

"Yeah."

He sighed. "Right. Let's do it!"

We carried the deer-heavy backpack up the stairs between us like a body on a stretcher, stifling laughs at the awkward struggle with so much weight on slippery steps, then down a still and stuffy carpeted hallway lit by dim lamps and smelling of mildew. As Sid fumbled to open his door, someone actually emerged from an apartment down the hall, but turned back abruptly without seeing us as if going back for something they forgot. Laughing like crazed schoolboys, we closed the door behind us inside a hot, tiny apartment, and standing before us in mock wide-eyed surprise was a diminutive, dark-haired White woman in denim overalls with two boys peeking shyly around her wide hips at us.

"So this is the Tom I've heard about!" she said when Sid had made the introductions.

"So this is the Isa you've been keeping a secret!" I said, freeing a bloodstained hand to shake hers. I liked her immediately. The fearless, solemn eyes of having taken on so much while still so young; the short but sturdy poise of a woman unafraid of manual labor, unfazed by grubby, snow-covered men carrying something big and smelly into her spotless home.

"Um, where are you going with that?" she asked as Sid led me past her. Sid only winked at me. Through the bathroom door we went and set the pack down in the bathtub. Sid kneeled and pulled off the poncho, untying the ropes bit deep in the hairy softness of the folded-up deer. The two boys crowded close at each side and Isa leaned over to see.

"I don't believe this," she said, but she was smiling.

"Hey, you married an Indian," Sid said, deadpan. "This is how we do things. Best place to butcher a big animal inside a house is in the bathtub." Freed from the pack frame, the deer's body sprawled stiffly on its back.

"Are you going to give him a bath?" one of the boys asked.

"Plenty of meat now. Bring me my knives. We got work to do, then we feast!"

"Can I help?" the older boy asked.

"And me? Can I help, too?" the younger one chimed in. Nothing like blood and gore to rivet the attention of small boys.

"Sure. Here, hold this leg like that," Sid said, turning on the water and washing out the clots of blood from the spread insides. Both boys struggled mightily to hold the hoofed leg against the tub rim.

"I guess I should say thank you for this, hm?" Isa said, returning with a handful of sharp knives.

"You're welcome."

Later, the main work of skinning and butchering in the bathtub finished, the boys asleep, a smell of venison cooking came from the kitchen where Isa (an old-fashioned Celtic name, she said) was making smaller cuts and wrapping meat for the freezer. Sid and I relaxed on the couch, sharpening dulled knives, rasping them back and forth on stones. The floor beneath our feet thumped to the rhythm of loud rock music booming from the tavern below—a Friday night drunken dance heating up so loud, Sid murmured, "Well, at least we don't need a stereo to hear good music. . . ."

"Sid," his wife called from the kitchen in a strange voice. "You better come see this."

I joined him looking over her shoulder at the sink where she was working on the deer's head. She'd broken the lower jaw away to extract the tongue, and was holding the rest of the head upside down. Something was moving at the back of the throat where the esophagus and windpipe met the opening into the sinuses. It looked like a cluster of small white slimy fingers wiggling slowly out from the interior of the head, but the tip of each finger had two black dots.

"Are those eyes?" Sid said, disgusted at the sight.

"Brainworms," I said.

"Brainworms?"

"Yeah, deer have parasites sometimes. Ticks, intestinal worms, heartworms. But the worst are brainworms. This guy's days were obviously numbered. No wonder he was acting so weird when I shot him. They were eating his brain away. That's probably why he was pointed out to me by the other deer. He could infect the others, so I guess I did them a favor. Like the wolves do, kill the weak and sick ones, keep the herd healthy and strong."

"Is it safe to eat the meat?" Isa asked.

"Sure, but let's not eat the head."

"Yeah, let's take it out somewhere and bury it deep in the ground," Sid said.

When we came back, we feasted. It was late when Isa went to bed, but Sid wanted to tell stories and catch up so we talked until I could hardly keep my eyes open. The only work he could find without being traced was temporary labor in orchards, and Isa had been reduced to part-time at the hardware store. She wanted to move to the Canadian bush where she had friends homesteading, but Sid hoped somehow to clear his name without doing prison time. He laughed about the destruction of heavy machinery on Mount Tolman and said he'd been but a small part of a big operation run by others. Yet because of his history of public prominence in other confrontations, the government saw him as an outside agitator and singled him out for prosecution.

Sid was not a timid man—the combat medals he'd earned in Vietnam were proof of that. I only hoped his going underground and getting married wouldn't lead him back into being the drunken recluse he'd been after mustering out. It had been nearly impossible to get him to leave his plastic and tar paper bunker in the Selkirk Mountains where his handwritten, cardboard signs promised C-4 explosive booby traps for those who dared disturb his solitude. Only his rage at the mindless destruction of the earth had brought him down to fight in the trenches of environmental activism. I hoped the enforced inactivity of hiding out from the man wouldn't put out his fire for living in the world again—and I told him so. Which led inevitably to stories of the war and the bad times adjusting to life at home.

"I don't get it," he finally said with an edge. "After all you went through, Tom, I listen to how you talk now, and I can't figure it out. How can you be so peaceful?"

"My war's over," was all I could think to say. "Maybe your war's not over for you."

But then as we sat in silence, I knew there was more to it.

"Maybe I should say *that* war is over for me," I went on. "Now there's a bigger war, the one that's been going on all along. The war to save the earth. The same as what brought you down out of the hills. But I'm in basic training for a different kind of role to play than yours. Not better than what you do, just different. Maybe it's like being more *for* the earth than *against* the enemy, ya know?"

"Maybe. You were always singin' your own song, even if you ended up in solitary. . . ." He was referring to how we met as prisoners in a military stockade. He stood beside me in formation when we were supposed to be singing, "I wanna be an airborne ranger," but I was instead singing a John Lennon song, "All we are saying is give peace a chance." Investigated for inciting the ranks to mutiny, I spent weeks in solitary confinement.

"I'll take that as a compliment," I said in a haze of fatigue. Then, inspired, I said, "For me it's like Neil Young said in that song—'it's only castles burning.' There's always gonna be castles to burn, but they just build 'em all over again, bigger and stronger. Sure, a lot of us know what's really going on, but who among us really knows the earth? The earth is always speaking to us, tellin' us how to live, how to be on her side. Most of it falls on deaf ears. I'm just tryin' to learn how to listen."

My ears began to ring. I'd adopted Clayton's point of view so deeply, I was beginning to sound like him.

"You sound like my grandfather," Sid said in a quiet voice. "On the Chippewa side. When I enlisted, he said, 'What good is a warrior if he can't hear what the trees are tryin' to tell him?' I used to hear voices in the jungle in Nam. I thought they were warning me where the Cong were, but I could never make it out. Now I think what Grandpa meant was: Be like the trees." He sighed. "But you get into this political thing and you just forget."

"I don't think you'd make a very good tree," I said dryly.

He laughed. "No—maybe a good grizzly bear?"

"In a china shop."

It was good to laugh so freely with him again.

"Yeah, but the tree thing, see, that makes me think about those hill tribes in Nam," he said. "And that bogus thing of winning the hearts and minds of the people. Those dudes really knew the jungle, better even than the Cong. And you could tell they weren't on either side, not really—not the Cong's, not ours. Their hearts and minds belonged to the earth, to the hills and jungle where they lived. They were helpin' us just because they had to deal with something they couldn't avoid.

"I remember one time when they dropped Agent Orange and all the leaves fell off the trees for miles—it was like the jungle was dead. The hill dude that was our guide on recon got this real bad look in his eyes when he saw it. Wouldn't set foot in the dead zone. The lieutenant argued with him, but he looked like he was about to cry, like he seen the end of the world. When he just up and disappeared on us, it made me wonder who the real enemy was."

14

THE FOLLOWING DAY WE hung out, ate venison, played with the boys, ate venison, took naps, ate venison, and in the late afternoon looked out and saw the snow had stopped falling. Sid was itching for action, hoping the end of the snowstorm meant he could work in an orchard the next day, but when Isa came home from work she said the weather forecast predicted more snow by morning. I said I better go while the getting was good. Sid told Isa he'd been thinking about her wanting them to move to Canada and he'd decided it was a good idea after all. Delighted, she looked radiantly at me like it had been my influence that had tipped the scales. She undid her hair, changed into bib overalls and peasant blouse, and danced barefoot around the room with a boy swinging on each hip, singing an impromptu song about leaving town behind and going to live in the bush.

"The only thing White about her is her big behind!" Sid said loud enough for his wife to hear.

"Well, the only thing *Indian* about *him,*" she retorted with a mocking snort, "is no butt at all!"

Another long drive, this time late at night, reluctantly taking my leave, and once past the city traffic of Wenatchee, it was a lonely run on a snowplowed and sanded highway winding north through the mountains. I had just enough gas to get home and no more money. I too was itching to do some work, and there were orchard pruning jobs waiting for me whenever the weather would allow it.

Somewhere between Chelan and Entiat, as the Ford Falcon cruised along without a hitch, there was a sudden flash of red light on the dashboard, like a warning light flashing on and off. I let off the gas and looked down to see which one it was, but where I'd seen the red flash was off to the right of where the gauges were—the bare metal between the gauges and the radio. I stopped by a snowbank, listening to the engine and studying the gauges. I could detect nothing wrong. At first I figured it must've been one of those peripheral optic nerve firings I have when I'm exhausted and staring fixedly for hours at the night road ahead, but then the other side of my mind kicked in. The side that knew when I explained it away, I closed the door on how the power has to work through me as I am, as I'm able to perceive at the moment. Maybe it was a warning. Maybe the power was taking care of me when I was unaware of something bad about to happen with the car—like the time I had been unaware of freezing to death.

I climbed out and carefully inspected things with a flashlight—tires, brakes, axles, driveshaft, exhaust. Then I raised the hood and studied the motor idling, the hot machinery moving in its slow rhythm as I crunched around on hardened snow, shining the flashlight on different greasy parts. Nothing was amiss. I turned off the ignition and looked at everything under the hood again, but it all looked fine. I was lowering the hood to close up and go on when my eyes fell on the generator's fan belt pulley, illuminated by the headlights reflecting off snow. My heart skipped a beat—the nut holding the pulley on the generator shaft was missing! It had somehow come unscrewed and fallen off, leaving nothing to hold the pulley on that turned the electric generator. At any moment with the engine running it could fly off, leaving me dead in the water, and probably damaging the belt, fan, and radiator to boot.

I looked in the back of the station wagon for something to replace the missing nut. As I rummaged around in the soft drink case I used for a toolbox, I knew it was useless. Generator shaft nuts are threaded differently from ordinary nuts, but I tried a few anyway, until I realized I might damage the threads and ruin them. With a sudden flash born of a lifetime of roadside quick fixes with baling wire and spit, I remembered the small used hose clamp I'd seen in the bottom of the toolbox. It fit perfectly, so I tightened it down with a screwdriver as hard as I could, knowing the softer metal of the clamp wouldn't hurt the hardened steel threads of the shaft.

Starting it up, wiping my hands on a rag, shivering from the cold of midnight in the wintry mountains, I jumped behind the wheel, cranked the heater up and drove on. There was nothing more I could do if the temporary clamp came off, so I just kept going, hoping for the best. As it turned out, I drove the hundred more miles home and all the driving in the week that followed with the hose clamp keeping the pulley on, until I finally bought a new replacement nut at the auto parts store in Oroville.

There was a new swagger in my step when I saw Clayton again. I was a little surprised at how lordly I felt, yet it was hard to resist how recent events infused each new day with a sense of purpose and invulnerability. It was one thing to be confident and fearless when the chips were down, when all seemed lost and the business of life seemed pointless. But this new taste of power and possibility was a little intoxicating.

I drove to the Woods place and found Clayton sitting on the front stoop enjoying the noonday sun, just as I somehow knew I would. I got out sporting a rakish yellow cowboy bandana (the warm Chinook winds were blowing from the east) at the neck of my new pearl-snap-button Western shirt, my thumb hooked in my new belt with the gaudy silver inlaid concho buckle. Greeting him with the Native teenager's slangy, English-influenced, broken-Salish expression *"Hast skulehált!"* ("Good day!") and formally touching hands with him, I noticed I was interrupting him plucking white chin whiskers with tweezers and Lucy's handheld vanity mirror. Everybody else was gone in his car to a Saturday gathering on the Inkaneep reserve in B.C., but he'd stayed behind, alone, he said, because he figured I might show up, and he wanted to hear how my power dreaming turned out.

When I sat down and told him about my experiences since I'd last seen him, Clayton seemed to share my enthusiasm, his wide face beaming like a proud uncle at the way his nephew was coming along with his self-training. He laughed at how long it had taken me to see the dream in my encounter with the three deer, and hinted ruefully that he'd had similar experiences figuring things out. He asked me how I picked which gas station to go to in Cashmere, and I said I went to the one that I happened to see when I drove past on my way up to Blewett Pass. When I was coming back and had to stop for gas, that was the one that drew me, even though there were others closer to the highway.

"Not the one have the lowest price?"

"No . . . the one that felt right."

"*Aaaa*. And you have only the little money left?"

"I wasn't worried."

"No . . . no worry about nothin' anymore, ain't it? And now we see the power man, have that look in the eye, see even the filling station with power eyes!"

He smiled and told me I reminded him of his elder, Old Baptiste, the man he talked of having a relationship with long ago that was like my relationship with Clayton. He said Baptiste was skeptical like me, and his power was always testing his commitment by revealing only a little, making him work for it. He had a spirit partner that worked through his everyday tools like mine did through my car, warning him when something was wrong. Clayton said the power he himself trained for under Baptiste's sponsorship always spelled everything out clearly in pictures, which made the older man "a little envy in his heart." Baptiste became more abrupt and demanding when he saw how easy the power was with Clayton.

It was amazing to have Clayton talk so openly this way to me, as if we were now equals, but at the same time it felt right and appropriate, too, like I had no more doubts about belonging in the same world he did. He said he wanted me to meet him even though "the old bugger" never had anything to do with White people and probably wouldn't like me. I was confused for a moment, not sure who he was talking about because it had never occurred to me that Old Baptiste might still be alive. Clayton always spoke of him as being old when he himself was young, and at nearly seventy now himself, what would that make Baptiste? Clayton said he lived way up north in British Columbia where he never budged from the foot of a certain mountain, beside a certain "fishing hole" on a tributary of the Fraser River. He said maybe he'd have a chance to take me to meet him. And even if Baptiste wouldn't talk to me, he'd have to see that I had something, and maybe he'd pass something on to me.

"Yah, to think about that and see what come."

Then he talked about how he could see I was ready, that if I agreed, we'd make preparations for him to send me on the long wander this summer as soon as the snow was out of the mountains. I shrugged indifferently. I was so full of myself I wasn't really registering the importance of what he said. I felt that whatever was going to happen would happen without me having to put much effort into it, and it would all be good. I was a power man in my own mind now, and I could handle whatever came my way. I barely noticed when his tone changed and he asked me with a serious look if I understood the sign I'd been given in my dream. I said I had no idea what he might be referring to. He said the fact that animals had shown themselves to me "in their true form" was very significant. Feeling a little impatient, I said I didn't see how since I'd seen them like that before, like the times in the sweatlodge and like the man who caught a robin in his hand, who Clayton himself had told me had to be the peregrine falcon who'd shown up to help me so many times in my life.

"Yah, but this time you doin' things with 'em as people . . . and then the *same things* with 'em as the animal," he said, gesturing first with one hand and then with the other.

"What's the big deal about that?"

"This the sign to say they no longer test you," he went on patiently. "This to say they now take you as the relative, no holdin' back. Very serious now, because they feel free to come to you. They feel they can depend on you. They know your feelings."

"They know my feelings?"

"Yah, sure." He said if I thought about it, if I compared how I felt toward the woman telling me to take "her strange boy," with how I felt toward the doe deer pointing out her sick yearling as food, I'd see what he meant.

"The same," I said. "The exact same—like I knew how she felt, and yet like I knew she wanted me to take him."

"And she know you *would* take him, eh?"

"Yeah, maybe. So what?" The rude words were out of my mouth before I could give some thought to them. Unfortunately they showed how tedious I thought he was being. Whatever he was driving at seemed unimportant compared to how invincible it made me feel. Clayton ignored my words.

"They know how you act as the man on what you feel," he said slowly, making me blush with how he could make a point about me so indirectly and respectfully. "This how it have to be. Only way for the power to work with you, with any person who have something. But maybe better if this not happen so soon. Better for this to come later. Even now, you feel the power crowdin' around, pantin' like the dog to do whatever you ask. Feel it, but don't see the danger."

I agreed that I saw no danger. Sitting in the Chinook-wind warmth of a sunny, late-winter day with him, both of us having had a feeling we would meet here, I felt on top of the world.

Clayton said such blindness was dangerous for someone training for power because I was acting with such conviction and assurance that what I had was coming at a run, just as if I was a seasoned power man. He wondered if I had the maturity to keep myself in check. He said he was concerned I was making decisions impulsively, like I was used to doing, and wasn't on my guard about my own unresolved feelings about people and what was going on in the world. That it was my deepest feelings about things more than anything else that gave shape to what my power showed me and offered me. He said power men and women who lived long lives and benefited the world were very careful about calling on their power, because power "had no morals." Having power was like having a devoted dog—the dog could attack people as well as save them. Whether the power used you or you used the power had to do with whether you really knew yourself. Whether the power made a person into somebody to respect or somebody to fear had to do with who the person was. He said there was always the danger that a person's power used the wrong way could "get to likin' the taste of human blood."

I laughed at what seemed like over-dramatic joking, but when I saw he was completely serious, I said it wasn't likely in my case. He said there was no way of knowing when it came to power, that there were too many people who thought power was only benevolent, and that such people were the ones who knew the least about themselves. The volcanic eruption of Mount St. Helens a few years earlier was an example of what he was talking about, he said. The eruption on a Sunday morning had been so far away, all we heard was a sound like dynamite exploding faintly far back in the mountains. By afternoon, the pall of ash was like a smog that left a gritty fallout on cars, leaves, rocks, everything. We'd missed the devastation in the Okanogan but other places like Yakima and the Toutle River valley weren't so lucky, not to mention the instant flattening of hundreds of miles of forest near the mountain.

"Why would we be any different than our mother?" he asked rhetorically. "Protect and give life with one hand, but kill with the other."

The only way to proceed was to know the lore, the "teachings of the stories," and act accordingly. He said he could tell that my recent experiences had changed me. That my slow, years-long awakening to what I had gained in childhood and trained for as an adult—which according to him seemed right for a White man unaccustomed to what Indians grew up with—had suddenly speeded up. His words painted a picture of me now hungering thoughtlessly for ways to use my power. He gently chided me for giving in to "feelin' so proud" of myself that I had no patience for "the wise words of your elder."

"Next thing you know, you be cuttin' me off, askin' me questions that don't respect my feelings. Like you know better, eh?"

The realization that he himself never did that to me, even though I'd always deferred to him as someone authoritative, instantly left me deflated.

"When our thoughts go high, then maybe a long way to fall," he murmured, sensing my sudden change in mood.

He said there were a lot of stories that told about people who "got something" and who "came out" proudly with it before they knew how to handle it. He told me one of them, about a young Indian man he named in Salish, *Ch'maistíselux Y'yat Swít,* or Everybody Knows It (that is, knows his name), who grew up in the Okanogan in the late 1800s. Clayton said this man was in the same predicament as me, only he was younger, maybe twenty. It was after the failed war of resistance against the Americans, a time when young Native men were coming of age for the first time in the confinement of the Colville Reservation and were faced with following the new ways being forced upon them by the Whites. Most things having to do with the old religion were suppressed and the young men were expected to accept their lot as Catholic farm and ranch hands, and submit to the domination and superiority of the Whites.

Everybody Knows It felt bad about being bullied into thinking he was anything less than the White men, so he quested in the mountains and received something powerful. It was soon obvious that he'd changed into a proud, outspoken man who thought himself not only equal to but better than the White men coming into the country in those days, and contact with him often led to bad words and violence. Everybody Knows It was a tall, strong, muscular man who seemed unafraid of anybody. He began to see that his power took care of him no matter what he did, warning and guiding him in ways that baffled the White authorities and allowed him to come and go as he pleased. The other Indian people became afraid of him and what his actions might bring down on them. They placated him with gifts and gave him whatever he wanted, urging him to stay away from the Whites. Some young men were attracted to what he stood for and began to follow him around and look up to him.

Clayton said Everybody Knows It was a true power man, that those who told his story said all the Native people could see he had the "hardness" and complete confidence in his power that made even Indian doctors wary of him. But the conviction of being invulnerable in one so young, inexperienced and unable to know his own feelings resulted in the events that quickly followed. Everybody Knows It killed a White man in an argument and was chased down by a sheriff's posse, cornered, and shot to death along with two of his unfortunate companions.

The story had the desired sobering effect on me. The terror of those times for the Native people was still palpable despite Clayton's dry, matter-of-fact retelling. Something in the story woke me to how untamed I'd been feeling, how I'd been having dark, unnamed cravings that I wasn't acknowledging. When I tried to examine what had been driving me, all that came was something like Yes! Give me more of this power stuff! It struck me for the first time since coming home how self-absorbed and out for myself I'd been. I told Clayton the story had a big impact on me, but I didn't know what to do with myself.

"Be like the *kw'áyluks* ('black dress' = 'priest') who can't help hisself, and all he can think about, his want to feel under the woman's dress," Clayton said dryly. "Not to give in to it, eh?"

I laughed hard at the unexpected aptness of his joke.

"Yah, now, time like this, to have the need for holdin' back," he went on. "We are just pitiful people, just common human people, *t'i kstel'skélux* (just come-alive persons). They are more powerful than we are, those powers of the world. Have to respect 'em, know how dangerous they can be. Show them they have to respect you. That you the one in charge of your own life.

"My advice to you, be grateful that they reveal theirself to you as they really are, people like us. But time to back away from the power. Let things cool off, take a breather, sit on your hands. You know—so you not be temptation to grab whatever they put in front of you!"

The gusts of Chinook wind blew harder in our faces. We were quiet, looking around at the world, at the snow melting away to muddy puddles in front of the doublewide. Clayton sighed and said you never knew how the power was going to work through someone, but something like this would have been better if it had happened when I was on the long wander, when he'd have been able to prepare me for it. He said he'd have to give me some of that preparation now, because I was in need of protection. Bailing off a runaway horse was good sense, but the ground comes up awful fast. It wasn't all the powers of earth and sky that had taken to me, only the Animal People, and he had just the thing to hold the Animal People at bay. Something I could have in place, at the ready for when they came to me in dreams, or even when I was distracted, like at work in the apple orchards. Something that would ground my mind in right relation to them, so I wouldn't just react to how well they knew my feelings.

He got up and led the way around back to the riverbank. We walked along the still-frozen Similkameen beneath the toss and sway of bare cottonwoods until we came to a little clearing. I sat quietly with him on a sun-dried log with the blindingly white summit of Chopaka Mountain in view. I knew he wanted the mountain to see and hear what he was doing. Choosing his words carefully, he spoke in even more earnest tones than before.

He said that now we were in the realm of secrets and what he was going to pass on to me was not something to tell just anyone. To be sure, as he was with me, that the other person already knew enough to understand it. He called it a "saying" that had been handed down for countless generations, passed down through families or purchased at great price by others wanting to use it, but nowadays ignored or forgotten by all but a few. He told it to me in Salish, and as I tried to translate it in my mind, he gave English versions of some of the words until I finally got the whole meaning in sequence.

It was obviously what would be called an "incantation" in English, words that cast a spell. In very metaphorical and even poetic style, the words stated that a desirable condition existed between the speaker and animals, and framed how to talk to animals—where the feeling was inside us that we spoke from, so the animals would know who the speaker was. That the speaker knew who they really were, people like us clothed in animals' outward appearances. As I said the incantation over and over, the words led me right to a feeling I'd only rarely encountered in my life, and then only at unexpected moments. The feeling came out through my voice as I said it, and persisted as long as I spoke the words. The only way I can describe the feeling (without revealing the actual words of the incantation) is to say that it was like a temporary but complete indifference to my own death. The words put me on a par with the animals, who know that death is just a change of clothing. For the first time, I understood why humans feel naked the way we're born into the world, that putting on clothes to mimic what the others in the world do doesn't hide us from our terrible fear of dying. The animals know their bodies are just clothes, something presented for feeble humans to see, and in that alone they are superior to us. When I told Clayton how different the words made me feel, he said it was because the saying was given by the Animal People themselves.

I told him I could see why it was a secret since nobody who hadn't already experienced the animals as human people would get it. He said that was all spiritual secrets were—things waiting along the trail for those who could understand and use them. But like anything else that had power, they could be used the wrong way.

When he was sure I'd memorized the saying, he told me to call it up and say it to myself as often as I could every day until it was a part of me. So that when I encountered animals I could speak to them and they would understand me. And especially when I was dreaming and had "the kinda feeling I had with that deer woman" toward any person I was dreaming about, the saying and knowing would come forward. I would have the presence of mind to hold back, and the animals would respect the power of the words.

I asked him why it would have been such a valuable thing for people to want to pay for it. He said there were a lot of other animals in the world than deer, and in the old days people were much more vulnerable to lions and grizzly bears—they were mauled or killed all the time. These were Animal People of the strongest power, he said, and their inclination to attack and kill unpredictably was an ever-present reality of life. He said in that circumstance, the most effective way, if there was time, was for the person to take off all their clothes and present themselves naked to say the words. Grizzly bears especially were angered by humans wearing clothes, but a naked human embarrassed them.

It was hard for me to see how the incantation would work in an encounter with a dangerous, threatening animal. It was one thing to feel how the words affected me saying them, but seemed risky to expect a grizzly bear to stop and listen, dressed or undressed. Clayton said I already knew the most significant thing in any encounter with animals was how I felt. That I'd told him stories of experiences I'd had when they knew what my feelings and intentions were and acted accordingly—like the deer knew if I was hunting, or horses knew I was afraid of them. So why did I doubt that they would know what the saying was making me feel? I said because just thinking about it at a distance made

me doubt being indifferent to my own death was sending the right signal to a hungry or alarmed or wounded, crazed animal. It seemed a
risky time to try it out. He said that was the White man talking. When
it came to power there was no testing things to see if they worked, that
I already knew if I went at things with that attitude then that was the
feeling I was putting out into the world, and everything in the world
would know it. Testing things to see if they worked to your advantage
was why White men were so cut off from power, he said, and only if I
was truly indifferent to my own death would the power of the saying
work.

For a long time I just sat there and Clayton said nothing. I sank into
a gloom born of an anxiety I couldn't fathom at first. The elation I'd
arrived with such a short time before seemed light-years away and the
pose of someone deranged and self-destructive. Odd phrases drifted by
in my mind like "drunk with power" and "pride before the fall." I saw
myself as lacking the necessary character and self-knowledge Clayton
suggested was necessary for withstanding the temptations of using
power, or for that matter, the dangers of approaching powerful animals
in the wild. I felt vulnerable, my own worst enemy, and had little confidence that saying the words of the incantation would protect me from
my own inner compulsions. It was the first time I'd ever been afraid of
what I was doing with Clayton. It was as if the White man in me
"knew" like original sin that I wasn't up to the path I'd chosen following Clayton into the world of power. The thought of going on the long
wander now filled me with dread.

Clayton's benign smile was not reassuring.

"Not long, and you be goin' to the places where those real powerful
ones still live and keep their secrets," he said with a mischievous glint
in his eye. "I be send you on a long walk to the faraway. And maybe
them animals don't like some White man come walkin' up unarmed
where they still in charge. . . ."

"Unarmed?" I exclaimed. But then I remembered, of course, you're
sent on a mission with nothing, not even matches or a knife.

"Sure. And maybe just outta nowhere some grizzly is breathin' in
your face. You know what to say, you have the words handed down,

why, that grizzly be just tame, and leave you alone. Maybe even give a gift to you."

Clayton seemed to enjoy my dubious look.

"Not worryin' about nothin', eh?" he said, mocking my earlier mood of invulnerability. "Well, maybe you forget what to say, the words don't come. Then you maybe find out why they take off their clothes to talk to grizzlies . . . or at least their pants, ain't it?"

15

THE SNOW DISAPPEARED SO fast in the lowlands under day after day of sun and warm Chinook winds, the promise of an early spring turned apple farmers into neurotic, driven men. Startled by the possibility that they might have only a few weeks to finish winter pruning, their competition was fierce for the few experienced men available in the area, like me. Cowboy-hatted old-timers in winter whiskers showing up in muddy pickup trucks at the Woods place where I stayed in Jim's trailer, men I hadn't really spoken to in years knocking on my door with unfamiliar smiles creasing their faces like we were old friends. Anxious-eyed owners of orchard acreage showing an unlikely interest in my personal welfare by asking me to come and work for them at twenty-five cents more per tree than previous years. An unheard-of jump in pay not experienced since the autumn, years before, when not enough Mexicans showed up at harvest time. The vision of apples rotting on the trees and consequent foreclosures on unpaid loans (there goes the new tractor and pickup) had resulted in a twenty-five-cent raise on every bin of apples picked.

But I had my handshake deals to live up to, negotiated at last year's rate, like Old Man Porter's forty acres of red and golden delicious trees on the steep heights above Palmer Lake. Balding Charlie Porter, skinny yet potbellied, was so nervously glad to see me actually show up like I said I would that he had to sit down in the kitchen and swallow one of his heart pills. Too jittery to sit and visit for long, he took my long-handled lop shears, pole loppers, and pruning saw out to his work shed and sharpened them up himself, then let me have the pick of his new aluminum three-pointed ladders. Leading me uphill where snow patches still wetted the flattened brown of orchard grass and the view of the lake below was like a picture postcard, he stood at tree number one in row number one. With him watching, I set to work around it, lopping limbs, sawing out the deadwood, taking down the crown, removing suckers, making big cuts for ladder-sets between the main leaders, opening the centers so the sun could ripen fruit on the shaded side. He sighed, grateful that his trees were in good hands, that he didn't have to train me or worry about the job I was doing.

"Well, Tom, I'll get outta yer way and let you get at it," he said, heading off down the rows for home. After a lifetime of laboring in his orchard, Charlie had an aversion to handwork that was almost comical. I knew he'd spend the days I worked on his trees with his feet up in front of TV.

Jim and, even in the old days, Clayton used to work in Porter's orchard, doing the seasonal work that came and went, picking apples or driving Charlie's tractor moving bins during harvest, thinning or propping fruit-heavy limbs with wooden poles to keep them from breaking. I was just another in a long line of low-paid contract laborers, bush monkeys who came temporarily out of the hills to make some cash. And like the others before me, picked for skill of eye and hand, not for any hope that I'd stay on as a steady employee. I was just another *shox'ḵwúlem,* a hired hand.

Orchard work in late winter leaves you so exhausted that by the end of the day you can't manage much more than supper and a long sit and stare before bedtime. The days are longer and you're out there from dawn to dusk, the whole turn of daylight spent moving from tree to tree under an open sky. Each tree is a new look at how something grows and what cuts to make to take advantage of the tree's inclinations. There's no way to explain why you cut what you cut—there's reasons and impressions and urges all mingled up as you go along. You jump in somewhere, do what obviously needs doing, one thing leads to another, and before long it comes to you that you're done and it's time to move on to the next one.

Porter's trees were so big and old, at only $3.25 apiece I had to keep moving, keep up the pace if I wanted to make good money. After a few days, my body's soreness and stiffness went away and I worked with a practiced ease, muscling the ladder into position without conscious thought, moving up and down the steps without looking. So absorbed in the task of pruning apple trees for another season of fruit, I began to feel like I'd been born wearing leather gloves and holding tools. Moving everywhere with a ladder to stand up and hold my weight, I found my dreams at night became rituals of reading trees and locating ladder-sets. The timeless, thoughtless, physical grind became second nature, my concentration so complete I'd forget it was going to get dark. I'd look up to discover ranch lights winking on down below. And see the Mexicans in the next orchard over filing out with loppers casually scissored over their shoulders, heading silently and wearily down to their row of shacks under the pines along the lake.

The metallic creak of the ladder, the chop of loppers shearing a limb off, the rhythmic back and forth of sawing through apple hardwood that leaves greenish sawdust clotting the saw teeth. The agricultural uniformity carved out of wild mountainous slopes where deer come down to taste the swell of buds. A snatch of Spanish song on the wind. The start-up of a tractor at the other end of the lake so far away all I see is the blue smoke of diesel exhaust rising into the breezy vacancy of mountain-held air. Training for power faded in the simple act of going back to work. I was once again content with the everyday things I was fully capable of doing well. There's a kind of confidence that returns when ordinary daily life resumes—the familiar self reasserted in known and predictable ways.

Working alone in an orchard, well into the swing of things, I found myself drifting away into the wild blue yonder of daydreams. Long-ago coming-of-age memories rising to the surface, floating on the still pool of my absent mind, presented themselves for inspection. I relived them without recognizing at first what was happening—that these particular memories buried in time and distance were coming forth from my deepest self wondering about what Clayton had said. Seminal experiences awakened by taking to heart what he said—how an indifference to death brought on the power, how my own personality and inclinations were the way the power worked through me. Episodes as life-altering as almost freezing to death, but having happened at a time when I was too young and ignorant and lost in the maze of events to really see them for what they were.

Like the time I was hiking in Zion National Park in Utah, full of youth's need for danger and daring after final exams and a long road trip. Striking off brashly from the carefully graded government trail, I set out to explore a sedimentary terrace above a deep side canyon. Hemmed in by multicolored slickrock cliffs, the passage was narrow, threading through fallen boulders, cactus, oakbrush, and shrubby pinyon and juniper trees. It was tough going, testing muscle and nerve, but the faint sign of a deer trail led me on, assured that the deer must know where they were going. Hours later in the shadows of late afternoon, long after any sign of deer had petered out on a rock shelf devoid of any vegetation larger than a tuft of grass growing from a crack, the end of the trail loomed ahead. The canyon boxed up completely in an echoing ring of cliffs.

Exhausted, sore, and thirsty, I sought for a way down to the trickle of creek I could hear but not see. Bouldering downward, hugging the rock for footholds, I descended to a smoothed curve of sandstone that appeared to offer a way down to the water, which sounded like it was just below, in a slot about ten feet wide. There was good traction walking in my sneakers so I edged over upright, on my feet, angling down the steepening grade into the slot along a rock joint, looking for the bottom to show itself as things opened up to view below. At the same moment I saw with horror that the narrow defile of the creek went down another forty feet, that it was all bare, vertical rock on both sides, my feet registered the fact that my steps were beyond the point of stopping. Gravity and inertia and the tilt of my lean allowed only a few, quick, dancing steps before what I suddenly saw was a fall to my death. In a blur of instinctive reactions that lasted only a few seconds, I used my last step to leap across the ten feet of air to the other side and scramble blindly upward to the safety of a rock ledge.

At least, that's how I always accounted for what happened. That's how it looked if I didn't inspect closely what I remembered. The event had the feel of unreality to it—I should have fallen to my death (or worse, survived the fall only to die slowly where nobody knew to look for me) but instead I came away virtually unscathed, marveling at how lucky I was. The years had passed, life had gone on, and although what happened stuck in my memory as something important, there were things about it that defied understanding. It was the unaccountable things I remembered that now surfaced in my daydreams.

What happened when I leaped may have taken only a few seconds but for me time stood still. There was something unreal about the momentous anticipation of stepping off into the void, but real enough that everything else was blotted out by my total attention to the moment. I remember clearly how I let go and accepted the inevitable. I felt it as a flutter in my guts, a calm, relaxed relinquishing of control, followed by a sudden split. My mind and usual self-awareness went blank but my body came alive like a ferocious animal that acted without my direction. My eyes shot across the chasm, instantly read the other side, and locked onto certain features that bulged out. My body leaped in desperation to survive, and in midair I ceased to do anything but witness what it did. The feeling of mortal danger in my guts expanded in a flash to a burning something shooting out of my navel, and everything that followed felt as if powered by it. There was a flood of feeling like an electric shock; a vivid, explosive blur of connection to some kind of support; and then I was experiencing myself in an unbelievable, panting, animal-like climb upward. It was so fast I only faintly registered something hoisting me up in a way that made my arms and legs seem like they had superhuman agility. Without knowing how, I was sprawled in a gasping, trembling, helpless pile of meat and bone on a safe shelf of rock.

It was my first real experience of the dark man who came forth to save me, the first time I was consciously aware of him doing the impossible. Gone as fast as he appeared, he left me a limp husk, barely able to hold my head up and look back across to where I'd leaped from. Through the ragged rips in my jeans and shirt I could see the torn skin and blood welling out but strangely not flowing. And yet my wounds were minor—nothing compared to a debilitating, excruciating trauma in my stomach muscles. They felt like I'd been gut shot with a bullet from a high-powered rifle.

Rolling over onto my back, I rested my hands on the dull, burning pain, and as it began to fade, I looked about the beautiful world I found myself still alive to see. Every form of rock and twisted bush and fleck of cloud in a deep blue-blue sky had an exquisite enchantment. When I edged over to look down, the creek far below was like manna from heaven. Unfortunately there was no way to get down to it. The telltale traces of my own blood marking my ascent drew my eyes. I studied the wall of rock I'd somehow climbed like a giant spider. I saw no way I could have done it.

When I finally stood up there was a searing, ripped feeling in my navel, like a razor-sharp thread leading back deep inside. Impending sunset was deepening the canyon shadows and I had to find some way back before it got dark. There was no way to cross over to the other side and go back the familiar way—despite narrow spots I theoretically could have leaped, I was too weak to do more than stumble along. I don't even remember how I got out of the canyon. All I remember was coming upon the government trail and feeling a sudden exultation—I ran all the way down the switchbacks to the bottom.

There under the dusk-released scent of cottonwoods I finally came to water. A deep-pooled creek where a woman and a girl in a bathing suit were purling for fish. Lying on the grassy bank with an arm in the water, hand open and motionless, waiting for the minnow-like native fish to touch their fingers. As I drank deeply and washed my wounds, their hands would come up with a splash clutching something silvery the size of a goldfish, and they'd swallow the wiggling little things alive. Anything that happened on earth seemed right and perfect and fascinating to me that evening. Every time I recall the first time I saw someone eat live fish, I remember that long after my scrapes and gashes healed, there was a lingering tender soreness in the muscles around my navel.

The vivid recall and sense of revelation led me to another, earlier memory. It was late, after midnight on a moonlit summer night in rural northern New Mexico. I was walking home down a dusty road from the house of friends to where I was staying in a small adobe village of Hispanic mountain people. They all kept dogs, mostly untamed mongrels who in daytime barked at me from their unfenced domains around each homestead, but this night they all came out onto the road in a wild, frantic pack to confront me as the late-night intruder. Usually just leaning over to pick up a rock was enough to silence them and make them slink away, but not this time. They surrounded me with such a din of rage, I staggered back to a crumbling wall, cornered and frankly fearing the worst.

Egging each other on, they closed in by ones and twos with bared teeth to get at my legs, and when I'd turn on them on one side, they'd come in from the other. It was something I'd never experienced before—me, a dog-lover about to be taken down by dogs—but my panic lasted only a few seconds. Something like anger at my own fear washed over me, and I had a moment of calm sobriety. It wasn't like letting go and accepting the inevitable, it was like I simply didn't care what they could do to me anymore. The me I was familiar with was no longer operative. I saw the dogs sense the change in me. They held back, suddenly reluctant to lunge in and close with me, but still crowded around in a bristling, deafening circle holding me at bay against the wall.

Then out of the shadows came a large, dark dog passing through the ranks directly at me, completely silent and low to the ground. I knew instinctively (watch out for the quiet ones!) that he wasn't mystified or cowed by my lack of fear like the others, that he was the real threat, the alpha male, and he was going to take me out. In a flash my indifference turned into fearless rage and I went for him, lunging to meet his approach head on. I was possessed with a pure animal bloodlust to close with him, kill or be killed, a rush of extreme conviction that had nothing to do with a few bad bites on the leg or a bluff of bravado to make a dog think twice about attacking me. Whatever took hold of me wanted only to kill, and the dog instantly knew it. Skidding in a sudden show of fear and a furious spray of gravel, the alpha male fled and eluded my snatching hands. I had a sudden pang of regret that he'd given up so easily. As I stood panting in the middle of the road with all the dogs scattered and barking in frustrated rage far out in the shadows, I felt myself as the only flesh-and-blood animal present who was devoid of concern about self-preservation. The dogs knew it in the way dogs know such things, in the way I then knew it. There was no way to fake it, pretend, bluff—the dark man was not the me that thought about things.

In those days the dark man was for me just an unrecognizable state of abandon, an experience of being alien from who was doing the doing, a crocodile-brained self acting on pure instinct. With the road open, I strode down the winding, narrow streets of the village, a few dogs still giving me desultory barks from behind cover. I began to shiver as I came back to myself in a kind of daze. There was an acid taste in my mouth and I found myself laughing a giddy, cackling laugh that somehow frightened me more than the dogs had. On rubbery legs I stepped inside the shack where I was staying and slumped to the floor, where I soon fell asleep.

The ground is cold and damp where I'm sitting under the apple tree remembering. One memory leading to another, more scenes from my past flowing by—seeing in my own experiences how Clayton was right. The power was always there, waiting to be unleashed in the face of mortal danger, and the trigger was that same loss of familiar self in a sober-headed, alien-feeling indifference to whether I lived or died. Would it be the same now that I was more consciously aware of how it worked? I had to laugh—there I was again, calculating things, assessing them to see if they held an advantage for me. There was really no way to test it. This wasn't spiritual metaphor dumbed down and pressed into the service of the marketplace. This was life and death. There were no assurances of surviving ahead of time.

When I thought about how I'd survived the things I did in my life there was no other explanation but the help of power. The car wrecks, the bullets that tore branches from the trees over my head, the speedboat that roared over me when I was swimming in the Missouri River at night, the exploding shell fragments that tore into my forehead— none of them harmed me the way they could have. Except for the scars everywhere on my body, I was in one piece, fit and full of life, complete in my own mind. It was simply the designs of power to save me and keep me alive to this moment. Arbitrary, unfathomable, not even fair when I thought about the ones I knew so well who died so young. And yet wholly acceptable; worth my time in training to unravel; the very stuff of what had brought me back to life since I landed in the Okanogan.

And for the first time it occurred to me that learning how to consciously bring forth the dark man was what this was all about.

16

WALKING TO AND FROM work now, because so many cars have broken down I've loaned mine out to the women of the Woods household so they can get by for a while. Along the river and beside the lake, then up to "Chicken" Brady's place where his failed egg business induced him to plant apples and try out the new "central leader" method of severely training the trees on one trunk, the line of trees crowded together like hedgerows. A different kind of pruning rarely requiring a ladder since the plantation is so young; moving much faster down the rows. The weather has gone back to cold and wet but I stay out in it, through sleet and cold rain, freezing hands and numb toes, making frogskins to pile up in the bank, taking whatever comes my way to accomplish what I agreed to do for Chicken.

Daydreaming about how I knew before it happened that Charlene was going to ask to borrow my car. How easily I accepted and acted on such things now. The day before, I heard her voice in my mind say, "*Kúhlintux inchá anp'wíhwin* (Loan me your car)." When Charlene came out to my trailer in the morning I was getting ready to go to work. I remembered the words I'd heard and just handed her the keys before she could say anything. She smiled and said only: "I got gas money. We be back Friday maybe."

One thing leads to another and I remember how I was first awakened to this way of communicating that my made-relatives take so for granted. The bad old days of my military career, close to the end, twenty-three years old and they finally caught up with me. When I refused to serve anymore and went off to Canada, it was like sealing my doom and forever giving up my right to a free life. But that's what it took to live up to what I felt at the time, and I lived with the consequences.

One consequence came when I dared to go home for a visit. The day before Thanksgiving when tipped-off FBI agents took up positions around my parents' southern California home and the wild barking of dogs was interrupted by an ominous ring of the doorbell. We got up from the dinner table and my mother opened the door. Shoved back by a burly suit waving a badge, she was brushed aside as he ran up and cuffed me standing by my chair. I could only smile sickly at my father at how inevitable it seemed.

On the ride downtown with the driver doing sixty in a twenty-five mile zone, I sat in back on my cuffed hands beside another suit who went through my billfold asking repeatedly if I was, in fact, Tom Harmer. Since he was looking at my driver's license photo and knew damn well I was, I said nothing. He murmured something to the agent driving. Instantly standing on the brakes, the driver squealed the car to a roaring stop and whipped around, pinning my chest on the front seat where I'd been thrown forward, and with his other hand jammed the barrel of his pistol in my mouth. I felt the shatter of one of my front teeth and tasted the gunpowdery metal as he snarled, "Oh, a hard case, huh?"

With his eyes inches away, I read his delight, his longing for what he might get away with doing to the likes of me. What had already happened to war-resister buddies of mine was about to happen to me—there's nothing like the rage of cops unleashed on handcuffed men they despise. I knew it was up to me.

"Yesh, my name ish Tom Hama," I managed around the gun barrel in my mouth. The gunsight ripped the roof of my mouth as he yanked it out. Smiling at my acquiescence, he let go of my neck.

"That's better."

He drove on. The agent at my side asked more questions, this time cocky and smarmy. I cooperated, swallowing blood and sharp bits of tooth. Assured of being the big dogs, they ignored me for the rest of the drive, casually bantering back and forth about how quick and easy it had been to take me. I didn't dare respond to their taunts, just went on alert, ready for anything.

They took me to the county jail where I sat in the drunk tank for hours with the smell of packed bodies and vomit. A pair of Marine MPs arrived and took me to the local detention cell filled with drunk Marines. The rules were you could sit or stand but nothing else. With two small benches, most of us had to stand for hours under the bright lights. Once in a while a guard would come in and kick with steel-toed boots whoever had slumped to the floor and fallen asleep. About two a.m., two Navy SPs took me on a long drive to the Long Beach Naval brig where I was held in a huge, damp, dungeon-like cell all by myself. Freezing in only a T-shirt, I paced back and forth to stay warm. Eventually two Air Force MPs took me in a van filled with other hand-cuffed men and drove to the missile base where they sat parked with the engine running in a remote, barren area. The constant snapping on and off of handcuffs had left my wrists bruised and bloody. A guy beside me murmured, "Try to tighten your fists when they put 'em on . . . then they're not so tight." I looked out the rear window at the fog becoming visible in the first light of dawn. "What're they doing with us here?" I whispered. One of the MPs in front hurled himself against the wire partition and shouted, "Shut the fuck up!"

Another van drove up, this one with Army markings. It backed up to the rear of our van and both vans' rear doors opened. It was a switch—their prisoners traded for us. Evidently I was to tour and savor the correctional confinement facilities of not only the civilian sector but those of all the services. Handcuffed to the iron bar behind us, we were off on the freeways, looking out from the stink and humiliation of our sardine can on wheels, watching the clean-scrubbed faces and nice clothes of rush hour drivers whizzing by on their way to work. By late morning I was being dragged around in a daze of sleeplessness, checked in and locked up in my own solitary cell at a base stockade. In the familiar military manner, I was nightsticked awake when I dozed off sitting on my rack, told that I couldn't sleep until lights out. Thanksgiving dinner was brought cold to my cell by a different guard, the greasy slime going down gratefully. The guard watching me wolf my food asked when I last ate. When I told him, he went for seconds and even brought me hot coffee. I had no illusions—I was being treated well. This wasn't Russia or Cuba. The casual brutality of American cops and military police was nothing compared to being simply shot in the head and my body dumped on my parents' doorstep.

The next day I woke to the lights going on and the rat-tat-tat of a nightstick banging along door bars. I sat up in complete resolve at what I had to do. In the clearheadedness after a good night's sleep, I knew I was on a one-way trip to ten years at hard labor in a federal penitentiary. Nothing I had done would be considered a serious crime in the civilian world—two counts of AWOL, escaping from the resulting stockade time, and then desertion because I left the country—but the military is a law unto itself. I focused on the fact that there was still a long way to go. There'd be more handcuffs and car rides, a jet flight to Texas, more car rides. I had to escape somehow. I had to be ready for any opportunity that presented itself. Give my escort the slip, book for the border, bury myself in the Canadian bush. And this time not come back.

Oddly, only one MP was sent, and when I was brought out, he stood by the tall command desk giving me a penetrating look. A lifer, so many stripes and hash marks on his sleeves I figured he was close to retirement, he quickly handcuffed me to his own wrist and led the way out. A motor pool specialist drove up and took us to the local airport with me and Sgt. Bienvenue still handcuffed together. At the airport, being in civilian clothes handcuffed to a full-dress, decorated military police noncom drew constant attention. We stood looking away beside each other when one of us needed to use the urinals. I was purposely as easy and bland and sheepish and cooperative as I could be, doing everything to put him at ease.

On the commuter flight he boarded us first, put me in the window seat and didn't take off the cuffs until we were in the air. Landing, he put them back on us both. L.A. International was crowded with holiday travelers and he was getting tired and more easygoing in our enforced intimacy. But everything he did was by the book. We boarded the jet first again and sat the same way as before. Once we lifted off, he undid the cuffs for the hours-long flight and I rubbed my wrists, feeling desperate. Despite the fact that we were beginning to exchange polite pleasantries, he wasn't letting down his guard.

In a moment of Coyote inspiration, I turned to him and said, "Man, I wish you didn't have to humiliate me with these cuffs in front of everybody. . . ." I told him in what I thought were very convincing terms that I'd already decided to turn myself in when the FBI arrested me. I said I'd come to see what a mistake I'd made, and that all I wanted to do now was go back and face whatever was waiting for me. I gave it my most sincere best, hoping that he would believe me and not use the cuffs when we got off the plane.

Sgt. Bienvenue listened to what I was so earnestly telling him, nodding his head with a sleepy look. When I finished, he said nothing. I sat there listening to my own thoughts silently continuing what I'd said to him: "Then I'm gonna bail the first chance I get." Almost instantly he took a deep breath, stirred, and turned to me.

"You're gonna bail the first chance you get," he said with simple conviction. The hair at the back of my neck stood on end. I looked out the window, knowing I was turning red. That he could read me wasn't a terrible surprise—after all, he had access to reports of my uncompromising determination to escape and evade capture. What was startling was the fact that he'd read back to me what had just gone through my mind. I wondered if it was only a lucky guess. Yet it seemed unlikely that a lifer from my father's generation would use a street-slang word like "bail." It came to me that the jig was up; there'd be no escaping from this guy. Since there was no point in further pretending, my awe at hearing my thoughts read back to me turned into sincere curiosity. I simply turned to him and said, "How did you do that?"

He smiled knowingly. He was completely frank and spoke in simple terms about it. He said he'd always been "sensitive" as he called it, and when the military started holding training sessions for military policemen to help those who wanted to develop it and use it in their police work, he signed up. The training he described for sharpening impressions, going into trances, and listening for the words held strongly in other people's minds—completely official and taught by an officer to what he said were mainly country boys from the backwoods like him—boggled my mind. He said he used his training to enter a light trance while I was talking and when I stopped he listened for what I held strongly in my mind. When he heard what I said to myself, he just "came out with it" so I'd know my subterfuge was useless.

As our conversation warmed to other things, he spoke of being a Cajun from the bayou country of Louisiana. He said he'd married and brought back to the U.S. a Korean woman he met when he was stationed in her country—she was the first woman who completely accepted his gift as something normal. He told me stories about how he did what he did, and I realized he was quite proud to be recognized by someone he'd used his ability on, regardless of the circumstances. He said nobody he'd "read" in the line of duty ever responded like I did, wanting to know how he did it. He said I was considered extremely high risk because of how successfully I had baffled them in escaping from the stockade where I'd been held. He was chosen to come after me because of his record of never losing a man in transit.

"I'm not gonna break that record with you, either," he said with a laugh. I realized I liked and admired him. I wanted to know more and pumped him with questions. Then I just listened to him telling stories like an older man to a younger. He told of how he and a buddy were in class one day, deep in trance, and his buddy "saw" his wife in bed with another man. His buddy got up, got permission to leave, and drove off base to home. He caught his wife in bed with the other man, just as he'd seen it . . . but I don't remember what else happened. By the time we landed in Texas, he was teaching me how to count to ten in Cajun French, and correcting my pronunciation of certain cuss phrases he said would break the ice if I ever found myself in Cajunland. When he got out the cuffs, I held up my wrist for him. He snapped them on with more care than he'd shown before. When he turned me over to the base stockade officer, he turned to me and said, "You're not as dumb as you put on, Harmer." He actually shook my hand and added, *"Bonne chance!"*

Ten years later, staring out over a rolling sea of apple trees under a gloomy northwest sky, I wonder whatever became of Sgt. Bienvenue. Probably retired to the swampy rice farm he and his wife dreamed about. There was one thing he told me, one little bit of advice that always stuck with me. He said if I stopped striving to make things go

my way and just let go inside, got quiet in myself and accepted whatever was coming my way, then things would come floating up that I'd
feel certain about, and I'd know what to do. Sitting for days in a seg-
regation cell, what he suggested came easily. What floated up was that
my meeting Sgt. Bienvenue was not accidental, that bigger forces
were at work in my life than I could see, and that I should do nothing. From then on I simply faced the music: enjoyed each day as it
came, planned nothing, worried about nothing, stayed ready for
whatever came. What I didn't know was that a new general had taken
over command of the base. His attitude was different in the changed
climate of the war winding down to withdrawal from Vietnam. "If
they won't serve, get rid of them" was his directive about cases like
mine. Instead of court-martial and hard labor, I was offered immediate discharge "for the good of the service." In a matter of days, I was
out on the streets.

Remembering my experience—so many years later and informed by
Clayton's lore—I now saw him as a power man. And I could see it was
his character and inclinations that defined how the power worked
through him. His stories told of a life radically different from mine. His
career of enforcing the military's power over its own was, to my mind,
a distasteful devotion to coldly using force on others. I was his exact
opposite, my own makeup and disposition leading me to resist and
evade that force however I could. And yet he saw something kindred
in me and shared what he knew.

From that day forward I never doubted that some people could read
minds. I never believed in such things before, and I didn't "believe" in
them now. When something is an experienced fact of life, there's no
belief involved. What I acted on in life was what was real—what I
experienced and knew happened. With practice, it became as natural
and recurring as the sun rising in the morning. I suddenly felt pity for
so many of my own people who were doggedly certain such things were
not possible. What could make so many reject such things without honest investigation? Then it dawned on me. I saw that it came from a fear
of death. People clung to a materialist view of life to keep death from
having any significance, any reality. There were just vague thoughts of

life "ending." What a way to make the thought of death nothing to fear!

What had become of my own fear of death? How had my familiar awareness of self become like no more than wearing a suit of clothes? Neither the essential me nor the dark man seemed to do anything more than wear the clothes. Maybe death was only a change of clothing. What was there to fear when you saw through the clothes? I realized I hadn't felt real fear of anything in a long time. Other emotions could possess me and drive me, but I really wasn't afraid of much. At least not of the things that others were afraid of. I was more afraid of what harm I could do. And that made me wonder. Clayton urging me to hold back from using power somehow made eminent sense, and yet I couldn't put my finger on exactly why I felt so convinced. Probing into my own feelings, I realized that if I gave in to my baser instincts or acted on thoughtless urges, the dark man who had saved me could be unleashed to terrible effect on others.

Then it came to me. A memory I'd purposely not wanted to think about—the kind of experience that only forced itself on me in nightmares. I couldn't avoid it anymore. I had to look at this one as calmly and willingly as I had the others.

Years after my release from the military, when I was lost in my back-to-the-land wander of North America's western outback, I found myself temporarily down and out in a damp and dismal coastal town that smelled of mucky salt marshes and paper-products factories. I had a hard time steeling myself for the few months of wages I needed to head off on another round of adventure. The life I was leading increasingly seemed like a pointless escape and the blur of places, people, and experiences nothing more than marking time. Working in a gas station next to the main West Coast freeway, I hit some sort of bottom at what my life had become. Yet I couldn't think what to do to change it. With a kind of self-mockery and without caring what happened, one day I started making the rounds of all the downtown taverns. I drank and walked and drank and walked nonstop all day and into the night. I remember something like a slow fuse burning inside me, and when I came home to the drab and mildewy walk-up where I lived on the top floor of a creaking Victorian-era house converted into tiny apartments, I was surprised at how sober I was. Awash in beer and yet unable to lose myself in alcohol's usual numbing, forgetful effects, I sat on a ragged couch, staring at the seeming pointlessness of my life.

Downstairs there was a wild drinking party going on, and the music was suddenly too loud for me. It was two a.m. and my indignation drew me to the window where I saw dim figures below yelling angrily at each other. A young woman tried to get into a pickup truck to leave the party, but a man yanked open the door and tried to drag her out. She screamed and I snapped. At first when I charged out the door and down the outside stairwell, I was an avenging angel bent on a vague notion of intervening and protecting the woman. But in a flash I felt the flood of pent-up rage released and directed at the unsuspecting man, realized with horror what I was really doing. The instant I changed my mind, something inexplicable happened—I was suddenly outside my body and seeing myself from over my left shoulder. It was a terrifying separation because the me that was observing myself racing downstairs was completely opposed to what he was doing but unable to have any effect on him.

I remember a mute, helpless anxiety seeing myself take three steps at a leap. I was awed by the contorted fury on my face, the demented gleam in my eye seen in profile. I felt I was being dragged along unwillingly beside what I realized was the dark man embodied for the first time in a way I could witness from the outside. I strove to somehow stop him—a kind of "No, no, no, no, no!" frantically but ineffectively beamed mutely at him like a boy trying to stop a man racing off in a rage.

I remember floating along over his left shoulder as he hit the ground floor and ran around the front. It was like nothing I'd ever experienced before. I was hovering to one side as he yanked the other man away from the woman in the pickup and smashed his fist into his face. I remember instantly reading the situation between the man and the woman—they were a couple, both drunk, and involved in a petty squabble. I had a moment of utter terror that the maniac punching away at the other man was me. I saw the dark man falter and waver. At the same moment I saw the other man, punished but rallying from his surprise, take the initiative and throw punches like an experienced street fighter. I sensed my terror had weakened the dark man's hold and the rain of blows was pounding on a befuddled shell of myself. I had a sudden burning need to "get in there" and help him, and without knowing how, I was back in my body directly feeling the pain and struggle of a fight with another man.

It was like waking up into a din of sound and sensations, and made me realize later how silent and unfeeling things were when I was split off from my body. Wherever the dark man went, he was gone completely, and with him went any conviction of kill or be killed. I went down in a frantic struggle as the ordinary, everyday person I was familiar with—a nightmare so real that what I remembered most was the look on the man's face, a rage revealed as the same as what had snapped in me. I remember rolling on broken glass by a curb, locked in a punching, kicking anything to endure the other man's relentless drive to punish me for attacking him. Figures loomed around us, strong male arms pulled us apart, voices shouted stop, that's enough, be done with it. I was panting, in a daze, and remember blurting out, "Yeah, okay, I'll quit." Relieved, I turned away from the hands releasing my arms. Then there was an explosion of stars and a vast black world opened up and swallowed me.

After a timeless nothingness, I begin to see something like a transparent balloon floating toward me and evaporating on me. Another one, exactly the same, comes floating and washes over me. My sense of things opens and sharpens. When I see a third exact replica of the balloon coming toward me, I realize there's sound, too—a certain rhythmic, nagging dah-dáh-dah-DAH? I feel I'm being shaken and a strange face appears looking into my eyes with concern. His lips are moving but all I hear are incomprehensible sounds in the pattern of dah-dáh-dah-DAH? Then with a start I come to the surface sitting on my couch in my apartment, some guy kneeling in front of me shaking my shoulders, saying, "Are you all right?"

My left hand instinctively lifts to touch what feels like the most unbearable, smashed-in pain I've ever felt on the side of my face. My fingers discover massive swelling and a broken jaw.

"Yeah, he snuck around and blindsided you," the man says. "After you quit and wasn't lookin'. You went out like a light. You remember me helpin' you walk up the stairs?"

I couldn't say anything. The man decided I was okay and left. When he was gone I began to tremble. I was consumed with the reality of what I had done. Something like not being master in my own house, of having been unwillingly outside my body while it went about acting on my unrecognized rage, became too devastating to bear. My whole body shook uncontrollably and I felt the dark man in me trying to come out again. My body hurled itself around the room in something like shock, an explosion of adrenaline-induced movement with no direction or purpose. It was like trying to stay embodied in an animal that was having a seizure and running amok. There was a feeling of revolt, of fleeing in terror of itself. I was little more than along for the ride as I found myself racing on all fours into the bedroom and crashing into things. There was a feeling of running to hide from something unspeakably monstrous, and then I found myself diving into the closet and burrowing under the pile of camping equipment and dirty clothes. Hidden and buried, I moaned and rocked, moaned and rocked. The taste of bloody tears only slowed the rigid lock of my muscles' rhythmic convulsions.

Then I felt a hand on my ankle and heard a female voice softly humming a childhood lullaby. A massive load of grief came sobbing out of me. Little by little I became a man again, became solid, of one piece—fully the same breathing, heart-pumping, thinking, consciously-in-charge person I was used to being. I knew who the woman was who held my ankle from the closet doorway and offered her comfort to me, humming in a small, brave, frightened voice what I heard as a child at my mother's knee. It must have been hard for her to approach the thing I had become hidden under the closet pile. Her gift of calling me back to human form will never be forgotten.

Reliving those events so many years later, what came to me was that it was just as Clayton warned about. The dark man had acted on my deepest, strongest, most unexamined urges. I had split apart because the best part of me tried to oppose him once he was already out, and of course, he was far stronger than a mere human soul. Brushed aside, I could only look on with growing horror until what? My lack of being there in concert with him induced him to turn on me? To melt away and leave me to face the man alone? To take the beating I deserved? And what happened afterward in my apartment seemed like a revulsion of my body against the mind that had come back to inhabit it. A body that knew the dark man as survival in peak experiences, as continued life, knew the me that usually ran the show as someone who was so feeble he had to be saved from himself.

I realized that everything I had done in the years since that experience had been unconsciously informed by a desire to keep the dark man in check because I couldn't trust my own feelings. I'd been seeking a way to live whole, to find a way that would allow the dark man to live through me without terrorizing me or others. That was what had been driving me to learn from Clayton Tommy, what always brought me back when I strayed away. And that meant, I now saw, exactly what Clayton had shown so deftly in his story about Everybody Knows It, and Sgt. Bienvenue had started me on the path toward. It meant being okay with whatever life offered and acting from the best of myself. Only then would the dark man's devastating power be something that I could live with and call up to use with the kind of confident assurance that Clayton had in calling on his own power.

I hung my tools in a tree and started for home. After a day of fog and sleet with the lake hidden in mists below, the sky had "gone back up high" as Clayton described it. The half moon overhead shone through a thin overcast and the world was dark, wet, and muffled as I walked the familiar miles. I recalled that I saw the man I had attacked one more time, days after the incident. We met on the street, my jaw wired shut after a late-night visit to the emergency room prompted by the woman who urged her help on me. His face was a mess—bruised, puffy, scabby, and his upper lip split. He laughed sheepishly, hardly remembering what had happened.

"Hey man . . . we were drunk. Forget about it!" he said.

He worked in a factory where his days were spent operating the machinery that made what he called "der-ders."

"Ya know, those cardboard tubes on the insides of toilet paper rolls?

That kids put to their mouth and walk around going 'Der-der-der-der'?"

We laughed and shook hands. I was glad I'd been able to abort the dark man's onslaught. Talking through clenched teeth and taking all food and drink through a straw for a month seemed like a small price to pay.

The moon's dim light came and went from above the cloudy drift over Chopaka Mountain. It was so still I could hear Cooksey's horses breathing even though I couldn't make out much more than their out-lines standing asleep under the crowded pine trees of their lakeside pasture. There was something morbid lingering after remembering the dark man, something like a bad taste in my mouth. My whole body ached and tingled in a way that had nothing to do with the stiff sore-ness of a hard day's work. The chipped front tooth I felt with my tongue, the tilt of my lower left molars where they'd healed back crooked, the way my many scars hurt when the weather was damp like this. And most of all, something I hadn't felt in a long, long time—a wounded feeling under my belt, in my guts. I tried to ignore it, but walking seemed to bring it on stronger.

On a whim, I decided to take a shortcut that would shorten my walk by a mile. The road curved in a wide bend around a raised benchland that was strongly fenced as a bull pasture by the cattle rancher who owned it. Bulls are usually no big deal for hands used to feeding and working with them as I had—at least the breeds used in that country as food cattle, the Hereford, Angus, Simmental, and Longhorn mixes. But this rancher kept only one bull in this pasture, a Jersey bull, and Jerseys are more aggressive and unpredictable. This one was known as particularly dangerous and for years I'd drive or walk by where he paced menacingly around his domain, bellowing and hoofing up clouds of dust even when it wasn't breeding season. Stuart had warned me not to be foolish and tempt fate by entering "Jersey Bull's pasture" on foot, but it was nighttime and I figured Jersey Bull would be standing some-where asleep near the lower-end gate where he was fed hay every morning and usually hung around. I could sneak across the upper parts and join the road again on the other side.

Climbing over the stout barbed wire fence, I headed uphill in the dark as quietly as I could, listening and watching for any sign of Jersey Bull. My eyes were adjusted to the moonlight enough that I could see pretty far. I appreciated the distraction from my aching body and gloomy mood—it took all my concentration to stay alert for anything and pick my way across a stretch of country I'd never been in before. The lower reaches of the pasture were open grassland but I soon discovered my path over the upper parts led through dense, tall brush and the deep shadows of occasional ponderosa pines. About midway across I came to an unexpected ravine and stopped to listen and study the dark shadows of the heavier brush below.

Nothing came to my senses to disturb the feel of free passage over the land that was slowly working its magic on me. Descending to cross the ravine, I was becoming the familiar night creature of other times, immersed in the instinctive moves of my body through an unknown, vaguely discerned landscape. Smelling the sagebrush that brushed my legs and hands, feeling invisible and at one with all I passed through. The dull soreness in my guts had been replaced by a comforting warmth, a feeling that my navel was opening, that it was an organ through which I was feeling my way along. It was a good hundred yards down the slope to the bottom, and along the way I began to feel the shapes and shadows around me for any threat. It was like some kind of muscled containment that reached out from my navel in a wide circle around me and "read" the feel of things. Remembering my long-ago leap and how this same feeling through my navel had saved my life, I gave myself over wholly to the sensation. I somehow "knew" that if Jersey Bull was near, I would know it. And there was nothing on the radar screen, no blips, nothing but empty night.

I felt a surge of animal fitness and poise, and I broke out in a run to cross over to the uphill slope. I literally danced across the dry wash in a release of joyful abandon, my eyes locked on the moonlit ground in front of me, confident of every step. The sensation of gliding effortlessly through a beautiful world that loved me was suddenly altered by a mass of dark movement seen out of the corner of my right eye. In a split second I heard the crash of rocks and thunderous charge of a huge animal through the brush toward me. Instantly my effortless stride turned into a frantic, blind, uphill sprint of complete panic. I heard the snorting, pounding, incredibly close pursuit of what could only be Jersey Bull behind me, and the thought of being gored by his horns spurred me into unbelievable speed. My eyes locked onto a pine tree with low limbs and in seconds I was going up it faster than I'd ever climbed a tree before.

It couldn't have been more than five or ten seconds from Jersey Bull's unexpected charge to me clinging to tree limbs ten feet off the ground. I was completely winded and my heart was pounding furiously but I was listening and looking for him below. Strangely, there was nothing to see or hear. The complete silence and lack of any sign of a bull was unnerving. At first I figured he was standing where I couldn't see him through the pine boughs. I listened intently for any sound of him. But there was nothing—not a breath, not a rustle, not a displaced pebble. I crept down and stood by the trunk, ready to dive up again if he appeared. Nothing. Passing clouds opened and closed above, bright moonlight sweeping the bottom of the ravine, revealing no sign of him.

The incantation Clayton taught me came to mind and I stifled a laugh. So much for being prepared. The panic of my flight dissolved into a wary good humor. I wondered if I should say it out loud now, to Jersey Bull silently out there somewhere. Would something so ancient and derived from the wild animals of the world work on a *skáha,* a domesticated animal? Clayton hadn't said anything about bulls, but something felt not right anyway. My mind was in full calculation now, and had concluded from the evidence of my experience that the proximity of the bull pounding after me would have left him no more than ten feet away from the base of the tree. Yet I could see all the way to the bottom of the ravine and there was nowhere for him to hide. I'd heard nothing, no steps of him walking away, no labored breathing from running uphill after me. A thousand-pound animal walking away so fast without a sound was simply not possible.

As each moment passed I grew more uneasy. My mind could not accept that there was no bull. I eased downhill and stood halfway to the bottom. The dry wash I was crossing when the bull charged was in clear view. My tracks digging into the soft, damp soil when I ran uphill were clearly visible. I tiptoed quietly around in an ever-widening series of circles but there was no trace of the bull and no whisper of sound to indicate his presence. The fact that the bull was not there and never had been finally sank in.

Returning to the tree I climbed, I sat down with my back against it and looked around with a strangely sleepy feeling that was like my mind trying to shut down to avoid the implications. Shaking the cobwebs out of my head, I thought: Well, if it wasn't Jersey Bull, what was it? I thought again about what happened. I realized I hadn't see anything more than a dark mass of movement to my right, that everything else I registered of being charged and chased had been in the realm of sound. There was no mistaking the sounds of a huge animal lunging through brush—the breaking of branches and banging of loose rocks had been distinct. Something pounding furiously after me as I ran toward the tree had been a blur, but I had no question that what I had heard was real and after me.

I inspected my memory of the dark mass I'd seen, trying to remember any features that would identify what it was. I began to feel nauseated. I looked over at the thick, waist-high bushes downhill, where I'd glimpsed the dark mass moving. A wave of fear swept over me. I felt a sharp stab of pain in my bellybutton and the full impact of unreasoning terror hit me like a stone. At the same time, I became aware that some sort of cloud had been seeping into me while I sat there. A sort of creeping lethargy had been draining away my waking consciousness and I was seeing a glimmer of the same whitish donut of vague light that I saw when I blacked out on the rock ledge at Naháhum Lake with Clayton.

This time it was like a movie fade-out, expanding to blot out everything directly in front of me, and then edging into the periphery where I could still see the details of the night hills. I turned my eyes to look at the things I could still see, but the white mass before my eyes moved with my eyes' movements. I had a blind spot directly before my eyes. I had a sensation of going completely still and rigid, and a conviction that I was losing consciousness. I realized the only way to look at what little there was left to see around the periphery of my vision was to use *wik'wst,* to shift my eyes and take it all in at once. The compulsion to do it was intense, but something made me terrified of doing so. Fighting off the urge to fall asleep, I blinked my eyes wildly and just turned and bolted uphill on all fours.

The sudden rush of movement made the white blur before my eyes fade, and I could just make out what was ahead. I clawed my way up and over the steep edge at the top of the ravine and gained my feet. I could see clearly again in the moonlight and ran as fast as I could. Only when I'd put distance between myself and the ravine did I begin to come back into my right mind. Slowing to descend the other side of the benchland, I began to look for Jersey Bull again, just in case. There was no sign of him.

Climbing the fence and regaining the road was an immense relief, but I strode toward home feeling more confused than ever. I knew something momentous had happened, but my inability to identify what it was left me with foreboding.

17

CLAYTON LEFT WORD HE was going to gather plants for Old Willie and wanted my help. On the appointed day he showed up at Jim's trailer at dawn. I hardly had time to tie on a red bandana before he let himself in, poured a cup of coffee, and sat down on the door chair rubbing the sleep out of his eyes. It was the first red bandana I'd worn and the first obviously summer-warm day of spring. Clayton spoke to me in Salish as he usually did when he first got up in the morning, as if it took him a while to remember communication with me was more effective if he turned on the English side of his brain.

I couldn't imagine what plants besides spring roots dug for food that Willie would want at this time of year, but Clayton didn't want to talk about it. He asked me how long I could be gone. I said I was done with orchard pruning and didn't have to start fence work with Stuart for several days. He seemed pleased.

"*Xast. Wai mut ƙwu'xóoy leƙuut. Loot stim ƙamém. Loot an'ƙsen'ƙa'íls* (Good. Then we can go a long way. Not for things to eat. Don't bother your mind about it, we'll just find some things for him, what plants an Indian doctor in his old age blows on and gives to others for their own good)."

Winters in the Okanogan seem endless, buried in snow under the gray pall of northwest skies. But when spring finally comes with its startling transformation into balmy, sunlit, Eden-like otherness, two different worlds seem to exist in the same place. The contrast is so

extreme it's like emerging from a cave out into the light of day. With
my orchard work finished, spring fever had hit hard. I avoided going
back up to the mountain cabin where the snow still lingered, and when
I wasn't doing chores for Charlene, I gave in to a lethargy that was little more than lying around in the sunshine like an old dog. It slowed
my putting together a camp kit and loading things into Clayton's station wagon. Clayton was in no hurry himself and drifted outside to sit
on the porch step sipping his coffee.

The magpies were back from wherever they went in winter. A flock
of them flew back and forth in the warming daylight of riverbottom
trees. We watched their ungainly black-and-white crowish clowning
made somehow dignified with long, iridescent, green-sheened tail
feathers splayed to land and drag behind them as they searched the
ground for the long sticks they nest with. As usual, Clayton called out
to them in their own language, displaying his skillful mimicry of bird
calls, his questioning *"An-an?"* (the Salish word for magpie) getting a
strident response. In a Chinese elm just budding out with soft char-
treuse green, two females bickered loudly over rights to one of last
year's nests, a two-foot ball of brush low in the dense tangle of limbs.

"Wai skaip'ch (Spring has come)," Clayton murmured. "Just in time
maybe. Take the thoughts away from how the Animal People come so
easy to us in the dark and cold. Take thought of plants wakin' up. To
dress the world in green. Well, this the time everything come back to
get busy and dress up in the fresh new clothes."

I sat on the chopping block and told him about the memories that
had come back while I was working in the orchards. I described my
early experiences and used the phrase "dark man" for the first time
with him, telling how "he" emerged and did things like coming from
my guts, through my navel. Clayton smiled knowingly and said the
way I talked about it sounded similar to other talk he'd heard in his life,
that some power men described their *shumíx* coming on them like I did.
It was reassuring to hear my experiences recognized as something old
and familiar to him. It made me feel more normal and not so isolated,
more hopeful that I could live well with what was inside me.

"But why you call 'em the 'dark man'?" he asked, brow wrinkled.

"Well, I guess because he doesn't seem like a very nice guy when he shows up."

My answer seemed to mystify him even further. Then his eyes lit up.

"*Aaaa!* You mean 'dark' like 'bad'!" He laughed long and hard until tears came. Then he sighed. "Yah, they not very nice, not the well-behaved dog come to do your business for you, eh? You such a card, nephew. A whole deck of cards. Next you be tell me the power is what scare you, not what you use 'em for!"

I told him no, I saw well enough how it was my own unexamined urges that scared me. He said my memories were valuable experiences worth exploring in other ways because every person with power had to "come to know for theirself" how losing the fear of death brought on the power to do impossible things. As he spoke, I had the odd certainty he was holding back, that he was leaving something important out about when indifference turned to power. Some indefinable something I myself had glimpsed but couldn't put a name on when I realized it wasn't Jersey Bull who charged and chased me in the ravine. Unlike the horror of seeing how my own failings could unleash the dark man to attack someone, this was a more inexplicable kind of dread—that what I was learning how to do unleashed something beyond my control regardless of how careful or self-knowledgeable I'd become. That what I was doing was attracting things at large in the world more dangerous than bulls or grizzlies—things I was truly defenseless against.

When I told him about crossing Jersey Bull's pasture on foot in the dark, he had another long laugh. His being so easily entertained was infectious. I saw myself through his eyes—how ridiculous a picture I must have made, running for dear life, scrambling up a tree, and then discovering no bull was chasing me. He said encountering a powerful spirit in the night was nothing new, his people used the same word for it as when somebody saw a ghost, *ḳuḳ'wíḳst*. The effect of it on me was a well-known, commonly experienced phenomenon for someone who had something; those inexperienced or fearful of power "just go out, same as a light switched off." He said it was just like me to "grab the bull on the horns," that as long as he'd known me I had a way of jump-ing in and pushing things to the limit. Not that I was impatient or foolish, but that I had an instinct for acting on things without really understanding why I had the urge. He said he himself would never go there or the canyon above the ravine at night unless he had some specific, important purpose in mind, some reason to call on the dangerous power that lived there.

"Why you think they call 'em Clockwillow Canyon, eh? Only the power man who know what he doin' ever go there," he said, shaking his head as if I should have known better. The way he said "Clockwillow" pronounced in a more Salish way made it seem like a familiar Okanogan word I should know, but I couldn't place it. The countryside was full of names that were Englished versions of Native names, altered enough from their original form not to be recognizable unless pronounced by the old-timers. Which was how I'd learned the city of Kelowna, B.C., was from *k̓iláwna,* "grizzly bear"; Loup Loup Creek from *hlup'hlup,* plural for the salmon that once swam up it before logging and mining ended a dependable fishery; and Chopaka Mountain from *chupákx,* "sticking up." But Clockwillow never seemed Indian to me. I always thought of it as another Anglo place name like Beaverdell, Two Strikes mine, Goodenough Peak and Loch Drinkie— that "clock" and "willow" must go together in some way I just didn't know the story behind.

I'd never been up Clockwillow Canyon, a short and narrow defile in the steep face of Grandview Mountain that descended to the broad glacial terraces lining the valley, that with seasonal water had carved the ravine through Jersey Bull's pasture. I'd heard there were lots of rock pictures up there, but nobody White I'd ever talked to had actually seen them. The Indians wouldn't talk about the canyon—if it came up, the subject was just dropped. What did Clayton mean that only power men who knew what they were doing ever went there? Then, I realized Clayton had said *tlak̓wílux,* the word for "power person." "Clockwillow" was about as good a way for an English-speaking person to say it as you could find.

"Yah, from all the time back, in story, the Indians know to stay away from there," Clayton said. "Just the ones who have the gift to call on, and even then, to know you take your life in your hand to go there at night and seek for somethin'."

He said that what the Whites had done in the world didn't change what was always there in the earth, what power manifested at certain places. He related with some disgust a conversation he'd overheard after a sweat, between "Uncle Coyote," a fortyish, charismatic, self-appointed Native guru to some prospective White followers. I remembered once sweating with Uncle Coyote and two young White guys he brought to Johnny Stemilt's, and was surprised to hear his influence and following was growing. As if imparting his deep wisdom of things to the White guys, Clayton said Uncle Coyote told them "things have power if people believe they have power." That sacred pipes and power objects and eagles and even Chopaka Mountain had power because people believed they did. In a way that sounded as if ushering them into the secrets of using Native power, he conspiratorially suggested it was this belief of people that Indian doctors (meaning he himself) learned to "hook onto" and do things that, really, the people were making happen themselves out of devoted belief.

Clayton said no real Indian doctor or power man would say that. Only Indians who grew up in the White world and "come back to the blanket" still impressed by White ways of thinking talked about things that way. Clyde Demoyne (Uncle Coyote's birth name) had gone off to boarding school as a child, then joined the Navy and stayed away in cities most of his life. Clayton said when no White followers were around and "Mister Coyote" was alone with his own people, he was quiet and timid because he knew "nobody ever hear him come out with a song." Clayton said Clyde knew nothing about the earth, that he spent his time indoors, watching videos of old war movies on television. Only with the naïve White seekers did he come on like a powerful teacher of old Native ways. He said the way he sounded talking to them was of someone who wanted power real bad but had given up hope of ever receiving it.

"Bein' the clever coyote, ain't it? Tellin' 'em what he think they want to hear, what sound like the great and wise teacher. You can tell he never feel the dark man come out and make him dirty his pants!" Then he sighed. In a pitying voice, he added, "But I know why he doin' what he doin'. Out there in the White world, all his life just the dumb Indian, and to feel just dirt to the White people. Now they come to him, eh?

Come from all over to sit at his knee and hear his wise words. How he out-White the White people, just like Coyote!"

He said the rancher kept Jersey Bull in that particular pasture because, whether the rancher knew it or not, it was a dangerous power place. Even the numbest Whites could feel what Indians felt in places like that, and the old-time landowners, the descendants of early settlers who'd been in that country all their lives, acted on such feelings, even if they rationalized it in other ways. Clayton said him keeping Jersey Bull there was a warning to keep people out, and that was how power worked, regardless of what people might think was going on.

"C'mon, I show you the proof," Clayton said, standing up and heading for his car. I got in as he started it. "We take a drive and you see for yourself how the power show itself for all who can see. The world wearin' the new White man suit of clothes, but even what your people do can't cover over the power!"

I rode shotgun as he drove placidly down the county road winding along the bases of grassy mountains beginning to green from the bottom up. The sun came over a timbered ridge and bathed the valley in arid brilliance as he pulled over on the shoulder by the steel gate into Jersey Bull's pasture. We got out and I saw the bull standing still in familiar indifference about a half mile off. Clayton led the way walking slowly along the asphalt pavement, head down and eyes searching the road surface for something. The springlike scent of pine and sage heated by the sun was a heady balm to my winter-starved senses. A pickup truck went by and we both waved back at Old Man Rutherford heading into Loomis. Clayton kept on, looking for all the world like somebody searching for a coin or key accidentally dropped on the blacktop. I studied the face of Grandview Mountain where Clockwillow Canyon was still hidden in dark hardrock shadows. From where we walked along, the ravine wasn't visible, but I could see where it had to be, behind a grove of pines lining the dry wash. Where the wash crossed under the road in a culvert, Clayton stopped and called out, "Here it is!"

I came up to see what he was looking down at. There was nothing but bare pavement as far as I could see until he brought his toe close to a large reddish pebble embedded flush with the surface of black asphalt. Looking closer, it was just one of many small stones showing, the gravel used as aggregate when they paved the road. But the one he pointed out had an unusual shape—it was the perfect form of an arrowhead, like the kinds the Indians used to make by hand from flint or obsidian, even down to the delicate notches on the back end. It stood out conspicuously also as the only rose quartz piece of rock showing, and it pointed directly up the line of the wash toward Clockwillow Canyon.

"See, the power work even in the White man's doings, what they lay down to cover the earth," Clayton said, gazing up where the arrowhead pointed. He said ever since the road had been paved the Indians had known about the arrowhead and tried not to drive over it. Before then, there'd been a certain red rock, repainted with Native red ocher every generation or so, to mark the place, but the bulldozers had buried it.

"Now you come along and you know maybe better than that rancher what feel dangerous up there, eh? You go and wake one of 'em up!"

"Yeah, I suppose," I said. "But I still have no idea what it was."

"They like a spirit, the old ones the stories tell about, but they got no clothes to wear, that we can see 'em like we do the animal, the pine tree, the mountain." We both moved onto the shoulder as another pickup flew by. We walked slowly back to his car.

"They live in just certain places, like that place is what they got— that place is their power. They the ones don't like it when the human people come alive on earth, want to kill and eat us because we so weak and pitiful, maybe just food for 'em. Just where Coyote kill 'em in the long ago, there they stay forever. But Coyote only kill what you can see. They still can take the life if somebody don't beware. Seem just an accident, like buck off a horse, or gun goes off by accident, like that.

"Only the power man, the hard ones, and the Indian doctors, like that, they maybe just test 'em. Have more respect because it's all power for those old ones. Then maybe learn somethin' real powerful from 'em. You try it again, nephew, my suggestion that you go in the daytime, when the sun shine and they hide inside the rocks."

We got in and Clayton drove on.

"My thinkin' of another power place," he mused, turning onto the road to Tonasket and the main Okanogan Valley. "Take the time to see how our mother show herself in the old Indian places, that a Sunday drive is the way to go. Be just the sleepy look-around on our way to dig bushes. Another kind of power place, *en'x'xá'em*. The kind bring to mind what make life good and strong. The livin' with power that hard to remember sometimes give a man the best of hearts, worth all we go through."

He glanced at me with a coy smile. He knew he had me hooked, had my complete attention and interest. He once said that it only took three things for a person to do well living in the power way: "That somebody have interest that he can't help hisself and is drawn to power. That he is brave, and don't give in to bein' scared. And that he don't suffer—nothin' really all that bad to him. Like the hard trails and go without food and water all the same to him as sit home and eat good." There was no question the first of the three described me.

"I wonder where that power place might be," I said, going along with him.

"Echo Mountain, they call 'em," he said, as if announcing a story. "But in another way, the elders used to say, 'Where they let 'em down with ropes.'"

Echo Mountain turned out to be a place south of Tonasket in plain view of U.S. highway 97. On the west side of the Okanogan River, the abrupt wall of highlands scraped bare and smoothed by thousands of years of continental glaciation are cut by narrow slot canyons, some with creeks rushing with snowmelt from the high mountains farther back, some just dry coulees having no observable reason for existing. Some of these ancient routes up onto high bunchgrass hills run parallel to the main north-south valley, and going up them the dominating features are a tilted block of bare rock mountain to the left and a gentler, terraced slope on the right. We hiked up one of these slot canyons, a dry one, one with just an old horse trail threading through a boulder garden of bitterbrush in the first greenish-yellow blossom of spring, the buzz of insects in the sheltered microclimatic warmth was unexpectedly loud in the stillness. Leaving the flatland orchards and greening alfalfa fields behind, passing the faint remains of pictographs as the only indication of the kind of place we were entering, we climbed steeply upward into dark timber that gave only glimpses of the ever-higher cliff towering in dazzling sunlight to our left. Spring-stupefied deer stared at us passing by, birds sang that I hadn't heard since the summer before, and circling above the trees, ravens croaked, showing off their feats of "lively difficulty"—the tricky airborne antics no other birds attempt, like flying upside down, that give them their Salish name, *yútelux.*

After a sweaty mile, Clayton turned right onto a fainter trail that led even more steeply uphill and out into brushy sunlight. He paused, brought a finger to his lips for silence, then went on. The trail climbed a series of cobbly terraces with tall stands of sagebrush almost closing the passage, and at each level the canyon opened up more to view below us. Along a rocky rim we passed a honeycomb of overhangs and hidden, ferny grottoes under giant slabs of banded granitic rock. I heard the first tentative nesting calls of a canyon wren from the cliff opposite, a series of descending flutelike notes that slowed to a sobbing halt. The bright yellow and orange flame of a tanager flew by. Mountain bluebirds perched on swaying limbs like bits of turquoise come to feathery life. Green plants of every kind were springing up from the rich black soil glittering with mica. The rim led to where all the terraces we'd climbed compressed into a steep promontory facing the sheer cliff of mountain about halfway up, across a dizzying vault of late-morning air.

We sat quietly recovering from our climb, I where Clayton gestured for me to lean against a prominent rounded glacial boulder, he against an old log, a twisted, eroded pine trunk with burned limb stubs and a vivid green coating of lichens on the north side. It was a spot free of brush, what looked like an old campsite showing traces of campfire charcoal behind where we sat close to the drop-off. The boulder at my back was shaggy with layered foliose lichens up to a bald top where dried white stains showed where hawks perched. Clayton dozed in the full force of sunshine, what his language called *ku'lal,* the hot stare of the male eye in the sky, the dreamy balm of solar silence nearly putting me to sleep, too. But then I noticed something vaguely acoustical going on, something that came and went in the breeze like a voice talking barely at the threshold of sound.

Opening my eyes and looking around made no difference. It seemed as if someone were murmuring in my ear, but turning my head in different directions, I could triangulate it as coming from the empty space between us and the cliff wall we faced about a football field's length away. It was startling to hear words I couldn't make out that simultaneously came from a distance and yet seemed to be whispered into my ear. Glancing aside at Clayton, I found him awake, gazing at me. Gesturing again to stay silent, he pointed with a jut of his chin to stay facing the cliff. Looking at it in detail, I saw it was rugged and fractured with deep holes and bulging outcrops, a kind of banded gneiss that ran in horizontal layers with tiny ledges and shadowy crevices where bushes clung precariously. What Clayton had brought me to without telling me what to expect seemed like an acoustical anomaly, a spot positioned to receive some focusing of sound that was like someone talking to himself in the hazy void of air between.

In the corner of my right eye I saw Clayton's hands making hunting signals, just like he used to do years before when he tested whether I was using *wik'wst* or not. He'd stand behind me off to one side, signalling something surreptitiously, then ask me what he'd signalled to find out how well I was attentive to my peripheral vision. This time he signaled, "Look, straight ahead, one thing."

Our use of hand signals, common for hunters trying to communicate at a distance without calling out (which carried so far and was a dead giveaway to animals that humans were around), was usually a source of humor for Clayton, and now was no different. When it was obvious I was still searching for whatever he wanted me to notice on the cliff face, he signaled, "In the middle, female, mating." I nearly burst out laughing—he meant the cavelike opening directly across at eye level. But not sure why he was pointing it out, I held out my right hand and waved a slangy, "Negative, what?" (Fist like a head shaking back and forth, hand held open, palm up, with a shrug.) He signaled right back, "Look, here," and I turned to see him predictably shaking with silent laughter.

He poked his finger into the dirt, gestured toward the cliff, then pointed to his mouth and made the sign for human speech, which he usually signed to mean he was hearing somebody talking. I looked back at the cliff understanding he meant the faint voice we heard was coming from the cave.

It made me think of a time when I was changing a flat tire on Jim's old yellow Barracuda for Grandma and Charlene to drive to town in. Thunder rolled off the top of Chopaka from the dark clouds massing above the summit, and after the prolonged bumping and muttering faded away, Grandma turned to Charlene and said, "Did you catch that?" Charlene shrugged uncertainly, then said, "Somethin' about the bugs gonna be bad maybe." "Better fix those holes in the screen door," Grandma murmured. The mosquitoes and biting flies were so bad that summer, horses and cattle stuck in the valley bottoms actually lost weight even with extra feed.

Another thought drifted by, how Kenneth the anthropologist had said to me one time when we ran into each other on the sidewalks of downtown Osoyoos that in his experience it was just a myth that Indians were more "mystical" than White people. He said most were just as "practical" and "logical" as most of any other kind of people. I said I agreed, that the problem behind the perception was that White people thought their own version of being practical and logical was the only one around, and when they ran into another version, they simply branded it as "mystical" and "unscientific." He said that's not what he meant at all, that he meant most Indians were just as inclined to "look for the proof of observable facts" in what was happening as the average White person. It was just a few who had mystical tendencies, he said, the same as among White people, but these few were taken as if they represented how all Indians were. Not being timid about what I saw as his usual academic correctness, I said the "mystical few" I knew seemed to me more practical and logical than the average White scientist, since they weren't afflicted with judging some kinds of evidence as not real. As an example, I told him how Charlene had told me the first time something happened that was exactly how she'd previously dreamed it. How when it happened as a teenager she took it as simple evidence of

how things worked in the world, and from then on paid closer attention to her dreams, becoming eventually skilled at anticipating what to
do when dreamed events came to pass. I said the only reason what
Charlene was doing was considered mystical and not practical or logical was because in the White version of practical logic, dreams weren't
"real." Kenneth got hot, said I was letting Old Willie, "that old trick-
ster and showman," influence my thinking, and stalked off.

So when my thoughts faded away I concentrated on listening for
whatever I might learn from the evidence of my senses. I had no pre-
disposition to discount the possibility that something in the world was
speaking in a way I might understand. After listening intently for a
long time it did seem, as Clayton suggested, as though the sound was
coming directly across to us from the cave mouth. It was naggingly
inconsistent, sometimes fading away completely in the breeze, sometimes so clearly the same as someone talking nearby on a windy day I
could almost tell what was being said. The intonation seemed
"English" to me, and sounded like mostly vowels framed by simple
consonants. My inability to discern what was being said seemed due to
the fact that only the low tones were carrying; the high tones were
barely suggested or faded out of hearing completely. It was a long quiet
time of listening in rapt attention. Trying to make out the meaning of
what was being said was a definite soporific; my head sagged and my
eyes dimmed to the lulling sound. In my sleepy daze, I finally recognized a word. Despite my feeling of hearing English, the word that
stood out in the stream of murmuring was *sin'ḳa'ils,* a Salish word hard
to translate but close to "something someone feels like doing" or "somebody's business." I automatically wondered what my business was
being there. In the absence of anything to go on from Clayton beyond
remembering him saying this was the kind of power place that brought
to mind what made life good and strong, I wondered what it was that
made me so unlike Kenneth. The words welled up silently from within
me: "I just want to know the world firsthand, not how those who seem
bent on destroying it say it is."

At the moment the thought passed through my mind, there was a
sudden alarm screeching of a single bluejay glimpsed in the timber
where I was looking down. Then the blur of a peregrine falcon shoot-

ing gracefully through the tops of trees. The falcon came out of its bar-reling stoop, slowed to land in a tree, and in an acrobatic splay of wings and tail, disappeared into dense fir boughs. The bluejay, instantly silenced, was nowhere to be seen. My heart skipped a beat. I registered its significance only after the fact. Such an inexplicable sign, a gift handed to me, a confirmation of something. I was touched and hum-bled by how their appearance instantly confirmed me in how I saw myself.

I turned to find out if Clayton had seen the momentous, unlikely glimpse of my two spirit partners calling my attention to them. He smiled back with a slow nod. Without thinking, I blurted out "Yes!" as if I'd been asked a question and was answering in fervent affirmative. After a heartbeat, my "Yes!" echoed back in eerie perfection exactly as I'd cried out. Suddenly reminded that this was "Echo Mountain," that I was supposed to be silent, I made an "oops!" gesture, but Clayton was laughing and murmured, "No, go ahead."

"Yes!" "No!" "Maybe!" "Hello!" "Who's talking?" I called out in succession, delighted and amazed at the most perfect echo I'd ever heard. The resonance and detail and pitch were so lifelike, I tried everything I could think of. Before long it was clear what worked and what didn't. A normal conversational tone wasn't echoed, only a defi-nite calling out, facing directly at the cliff. Low tones were echoed per-fectly, high tones came back as a whisper, or not at all. Three syllables was the right length—any longer and something was lost, run over in the return, and any shorter seemed oddly delayed and like abusing the privilege.

When I called out, "Here we are!" and it immediately came back with my deep bass of playful announcement, Clayton stood up, and I suddenly felt ridiculous. Apparently unwilling to make his own echo, he hand-signaled for us to leave. I followed him through the sagebrush taller than me along the rim where it continued around the promontory and into a deep foldback in the mountainside. In a dry ravine out of sight of the cliff, I joined him where he sat and pulled out his pipe bag. He seemed serious and thoughtful as he filled his pipe, lit it, and smoked without saying anything. He rarely smoked his pipe outside public or private ceremonial settings, so I sat still and tried to be unobtrusive. The wisps of smoke drifting by smelled strong and acrid—he was puffing on "twist," the mind-bending Native tobacco that always made me dizzy and sick to my stomach to inhale as he was doing. Then he tapped out his pipe and put it away in its beaded leather pouch, showing no more sign of the powerful nicotine dose than slightly watering eyes. With a quiet, matter-of-fact voice, he told me the story of Echo Mountain.

"*K'saaaaapi,* long, long ago, in the time of the Animal People, why, there's this *pk'am',* this here Bobcat, Wildcat, but he just a young man, a boy. In his heart, he is bad about everything. He don't care about whatever the . . . the other people say to him, his people, to prepare him for the grown-up life to come. He just angry and he don't care . . . don't care about hisself. So he go off to be alone. He just walk along the river and feel bad. He get the thought in his mind, not far, and he can go up to Echo Mountain and tell off the world. And so he come up like you and me, he come to that there *xkl'oot,* that rock, that boulder. He cup his hands and he shout: 'I hate you!' Just then, the deep voice of the mountain boom back to him, 'I hate you!' This powerful voice strike 'em in the heart, that Wildcat, that the earth hate him, and he run away, just frighten. He run all the way home, down the river, to his folks' place. He come in feel so bad, and his mother look up. Says, 'What is it? What scare you so bad?' Wildcat tell her what happen, and his mother just smile.

" 'You go back,' she say. 'Go back up to Echo Mountain, but this time you call out what I tell you to say. We can't be thinkin' we know what is best for ourself without we find out how the earth feel for us.' She whisper in his ear what to say, and that boy, that Wildcat, drag himself back up to Echo Mountain. When he get there, he cup the hands, and this time he call out: 'I love you!' Just like that, the deep voice of the mountain boom back to his ears, 'I love you!' All at once, his heart fill up. He come to the top, he smile, he feel that welcome to be here in the world. *Wai i hwi.*"

A long silence followed. The lesson sank into the fertile ground of my own experience. Clayton finally stirred and began to speak again. He said the voice we heard when we were silent at the "hawk landin' rock" was *sp'íwchens i pk'am'*, "Wildcat's echo," something most people who came there to hear their own voice echo back from the cliff didn't notice or pay attention to. He said only those "who know somethin' from have the ways handed down" knew to listen silently. Wildcat still lived inside the mountain, in the cave he pointed out, and would tell you and show you things about your life if you knew how to ask.

He talked about Echo Mountain as a well-known place to send young people on a mission, to fast and seek a spirit partner in the days before the Whites came. Those seeking "great power" were let down by ropes from the top of the cliff by relatives. Once in the cave mouth, the person untied the ropes to be drawn up. Left sometimes "for weeks" without food or water or anything more than a blanket, those who suffered in the cave always got something *kwich'kwácht*, "real strong," from "Legend Wildcat." Clayton said when the ropes were lowered to retrieve the person, they usually clambered up yowling and spitting like a cat and had to be "smoked" with *xas'xas* root to gentle them back into being human. One girl once actually climbed up and out without ropes, he said, and ever after was known for her ability to climb anything, trees or cliffs that nobody else could scale bare-handed.

"She climb up things with power," Clayton said, looking significantly at me. "Maybe you know somethin' about that, eh?" I thought about my leap and climb in Zion Canyon and figured maybe I did.

"And so we come to the end. The last thing I tell about Echo Canyon. What the elders talk about only with the ones who got somethin', who know somethin'. That they say that cave, *ixí en'tlwínk,* that *en'tlxúlaux,* that opening into the earth—that's the bellybutton."

He rubbed his belly and smiled.

"Not an 'outie' like I got, but an 'inie' like you, ain't it?"

We laughed at his playing with the new English terms he was always picking up in his travels.

"But the navel, eh? The place in the middle, in all of us. Where we come from, how our mother give us life. And like I tell you before, *en'kak'a'íus,* like 'middle, center, in between,' this the spot where just the ordinary meet the power. Where they touch. Where we can know the power. Where the power man wake up and live.

"That how the elders talk in the long ago: That cave is our mother's navel. And so they come here and do like that, maybe like the echo, like we say, *p'iwt*. To send out the voice and have that come back. But somethin' else sent out, the child to the mother, reach out from the navel and have that reach back to us from our mother's navel. Right there, where that boulder sittin'. That how they know how the earth feel about 'em, feel for 'em. What they reach out with and grab, why, same thing reach back and grab from the earth."

18

W<small>E DROVE SOUTH AND</small> left the Okanogan, heading across the Columbia Basin dryfarmed wheat fields studded with lone lava rock sentinels, to Dry Falls, one of Clayton's favorite places in the world. The afternoon desert spread away to the infinity of a flat horizon. It was already hot there; hot with an interior, dusty, sagebrush smell to it; the heat of baked volcanic dirt. A heat without the Pacific coast's chill of sea or promise of nighttime cooling. Just what the refugees from rainy Seattle and Tacoma drove desperately 200 miles to find so they could lie out like beached albino seals on the shores of cattail pondlike lakes. Where we saw them from the state park overlook, a thousand feet below the cliff edge where the Columbia River in ancient times thundered over and carved out twisting canyons in layers of basalt. Clayton paused in his study of shimmering heat waves to hand me his binoculars, grinning, amused, mumbling something about "the ones with big eyes staring up at the sky." When I scanned the view with powerful magnification, I focused in on the bathing-suited bodies on beach towels. Some of the women were topless.

It was a time of far more concentration on plants than I had ever experienced before with Clayton. I'd already learned plenty from him and others about the Native uses of plants, but now he seemed bent on keeping my attention away from animals. It was already full spring in the protected, sun-drenched canyon bottoms, with wildflowers blooming on every side. The remote campsite we packed into was far from the motor homes and crowds of tourists, a stiff hour's hike over tortured, hummocky badlands into a braided maze of side canyons, each careful step over unstable screes accompanied by the familiar dull knocking sound lava rocks make.

Set back in a hollow of towering cliffs near a weedy pond, a green oasis in the starkly arid rock and brush, the old campsite Clayton asked me never to reveal how to find showed little sign of use beyond the charcoal remains of a campfire and an old sweatlodge framework. We lit a fire only at night so the smoke wouldn't attract attention, the stinky resinous flames of rabbitbrush to get it going, the crisp balsamy cottonwood for light, the long-lasting brown birch for hot coals to cook over. An endless soughing of wind high up on the cliffs lulled me to sleep where I made my bed in the crickety stillness under stars.

For two days Clayton led me around in the bake of sun to gather the plants he was looking for. What he instructed me in digging up or cutting away or pinching off to bring back to the pond and wash or lay out in the shade to dry were mainly things that didn't grow up north or were not ready as they were here. It was an oddly contradictory place, limpid lakes and barren cliffs, canyon wrens and seagulls, desert brush and springs hidden in groves of aspen. Stretches of brown ropey solidified lava that tore at the soles of our shoes gave way to bowl-like swales of deep soft white powdery soil. Stands of desert brush and prickly pear cactus to greening thickets of wild rye grass, cheatgrass already going to seed, and a riot of penstemons, yarrows, and wild parsnips coming into bloom. Woven into boulders covered with multicolor lichens at the shaded bases of cliffs grew elfin forests of serviceberry and mock orange covered in shrouds of clematis vine. Quail ran ahead of us over the bare rockslides where poison ivy grew in clumps, and hid in the sun-warmed gromwell showing their first creamy yellow flowers. Along the clear depths of lakes, thin fringes of birch, willow, osier dogwood, and wild rose were aswarm with flying insects. Hot, dirty, and sweaty from our long hikes and hard labors, we swam in the "soapy" alkaline water of the pond and lazed in the shade of stunted prickly hawthorn trees listening to the blackbirds and meadowlarks singing in the solitude. It wasn't quite the desert of my youth in the Southwest, but it fed my winter-starved craving for heat and light.

The main plant Clayton sought for me to dig was the medicinal Indian balsam, a species of perennial buckwheat with whorls of narrow wooly leaves at the base and stalks of creamy white flowers similar to the more common wild parsnip. The scented taproots sank deep into the rockiest soils making it hard work to pry them out with the length of iron rebar I used as a digging stick. Tea from the root had been the fastest, most effective remedy for diarrhea I'd ever experienced. As we worked digging up a number of them, Clayton revealed a long list of uses for the stronger doses, from different locations on the roots, boiled to certain colors of water, that made it such a widespread, revered, sought-after medicine. He described cures of people suffering from cancer, lung infections, "poisoned wounds," and even the common cold.

We gathered the different "sages" as he called them, *Artemisia* species having such tonic life-giving powers just their smell alone made me feel good. Especially the raggedy, stemmy clumps of wild tarragon which were steamed with stinging white clematis vines for a poultice Clayton said healed sprains and broken bones faster than anything he knew. He said the big sagebrush that grew everywhere, *sḵwa'sḵúl'stin,* was the "boss" or "head doctor" of all the other stiffly shrubby things with small dryland leaves like bitterbrush, rabbitbrush, saltbush and others, and had determined for these others how they were to make themselves useful to come-alive people.

The rules of gathering emerged from the routine itself and occasional things Clayton said: Take plants only when the sun was up, early morning was best, midday not good for anybody's sake, afternoon was okay, but don't harm the plants after the sun went down because then their power was "seeping back down into our mother where it come from." He patiently explained all I could imagine wanting to know about the plants we gathered or the plants we encountered that he felt like talking about. But any question from me like "What's this one called?" or "What's that one good for?" was ignored as if I hadn't even spoken.

Dawn and dusk were difficult times for me, the long northern glimmerings of twilight when nothing needed to be done. Especially dusk when a moody unease came over me in the shadowy transformation to night, my thoughts stilled by the owl I never saw calling *hoowoot-hoot-*

hoot between lonely, patient pauses. A movement in the brush that signaled a sudden breeze scouring through to hit me with a chill. Something on the ground where I walked that seemed to be an animal shivering but then seeped away like a bad dream into the bushes. Somebody glimpsed standing in the rustle of cattails by the pond, somebody who wasn't supposed to be there and gave off a feeling I instantly turned away from, but still reached me in the language of bat's wings, their faint fluttering around on silent patrol at the very moment the last light failed.

Drawn back to the fire where Clayton sat telling me stories late into the starry night, instructing me in making the different kinds of plant preparations used in the sweatlodge. The washes and rinses and drinks and potions to splash on the rocks for the needs of people who sweathoused to live the best of lives. Even the plants used to harm the power and health of others, and the ones used as protection from their use against me.

My head so full of the lore of plants as persons who want us to use them that when I finally went to sleep on the hard ground on the last night, I dreamed of a certain tree leaning over a river that looked like a giant man frozen in place. I realized my seeing his human form had drawn his eyes, seeking for whoever it was who dared penetrate his secret self. His great, bushy, wooded head turning, eyes locking on me with a baleful stare. Suddenly afraid of being so exposed in the split-second of his power-beam eyes, I woke up with a start, knowing he was judging my worthiness, my fitness to know and use plants. Recovering in the dark of my blankets, instead of relief I burned with anger, a desire to leap up and run someone down. I climbed out and put my shoes on and wandered in the darkness until dawn, brushing the passing bushes with bare hands. Until I calmed down and smelled the coffee and campfire smoke of Clayton calling me back.

"That there one we don't talk about," he said after I told him about the dream. "He keep the secrets of the death plants, the ones who kill us so easy. The most powerful medicines of all. Only the Indian doctor get past him and learn how to use the death plants to save the person who is lost. Gonna die from the cancer, the stroke, the fall apart from diabetes that the White doctors give up on."

One cup of his thin coffee and my heart was pounding. I didn't want to eat; I only wanted to know more about the treelike man with powerful eyes I'd dreamed about. Clayton refused to talk about him.

"See, he already make you so angry, you want to go to war, want to kill somebody. My hope that we come here and camp out to gather plants, you maybe see somethin', learn somethin' from some plant. Have a dream like this give to you, that some plant person show you how to use 'em, cure what ail you, bring you back to your right mind about your power. Maybe somethin' to be your own special medicine. But not this one. This not a good sign. This pretty bad one to come in the dream."

He wouldn't say any more about the man so I asked him what he meant by "death plants." He mentioned the commonly known wetland plants we were careful to avoid "who stand by water," the poisonous hemlocks, baneberry, monkshood, and "the boss of them all," corn lily or false hellebore. The thought of their attractive deadliness, these plants I'd been aware of and afraid to do more than study, touch, and smell all my life, instantly cooled my interest. I knew that some of the plants he'd been teaching me about had poisonous properties, and all had to be prepared and taken with care, but these others were the ones that could sicken with a taste and kill with a swallow. The thought of them somehow being made fit to save the lives of people already close to death mystified me, yet Clayton said they'd been known for that use long before the Whites came. I asked him how their use or the use of any plants for that matter as effective remedies, had been figured out in the old days. He laughed and rolled his eyes.

"I know how the *Suyápi* think we done it," he said, shaking his head in disbelief. "That we done like they do, test it on a person. We make the sick child or the elder about to pass on drink somethin' and see what happen! Or just happen to notice somebody die who eat this one, or somebody get well who drink the tea of that one.

"No. First, to come alive on this earth, all like a dream, all power. The first teaching about the plants come then, they take pity on us and help us stay alive. So then the world get more solid and we grow more hard, and we know to go back into the power, into the dream to ask the plants to show us how to use 'em for the other things. To give instruction of how to prepare the cure.

"That's how we know what they good for, how to use 'em. They show us. And they still showin' us. The new thing that come along to sicken us, try to take our life, why, then the different plant come in the dream, come to the person in the sweatlodge, say 'Use me, I'm good for that. That's nothin' for me to fix up.' And they show what part to use, how much, how to prepare 'em, how much to take.

"But now, only the Indian doctors know how to use the death plants. The only thing I know about 'em is how they push you into the power, because you dyin'. They take you where it's all power, and only power keep you alive. Somebody like Old Willie, now, I see 'em chew up and swallow that root of the old lady who smell so bad." (Clayton called corn lily simply "old woman," *peptiwínaux,* or "the one that smell like somethin's dead.")

"That old bugger just smile and nothin' happen. Maybe because he already die and come back. It's all power for him to be alive now anyway."

Clayton said we'd gathered enough. We abruptly broke camp and packed everything out. The only other thing he did was stop along a side road where rounded cobbles of lava rock perfect for use in the sweatlodge showed in a cutbank and we loaded so many, his car sank low on the rear springs. Then he had me drive with hardly a word all the way to Old Willie's house in B.C., passing by the Woods homestead without stopping, using the cut in the boundary fence that came out into the Similkameen reserve to avoid being inspected by Canadian Customs. We arrived late at night to find Old Willie sitting up in his long johns, expecting us.

It had started to rain at Keremeos and the mountain coldness made his woodstove fire a cheery welcome for his sunburned visitors. Without a word from us about what we had brought, he said in Salish, ("So, you brought me some rocks to heat. That's good because I'm all out.") Clayton, who'd slept on the drive up, sat down with a cup filled from Willie's ever-present pot of hot coffee, and they began to catch up in a lively exchange of Salish anecdotes and humor. I made a bed on the floor of Willie's screened-in porch and fell asleep to the distant sound of their voices.

The endless *bedelerp! bedelerp! bedelerp!* of roosting robins singing in the rain woke me after daylight to the evergreen-scented wet of the mountains. I was still lying there in the warmth of my blankets thinking the old men would probably sleep in when the door to the house opened and they both came out dressed in rain slickers and stepped around me. They propped open the screen door to carry in the gathered plants, so I quickly got dressed, and went to help. Old Willie was all business, directing us in where to store the fragrant bags and bundles in a small back room smelling of cedar smudge and the green, dried plants hanging along the walls.

Everything but the rocks had been taken inside and I was studying his hanging plants, identifying what they were, when Willie turned and fingered the black bandana I'd tied around my flannel sleeve. He asked me who I was in mourning for. Clayton left the room laughing and Willie went on with his deadpan tease, saying it was all right if I didn't want to tell him who died, but that if I wanted to be such a good Christian White man I should always cross myself before coming into his house. I was in stitches at how serious he looked when he abruptly shifted and asked me if I was willing to die to learn about my power. I didn't know what to say.

"I guess, if that's what it takes," I said, thinking along the lines that anything could happen and I wasn't going to give up just because things could get dangerous.

"Maybe you just say that," he said. Clayton came back with a cup of coffee. "Maybe just say the words, how the White man pretend, and not say what is in your heart, eh?"

Clayton sipped, listening, and I shrugged.

"I don't see why it has to come to that."

"Somebody scare you off, make you angry at yourself." He looked at Clayton.

As if prompted, Clayton spoke up, saying that after I went to bed last night, they discussed my dream and what it might mean. The memory of seeing the tree revealed as a giant man came back, his fierce eyes seeking out whoever was looking at him, locking onto my gaze like power beams that flooded me with fear, and then startled me awake into anger. Now all I felt was a strange discomfort, like I didn't care to remember about him. Clayton said they wondered if I was really willing to "risk all for a better life," that maybe this dream was a warning, to show me there was something "small in the heart" about me.

"I don't know," I said. "How could I stand up to something like that, like him? He was huge and just his eyes were enough to . . ."

"To hurt you?" Willie said after I trailed off, finishing my words with a quizzical raise of his eyebrows.

"Yes." I knew immediately what they were getting at. Regardless of how many times I'd thrown my life away and come through, the urge for self-preservation in the face of something more powerful than the ordinary man I was used to seeing myself as made me react with timidness. It was also difficult for me to credit dreams with the force of waking experiences the way they did. I realized that some part of me was always rising to discount whatever power experience I might have. Yet there was no doubt how humiliated I felt at my fear upon waking from the dream.

"My want to know, what for you fastin'?" Willie said out of the blue. I thought back. I hadn't eaten since the night before we left Dry Falls, hadn't drunk anything since the coffee I sipped telling Clayton the dream the previous morning. Here it was the next day and I still wasn't hungry or thirsty. In fact, the thought of eating or drinking was the farthest thing from my mind. I figured Clayton must have mentioned something to him about it.

"I didn't know I was," I said, and shrugged. Willie looked at Clayton.

("His power wants him to drink it,") he said in Salish. Then in English to me, without looking at me, he said, "Magic tricks not work for you, eh, Bluejay-eater?" He moved to the far side of the room where he turned to face me, his back against some dried corn lily plants hanging upside down by the roots. Clayton sat down with a resigned sigh, and I turned to him wondering what magic tricks Willie might be referring to. He carefully set aside his coffee cup and looked up at me.

"*Loot inchá,* I not say nothin' to him about you not eat or drink."

The dry plants rustling drew my attention back to Old Willie who was swaying where he stood, singing a faint, wordless song that was unfamiliar to me, and making motions with his hands in front of him like someone would make digging in dirt bare-handed. I was tired of standing and wanted to sit down, too, but forgot about it in my surprise. His transformation from the wispy-haired, frail, and somewhat horse-faced and contentious old codger I was familiar with into what looked like an experienced performer working an audience was complete. Bent over at the waist, swaying in time to the song he sang louder and louder, he stared fixedly but indirectly at me while pantomiming digging like a dog. Clayton picked up his song and sang with gusto as if helping Willie call on his power, and soon Willie caught the power of it with sudden spasms like he was going into an epileptic seizure. He seemed to sing to keep from falling to the floor and finally grabbed his knees to slow his jerking.

What had been mildly embarrassing to witness now became stirring and mesmerizing because whatever was embodying him turned his movements into a nose-up, swaying side-to-side that for all the world looked exactly like a heavy-bodied bear weaving back and forth, getting agitated, and sniffing for the scent of something. Willie's eyes, which had been staring with a wide, otherworldly blankness, now narrowed to a beady, darting, myopic search around the room. I realized he wasn't singing anymore and only Clayton's voice filled the small room with the simple melody repeated over and over.

The power of what Willie was doing drew me into his spell—I felt a shivery, floating sensation, and then like something dropping down inside me. I could tell whatever was happening to me was something I could stop if I wanted to, but it felt so good, so consuming, so attractive—sort of a cross between unimaginable grief and joyous ecstasy—that I let go completely into it. The way he lifted his left hand off his knee when he swung to the right, then his right hand when he swung to the left, was so utterly bearlike, I was enthralled and wanted only to see what the bear would do next. In a daze of complicity, I could tell the bear man in front of me had caught the scent of my willing participation to bring him out. He couldn't seem to see me, but he huffed and clicked his teeth, warning me he was there, that he was aware of me.

By the time the bear stood up on its hind legs with its paws hanging in front and its eyes focused on me, I was rooted to where I stood, unable to think or have any sense about anything but the bear looking into my eyes. I felt hypnotized, unwilling to let go of the bear that seemed to be seeping away from Willie, whose hands were slowly dropping to his sides. Only his squinting eyes seemed bearlike, and they held my gaze. Willie spoke to me in a dragging voice and I couldn't tell if it was English or Salish. But I could tell what he was trying to convey to me—that he wouldn't let the bear harm me, that he was only showing me that the power was real. His eyes had the same fierce, power-beam effect as the tree-man's, and I realized he was saying that if I could see a spirit looking at me like that, then I was "in the power" myself and so, what could harm me? It all made perfect sense at that moment. Even as he spoke I knew I could look away and stop whatever was happening. Then Willie dropped his eyes with a sharp clap of his hands, and I came back to myself with a shudder.

The room was flat, bleak, and unappealing. I had a feeling like waking up from a disturbing dream and my navel stung dully. Willie looked listless, scratched himself, and yawned. I bristled for the first time at the old Indian doctor who had always seemed so unthreatening to me. My ears rang and I cleared my throat, trying to formulate my angry feelings into words. Casting around for why I should be in a rage at what I felt he'd done to me, I saw Clayton looking calmly up at me from where he sat, sipping his coffee again. My anger melted away in an instant. The thought occurred to me that nothing frightening had taken place, yet I had still reacted with anger, with a desire to say something mean. Feeling contrite, a wave of warm feeling for the old doctor surfaced and I blurted out, "Thank you, Grandpa."

He smiled wearily and came up to me.

"You okay now, Bluejay-eater? You in your right mind?"

"Yeah."

"You ready to die to learn about what you got?"

"Yes."

"What gonna happen when you die?"

"I don't come back to this body anymore," I said, wondering where my answer so instantly came from, but certain it was true.

He nodded slowly, looking at me long and hard.

"We have the way, handed down, how to come alive again," he said like stating a simple fact. He turned and motioned for me to sit down. He seemed utterly exhausted by his labors, and sat leaning against the wall by Clayton, sighing and rubbing the muscles of his thighs. The floor was covered in linoleum that was cracked and missing in patches where I sat, and for some reason the hardwood floor showing through fascinated me.

Willie said the dream given to me was a power dream about what plant medicine I needed, just like Clayton hoped I'd receive. He said my power knew best what I needed. Getting angry after seeing the tree-man looking at me was the reaction of someone holding back from full commitment to living with power. It meant I had "something bad" in me, something I "picked up" in my life and let live inside me to the point that I felt it as a natural part of me. He said seeing a powerful spirit like I'd seen in my dream and seen coming on him was like opening the door to what was down deep in my heart. Some bad thing like I had in me was what was being threatened, because it had found a home and didn't want to leave what it was slowly taking control over. If I didn't do something about it, I would become mean and heartless, and sabotage every effort of the "real" me to live in the power way. He said a man who was "small in the heart" like that only made enemies out of the spirits he encountered, and the truth was, "they don't want you to hurt yourself like you doin'."

I can't say I followed what he said, despite my hanging on every word with a rapt feeling of warmth and gratitude. His words, never easy to unravel from his Salish-influenced grammar, and always slurred, went in circles, and before he'd come full circle, he'd swing out in another, related loop that never quite came back. Yet what he said rang true. He implied that a lack of conviction about power was a form of illness. That resistance to that side of ourselves that sought for a powerful connection with the mysterious source of our own living here in the world was a sign of something wrong in us. And that full health, especially mental health, was restored only in a dreamlike acceptance of what could be felt and known but never really put into words.

He finally said it was up to me, that maybe now "in my right mind" I could see why my power wanted me to take extreme measures and "face down what have such a fright of power" in me. It became clear that he meant he was willing to prepare a medicine from the tree-man's death plants for me to drink if I wanted him to. All of a sudden, not coming back to my body took on a different light. It was only a momentary twinge of fear, quickly overcome by my confidence in him, and my conviction that he was right—there was something wrong with me. I had to do something about it. After he stopped talking and just stared at the floor, I asked him what his fee would be for doctoring me. A crafty look came into his eyes.

"How much you got?"

His reply was so out of character with the indirect way he handled such matters, I knew he was mocking White ways. Clayton and I both laughed, and Willie's face softened.

"No, what you done, that just make me stand behind you," he said, gesturing toward the plant parts we'd gathered and brought to him. In Salish metaphor, he was saying he was in my debt and owed me some obligation. "My want to doctor you for free, Bluejay-eater."

That settled, I said sure, let's do it.

19

Clayton's car got stuck in the mud halfway down the hill and I had to carry the rocks the rest of the way in a milking bucket. Willie had said in Salish either "Go take it to the sweatlodge" or "Go take them . . ." Contemplating the endless pour of rain from watercolor clouds wreathing among the mountainside firs, I'd chosen the driest, easiest interpretation and I drove the old Ford slowly down the parallel tracks to the river. On the steepest part the tires began to bog down in the mud of deep ruts and I gunned it, careening downhill until the car high-centered and slid to a stop, the tires spinning uselessly. Once all the rocks were piled by the fire pit at Willie's sweatlodge, I headed back up to the house, passing the car sitting unnaturally low, at a steep, nose-down angle, fenders deep in muddy water washing by. It wasn't going to be easy getting it out and back up the hill.

Clayton didn't say anything when he saw his car. He went down alone to build a fire and heat rocks in the rain. Old Willie took me with him for a walk along the base of mountain upriver and then turned into a dry canyon. Following a stock trail through two fence gates, we came to a marshy spring fenced all around to keep cattle out. Dominating the enclosure was an enormous brown birch tree, multiple trunks leaning out and up in every direction, and most of the swampy ground was hidden under it. White granite boulders stood around everywhere. We'd walked only about a mile, but after we slipped through the barbed wire,

Willie sat on one of the boulders under the spacious low roof of birch limbs, gasping as if we'd just finished a mini death march.

"Too much donuts and coffee!" he wheezed, then laughed.

The horizontal, snaking, foot-thick trunks of birch gleamed like wet bronze in the rain, and the first oily looking green leaves were coming out tenderly. Here and there were dark green clumps of juniper impossible to see into, and stinging nettles shooting up along banks. The bare skeletons of last year's water hemlock, baneberry, and cow parsnip stood in the lower-lying black muck, and farther uphill, the first shoots of corn lily were emerging like fat green thumbs from mats of brown marsh grass. Willie stood up with a sigh and put his hand on a birch trunk.

"This the one you dream about," he said as if stating an obvious fact. Brown birch seemed like an obvious candidate. It was also called "water birch" because unlike the white or paper birch that grew generally in forests, this one usually grew in wet places in the more arid, open country. Willie gathered a handful of stringy hair lichen hanging from the birch's limbs and made a round, cuplike nest of it. Then he strolled around, studying the various corn lily shoots, careful not to step on them. He chose one and had me carefully dig down the side of the stalk with a stick. The mucky, organic soil was hard and fibrous and I used my bare fingers to pull out root-bound masses. About a foot down I came to a sandy, watery substratum where the dark, slimy rootstock turned into fingerlike rootlets radiating away horizontally. The marshy stink of exposed corn lily roots was a little nauseating.

Willie knelt and spoke in his mumbling, slurred Salish, addressing the plant, like Clayton, as *peptiwínaux,* "old woman," and saying something about taking only some fringe from her dress. Feeling around in the hole, he broke off some of the tough runners of secondary root, and when he had enough, dug in his pocket and tossed some coins in the hole with a brusque, *"Limlempt."* He had me fill the hole back up and then he washed the pencil-sized roots in a spot of open spring water, peeling off the previous year's rotting sheaths down to pale white living tissue. Shaking off the water, he nestled the cleaned roots into the mass of lichen, closed it around them like a ball and slipped it into his shirt pocket. We washed our hands where the spring emerged at the base of the birch tree, Willie saying we had to use water upstream from the death plants because downstream the water was "poison." He said if I put my finger in my mouth after washing in water soaking in corn lily roots, it would make me sick.

On the way back, Willie went into a grove of pines on rocky ground and picked a handful of tiny, heathlike, leathery leaves from the creeping mats of common bearberry or kinnikinnick. In the rain, the deep evergreen shine of the leaves and bright red, mealy tasting berries still clinging to twigs just inches above the ground stood out brightly. He put the leaves into another pocket and we headed back to his house. Inside his herb room he opened and dug around in a feed sack full of dried, aromatic, evergreen-looking leaves and dried flower tops that I immediately recognized as Labrador tea. Picked in high-mountain swamps in summer, this had to be last year's gatherings. He selected a handful of leaves and put them into yet another of his pockets, and putting away the bag, asked me if I knew what plant it was. I told him what I thought.

"Yah, what we say, swamp tea, but not the one White man drink," he said. "This his bad brother. Look kinda the same, but not brown on the bottom." He produced one of the leaves with edges curled stiffly underneath and turned it over. Instead of the usual rusty-colored hairiness on the underside, it was a fuzzy white and had tiny crystallized droplets hidden in the fuzz. Yet the leaf had the same look and feel and spicy, unmistakable smell of Labrador tea.

"This the one we call *k'ácha'*, the one who hit you. The one you go to for him to hit you," he said, then tried to explain in Salish what he meant. All I could glean from his words was something like "delivers a blow," pantomimed as someone hitting with a fist. "These three go together," he added, touching the other two pockets. "Well, maybe two more, the five that the Indian doctor know. But these three for you enough, eh?"

He sent me back out into the rain to carry down some things to the sweatlodge—two old blackened teapots, an equally fire-encrusted tin lid to a lard can, and an old coffee mug with the handle broken off. Later he joined me and Clayton at the warmth of the roaring fire, our wet clothes steaming in the rain. I watched him "stick" to one side of the lodge door—set up his power stick like he always did when he was going to doctor somebody. His gathering of *sen'ch'ch'wistem*—bits of feather and fur, a brass bell and a stuffed nuthatch tied to the top of a four-foot dance stick—looked unchanged after so many years, maybe a little more worn and bedraggled than usual. He fit a plastic bread bag over it, to protect it from the rain, keep it dry, and it looked silly, like litter on a stick. Clayton muttered something droll about "callin' in them Wonder Bread spirits." Old Willie looked sharply at him, and at me daring to laugh.

"I know some guys gonna burn up once we get inside," he spat, hiding a smile.

"Huh, well, maybe none of us gonna get out alive," Clayton said, pointing with his chin at his car stuck in the mud facing down at us. "Seem like my car move a little since I last look. . . . Maybe we go in and next thing you know"—he made a slurping noise and slapped his hands together—"Come free and run us over!"

Willie laughed hard. The two of them joked back and forth relentlessly, and soon turned to teasing me as the main topic. My car-parking skills, doorway-sleeping inclinations—every quirk and foible they could think of—was examined in detail, exaggerated, twisted to absurd lengths, and then pronounced upon with "But that's his way!" as if such trivial things were the serious requirements of my power. By the time the rocks were ready, I was giddy from laughing so hard. Only when I saw Willie empty his pockets and carefully place the ball of lichen at the base of his power stick did I sober up and remember what we were about to do.

But nothing more was done or said about it, and we undressed and went in with about a third of the hot rocks. The first round was a joyful return to the burning steamy darkness of earthy smells and songs sung, this time shared with the two old men whose sense of humor and loud cries were like we were celebrating something wonderful about being alive and together at that moment. When we emerged like cooked lobsters to swim in the icy river yellow with snowmelt, the rain had faded to a mist and the early afternoon sun was trying to break through the layered drift of clouds. A pale sharpness of light suffused the air, turning the droplets of mist into glittering pinpoints falling on the river where we bobbed silently. Once out and standing on the bank, I instinctively looked at the surface of river to see the reflection of light coming through the clouds. There was a distinctively female loveliness in the vague image I saw wavering by on the current. And there was a particular color and feel to it, something I'd seen before, that I recognized as meaning this was it, the rain was over, it was going to clear up soon. It seemed to me at that moment that every turn in the road, every new experience with these men was another opening into how the world was aware of me, showing me sign of itself, teaching me the lore of itself. Each revelation like this filled me up completely, sang inside me, held me spellbound. Each new certainty, like this one about the weather clearing up, solidified inside me even as the ephemeral sign passed away, leaving only the memory of it for the next time I would see the woman in the sky show herself like this. Shivering on the bank of the Similkameen, I knew something profound was changing in me, that I could never go back to the way the world used to be.

More glowing rocks were pitchforked into the sweatlodge, and Clayton piled fresh firewood on the remaining rocks in the pit of coals. Old Willie with a dreamlike look in his eyes, softly talking to his bread-bag-covered powers and the ball of lichen tucked against the stick. Speaking to his spirit helpers with the same childlike, furious pleasure he always used talking to them, as if they were his true relatives in life, the ones who actually kept him alive. Then he told me to *kw'ówintem,* "pray over her," gesturing to the roots hidden in lichen, and crawled inside with Clayton.

A sudden wake-up call. A tiny lump of fear in my guts as I spoke to the lichen ball, the poisonous roots, feeling exposed and fragile in my wet nakedness. Speaking to something I was afraid of, that was more powerful than me, that I had no understanding of. Blurting out how I was asking for her help, how I wanted to be a real person in the world, somebody the forces of nature like her would feel belonged here. Then Willie had me hand it in to him, and the other things sitting around outside, including his small pipe and the kettles of water he had boiling on the fire. Once inside sitting with them, I smelled the swamp tea in one kettle, boiled and steeping now, and watched Willie place the fresh bearberry leaves on cooled rocks so they would slowly toast in proximity to the hot, glowing ones. He then arranged some of the glowing, molten-looking rocks in a flat pile close to his crossed feet. He used his bare hands, the sizzling sound of skin touching incandescent rock just blowing my mind how he must be burning himself, but Willie appeared unaffected and placed the lard can lid, rim up, on the cluster of rocks. He opened the lichen ball and placed the white slips of root on the metal, where they instantly began to sputter and smoke. The aromatic scent of steeping Labrador tea and husky, toasting smell of bearberry leaves that perfumed the inside of the sweatlodge was quickly overpowered by the stench of roasting corn lily roots. I was grateful the door was open; the acrid smoke was so thick at first we were all heads-to-the-floor to avoid the way it stung our eyes and noses.

With the door left open, Clayton sprinkled some water from the bucket on unused rocks to clear the air with fresh steam and keep things hot and humid inside. I wasn't nervous, just curiously focused on everything the two men did and said with a sense of inevitability and hope. Willie kept things light, clearly trying to keep me at ease, and prompted me a few times as he "cooked up some medicine," encouraging me to ask questions if I wanted to. I was strangely blank, but then I remembered how they talked of corn lily as an old woman and swamp tea as a bad brother. I asked him who bearberry was as a person. He said just an old friend, somebody anybody could find everywhere in the world, always the same. He was *xast spu'últ,* "good smoke," somebody who was always there to smoke and feel good about the power. Willie said that was how plant medicines were used—you started with the closest and most familiar and worked toward the more rare and unfamiliar, each one introducing and getting you ready for the next one. The two more he wasn't using with me he said were so rare and hard to find, few people knew they even existed. One was evidently a mushroom by the way he described a "slimy old man who pop up out of the ground after the rain," and the other sounded like some kind of swamp orchid, "the painted face of the woman stand in water."

I asked him how it was that the corn lily roots could be prepared like this so they didn't kill a person who drank them in a tea. He laughed like a little boy with a secret. He didn't speak of it like drinking a root tea, he called it "drinking her," and said, "But she *do* kill 'em, the one who drink her!" He gazed at me with shiny eyes, as if wondering why I wasn't getting it. I had a sudden image of myself bolting outside and escaping. My question had revealed I was assuming he had some way of preparing the roots that removed the poison, and now I could see with a kind of appalling dread that he was perfectly serious. I cleared my throat.

"Maybe you could help me out here, Grandpa," I said, feeling trapped. "Take pity on me and tell me what to expect. What's going to happen to me?"

"*Kmátem!* (Certainly!)" he said, picking out and setting aside the bearberry leaves which were curled to a crispy brown like tiny leathery potato chips. As the corn lily roots slowly glowed and shriveled to ash on the metal lid, he sat erect and spoke like telling a story.

"My wonder, who hear her callin', *k'wúytet* (our mother), the earth? 'Come and get to know me, your mother,' she say. Some she reach out to. *Hoo, 'ax, 'ax, 'axel, swit pukwelhtís kul swit.*" (He was motioning like pouring his words onto the rocks and saying, "Hoo, do like that, somebody pouring something hard of hers into somebody.")

"Put in 'em some little bit, somethin' make 'em quiet and just listen. So they can hear *choochín*." (*Choochín* was how spirits talked to people, the sound of their voice. Willie was prefacing things by recapitulating the process of becoming a power person.) "So they can feel things, know somethin'. Somethin' that don't matter how they make 'em wait in line and keep 'em like walk in their sleep. All the White world now, and to have what the Whites put in front of their eyes, have somethin' glitter in front of the eyes. Seem like everybody got 'em, the shiny piece of rock, hang in front of the eyes, and just stare at that."

He said something I didn't understand in Salish, and Clayton interjected, "He mean like the quartz crystal."

"Well," Willie went on, "they few of 'em like that, the power mans, hear *choochín*, and pu! The shiny glitter gone! Look around and everybody else asleep, still starin' at the bright before the eyes. But not the few. And she call to 'em, our mother, say, 'Be the hero-man, be the hero-woman, and not have the fright!' She say, 'Look, look how they hurtin' me. All starin' at somethin' else, but not me, and still take all my fine children, the flower, the tree, the rock, the animal, the water. Kill 'em and use 'em all up! Look how they stare and just walk in the sleep. *Psxúyux amút alá'!* (Come here and sit!) Learn, know somethin', let me pour more of my hard into you!'

"Even the *en'pamíntales* (environmentalist) they hear her callin'. They come around, come around. And my have to say to 'em: 'Where you think that come from? You White people and you feel for the earth, how she hurtin', and where you get that? From Native people, what they been sayin' all along. Only you take just the thought and make 'em into somethin' else. Call our mother *en'pament* (the environment). Take only the thought, and not where it come from in how we always live in the world!

"My wonder, just almost nobody nowadays look around and see without the bright before the eyes. They put 'em there when they just the child, and pu! *Waí'payem!* (They go White man!) Like that, and think they gotta wait in line to know somethin'. The old boys, they tell me in the long ago, they seen it comin'. Long, way back. Somebody tell what they see, the long line of people walkin' by, walkin' by. And every one have that bright glitter to stare at, like hangin' from the hair, in front of the eyes. Walk along in single file and don't see where they are, where they goin'. And the one who see this, see 'em walk by in the long line, he sittin' in the house in the ground, *kikwúli* (the traditional winter pit house), and they don't notice him. He think he's maybe dead, and that why they don't see 'em. But then he come alive again, and he tell about it. Tell that what to come, who comin', how that gonna be. And now we see, all around, and even the Indian got the starin' at somethin' bright and stand in line. Nobody see what look out from the shadow, from the rock, from the sky, from the water. Just the few. Just the one or two, somethin' poured in for how she pick 'em, maybe the more if they have the heart for more.

"Maybe somebody have the heart for more," Willie said, moving the lid off the dimming rocks and setting it aside to cool. The roots were nothing but ash in the fragile form of slumped squiggles. "Somebody tryin' to eat bluejays, but can't catch 'em. Can't hold 'em in the hand. Not easy like to grab the robin, eh? But he the one have to hold birds in his hand!

"Well, okay, so . . . first thing to see, when the bright spot in front of the eyes go away, the bad thing in the body. All like dirt, the piece of something alive, maybe the chunk of somethin', *uhl sk'aps* (and it moves). What come in and live inside from the bad. Stuck in there, maybe here, here, here" (touching spots on his abdomen). "And it's all power, easy to feel 'em and see 'em, and pu! Kills 'em, that bad inside. Just nothin' for that old lady to kill. And come out, like to drive out what can't live inside the body no more, because it's all power. That when you do like the boy say when he sing to call on his power, that wind. Because it's a mess!"

(He meant the sweatlodge power song that went, *"Ka'k̦ín sniwt wai k̦in xooy,"* "Toward where the wind blows, well, there I go." I presumed Willie was telling me some vomiting or defecating was to be expected, and was suggesting I go outside, downwind.)

"And then the number two thing, they have to come. Whatever you got have to come and see what so clean, so pure, nothin' but power now. They have to come, and they comin', they here. They the ones show themself to you in life. See, he fond of you, he choose you to be power in the world, like through you. And he don't want that you die. Not unless maybe this is your time to go, but then, nobody can do to change that, eh? So like I say, he don't want that you die, so just like that, the world get soft. Not like we see now, but soft, like go right through.

"This the number three, how everything of our mother become like the bubble on the water, soft, and kinda like fog. The only hard is who you got, right there with you. You know when the world turn soft, that is how you dyin'. You know when all soft but the *shumíx* person who is with you. You dead, gone, and nothin' left but the *shumíx* that love you. But let's say you don't got nothin', eh? No power, what then? What happen to the person who don't have no gift from our mother and drink the old woman? World turn soft, then what?"

When I said nothing, Clayton murmured, "Time to kiss your ass goodbye, ain't it?"

We all dissolved into laughter, mine more morbid than theirs.

"But you the power man, Bluejay-eater. You have somebody always waitin' to give instruction. You hear *choochín,* you know somethin'. You do what they say, how to come alive again, start over. For the one have that heart for more, the world is soft, and so you know how the world was at the beginning. How the world still is, when you nothin' but power. And the power, that's hard. So with the power, you make the world hard again, and pu! You come alive again, the pure, the healthy. They show you how, what you got. Tell you, show you, and then you come back. You come to the top, you see it's all hard again."

After a pause, he added, "Then the four and the five, but only for the one who blow. Who come back and blow with power. Only for the one she choose as the doctor, the Indian doctor. So we not doin' that part. Just the three to wipe off the White man, the Bluejay-eater, wipe off all that bad."

Willie began crumbling the bearberry leaves into the palm of his hand and loading his pipe with the tough, crushed fragments, tamping them down with his little finger. His pipe was small, a greenish stone drilled and carved in designs, with a wooden stem about eight inches long fit into the side at the base. His mingling of metaphors with the words "hard" and "soft" was a little vague, so I asked, "Grandpa, what do you guys mean when you talk about 'getting hard in the power'?"

He finished and held the loaded pipe on his knee.

"See, when the power man get hard in the power, the world get soft. Kinda how he have to be to live in it, soft like that. Somethin' come on a person over and over that stiffen in him, make him like where the power come easy and stay longer. When that happen, everything else, all around, get soft. Can see right through things. Like awake in Legend time, and everything kinda oozes. Whatever he see, well, that how the power make it that way, and we can see that, because not so solid anymore.

"Like that mountain there, how the power is what make the mountain stand there like that. But soft, not so solid anymore, like we see there on the river, like in the mirror. Like thin and hollow, can go right in, pass through, like go in a big bubble. Get kinda vague and misty, and then you see what's there, what don't fit. Maybe the person in the mountain, the power who is inside. Maybe the dark spot, or the color, or the *choochín,* the voice speakin'. Whatever how things really are under the surface when the world not so hard, so solid anymore."

He waited impassively, gazing out the door of the sweatlodge for anything more I might want to ask. There wasn't.

"*Wai i hwi* (So be it)," I said.

He smiled kindly and lit his pipe with a cigarette lighter. Inhaling a few puffs, he handed the pipe to Clayton in the counterclockwise way he circled his pipe among people. Clayton puffed briefly and handed it to me. Willie told me to inhale and finish everything in the pipe. It tasted sweet but strong with a musty "kinnikinnick" bite to the smoke that began to build up a sour-tasting saliva in my mouth. I'd never smoked it before but knew it as a safe, mildly relaxing addition to smoking mixtures. Smoking the whole pipeful took a long time and inhaling every puff became difficult as the smoke began to sear my throat and lungs. I began to get dizzy and increasingly stupefied. A kind of vertigo began to build; I had a sensation of the floor falling away and whirling around. This was strong stuff and before long I was swaying, finding it hard to keep from toppling over. I wasn't quite done smoking all that was in the pipe, but I was struggling not to pass out, and when my hand holding it fell onto my knee, I couldn't seem to lift it back up to my mouth.

Willie reached over and took the pipe from my hand. I vaguely heard him pouring something liquid, and then he was putting the hot mug in my hands, fitting my fingers around it.

"Here, drink this," he said. I was unbearably thirsty and the sweet aromatic steam of swamp tea filled my nose as I drank it all down in a series of gulps. Instantly feeling better, I held out the mug for more, and as he filled it from the kettle, I saw why the tea tasted so much stronger and more "mediciny" than I was used to—the liquid was almost black from having been boiled and steeped so long.

The relief and stimulation of drinking something gradually paled by the last few swallows of the second mug. I was beginning to detect something more than just refreshing liquid gurgling down into my empty insides. What had cleared my dizziness was now causing shoot-ing pains in my stomach, faint at first, then strongly uncomfortable, then almost incapacitating, like someone hitting me there with their fist. It was accompanied by something like a mild electric shock. My guts began to cramp, my heart began to pound furiously and erratically, and I felt mildly delirious, like a really bad case of the flu was coming on. Little by little the cramping faded, and I began to feel euphoric and drowsy. It was like the pleasant effects of Labrador tea magnified many times over, perhaps somehow augmented by the effects of bearberry smoke in my blood, but in any event closing me off in a shroud of sleepy well-being. It worked to anesthetize me to the grim side effects of swamp tea's bad brother—my heart still palpitating and my body jerking spasmodically. I could tell something was going wrong with my insides, but at the same time I was so disconnected and floating, I was completely uncaring about what was happening. I was losing external feeling, going numb, and yet sat rigidly erect.

It was like falling asleep with my eyes open as I watched Old Willie pry the mug from my fingers, hold it under the tilted metal lid, and carefully tap the corn lily root ash into the mug. I could tell I was losing track of time, because I didn't see him fill the mug with boiling water or set it aside to steep. I only "knew" that's what he'd done when he finally dipped his finger into the ash tea and then licked it. He pursed his lips, judging the taste. Something flickered in his eyes and his face softened. He held the mug over the hot rocks, let a tiny drip fall, which instantly vaporized in a hiss, and spoke some words. As he pulled a small wooden mug out of his pipe bag, and carefully poured the liquid from the mug to the cup, leaving the ashy residue that sank to the bottom behind, I knew what was coming. I was completely unafraid. Whatever was in "good" smoke and "bad" swamp tea had erased any emotion, any thoughts. I was a blank slate, ready for anything.

Willie leaned over and held the cup to my lips. With great effort I managed to drink the few sips. It tasted like wet ash, but as it went down I felt a burning ache. Nothing else seemed to be happening, but by degrees the stiffness of my body loosened and I slumped back against the willow framework of the lodge.

Clayton said later that they both sang songs almost continuously after I "drank her," but if they did, I have no memory of it. I remember being completely absorbed with something growing hard in my guts. In the dim light, the open doorway was blindingly bright, and the two men, the interior of the lodge, the rocks, everything became a glittering blur that I avoided looking at. I could feel the blood moving everywhere in my body, but by degrees it felt like it was slowing down to an almost imperceptible trickle. As the pulse of my heart slowed to a faint pulse, like a wave at the seashore taking forever to come in and go out, the brightness of everything began to dissolve. I'd had the impression that everywhere I looked, my eyes had been lighting up whatever I saw so that it glittered too brightly to focus on; but now, as my heartbeat slowed to nearly a standstill, whatever light there was began to dissipate. Everything became murky, but at the same time, I found its vague flatness somehow reassuring.

A pain began to grow and consume my attention, something terribly wrong in my guts, and as it reached unbearable proportions, it seemed to focus on the hard lump I felt high on the left side of my abdomen. I could feel it moving, like a mouse trapped in a tight spot, struggling to get free. I became aware that my heart was not noticeably beating, that I was barely breathing, that there was something foamy dribbling from my lips. I felt my hands and feet going cold and my jaws going rigid. There was a faint flicker of some part of me that was clinically monitoring the symptoms of my body shutting down to a low ebb, but it wouldn't be until much later that I identified what the poison exactly was. Powerful cardiac glycosides simply stop the heart from beating, so my description of how Old Willie prepared the ash tea is purposely vague and misleading so others will not be tempted to try it. There is nothing visionary or hallucinogenic about corn lily, just a vividly experienced descent into death, into a realm where your heart stops beating. If you survive, it's true what they say, you come back to life more healthy than ever before—in fact, a state of healthiness previously beyond imagining. But I want to state here that many people have died drinking this tea. The only reason I'm telling about it is because it actually happened and the events that followed would be hard to understand without knowing what I went through.

I remember that I was aware that I was dying, but it seemed unimportant. It was the building pain that consumed me, and it finally reached some kind of peak. I felt the hard lump go still and begin to soften. I "knew" whatever it was had been killed, rendered inert, and whatever had killed it was now spreading fingerlike all through my guts and up my esophagus like liquid flame. It was like acid burning its way through all passages, through all obstructions. The hard thing was dissolved in it and seeking a way out. All of a sudden I was moving, jerking, flailing, vaguely aware my body was trying to do something without my volition. I felt hands pushing me, guiding me; heard rude laughter; bumped into things. Then I found myself looking at a murky world that only somewhat resembled the outside of the sweatlodge. The sensations of vomiting and defecating a runny fluid were like being inside someone else doing it, yet I recognized the familiar shape and feel of my own body making a mess on itself from both ends. The convulsions continued in a dry retching that went on and on, but had the effect of bringing me back to some semblance of normal awareness. Gasping for air, the cramps in my guts nearly paralyzing me, I crawled to the river's edge, slumped down in the soggy grass, and feebly washed myself off.

Feeling grateful that it was all over, I was no sooner finished and dragging myself back to the sweatlodge when a crushing lethargy came over me. It was like every ounce of energy slipped away. I fell on my side with just enough effort left to turn onto my back, and found my hip pressed against the bark of a large cottonwood tree. All I could do was lie still and look at the dim and murky world. I felt something alien pulsing in my blood, and my slowing breaths smelled rotten. I realized it wasn't over, that I was dying again. I felt my heartbeat slow to a halt, and my breath slow to a windy opening, no longer moving in or out. I was floating in a sea of nothingness, but I could still see my bare knees. They jerked when my body took a sudden breath. But I'd killed enough animals in my life to know such involuntary gasps for air were fruitless when there was no blood circulating. Another straining gasp for air, and I thought my head must be turned up somehow because I could see my body stretching away on the ground, wet and sunburned and hairy. Without feeling it, I saw my left leg jerk in a muscular spasm like I'd seen deer do after I'd killed them. The only sensation I could feel was something like dissolving into the world around me, an undifferentiated blending into the ground and the tree that slowly faded away.

Another spasm in my left leg, and I saw my left foot cross over my right. Dear, sweet body, I thought with regret. It somehow pleased me to see my feet crossed like that. This was always how I liked to lie on my back, with my left foot crossed over my right. Something tore loose in my perception of things, there was a feeling like a veil lifted, and I saw myself as a little boy, my tiny feet crossed just like this where I lay between my parents, their giant feet crossed the same on either side. It's a shattering memory, and I feel myself floating away on a bittersweet longing for the experiences that made me uniquely me. It's as if dying for me is leaving a string of familiar memories behind, and they march inexplicably past like emotions felt in sequence, all while I begin to lose sight of my body.

But before it all fades away, a bird flies down and lands on my left knee. Why not? I'm just a cold log for a bird to perch on now. But then the bird begins to walk down my thigh and I'm surprised I can feel his claws. I feel drawn to look at the bird, see what's going on. Instead of a bird, I see a tiny man, no more than five or six inches tall, walking down my thigh, yelling in a small voice at me. I can't figure out what he's saying, but it doesn't matter; nothing seems to matter anymore. But he's stamping, I can feel his foot, I can see how bright and hard he seems. Something floats by—a memory—the time in my first sweat-lodge when I was on retreat, alone, when I saw through a hole that appeared in the ceiling, bluejays perched on the edge, looking down, *kwash-kwashing* to each other. Then I heard what they were saying in words, superimposed on the racket of their bluejay calls. And suddenly I understand what the tiny man is saying to me.

He's telling me what's wrong with me. That I've been slowly killing myself with some dark fantasy of what life is like. That I "smelled dead" long before I "drank her" and came to this. That everything that happened to me in my life now means nothing. "Look! Look!" he says, gesturing for me to look around. The world is misty, transparent, beautiful beyond belief. I ache at how the sun seems to float in the clouds over the mountains, how it illuminates the mountains' insides, making them look like churning masses of swirling glitter, how it makes the cottonwood limbs overhead shimmer in a yellowness I can see through.

"Look!" he says. "There's nobody here! You're all alone. Nobody's going with you!" I instinctively know he means nothing and nobody in life has a hold on me, that I'm right back where I started when I was born—that life and death is ultimately just between me and the world

I find myself in. He does something with his hands, grabs something I can't see, and I'm suddenly flooded with a feeling of love, but not for my body or for myself—for this place, this world I seem to still be lingering in. I suddenly understand why these Indian people I'm close to live with their feelings on their sleeve and have such passion for experiencing whatever is happening. It's all right there in a crisp, single ache, a desire, a lust for being wherever I am.

I have to get up. I have to move, go, do, live. The tiny man leaps, flutters up as a bird into a niche, an opening in the side of the cottonwood tree that wasn't there before. He perches there for a moment, giving me one last look that says it all. Yes, that's what brings me, he seems to be saying. That. The rearing up on your hind legs, knowing it's all there in you, in the burning for the beauty, the mystery, the feeling. When you're like this, I am close. This is what power is attracted to, living the power that gives you life and breath. Not the confused longing, the self-pity about what cards you've been dealt in life, the escape into mindless work, insanity, loss, and meaninglessness.

I struggle up like waking from a dream, like slipping into my body already in the process of trying to stand up. I have the sensation that I've been witnessing the dark man easily getting to his feet, but as I become completely aware of myself standing and leaning against the tree, I lose him and am so weak I can hardly stay up. There's a dreadful feeling of dizzy sickness, but my heart is beating, I'm breathing. I sway and hold on, feeling the spot in unbroken cottonwood bark where I saw him go in. It occurs to me that the world is not so soft anymore, that it's becoming the same solid world I remember from before. Looking around in slow, animal appreciation, I don't feel like myself, but I don't care. I don't even mind the world growing hard and difficult to see into anymore. I know he's always there, underneath somewhere.

I'm not really sure where I am, swaying unsteadily in unfamiliar surroundings that I know somehow should be familiar. There's a low-grade exultation going on, and everything I look at seems to contain an innate perfection of being that when I first set eyes on it—like the river, the brushy shore, the boulder, the clump of rye grass—has some kind of voice speaking. It's as if my eyes seeing something in the hardening world, recognizing it, kindle a sputtering kind of hearing that "tunes in" to the sound tied to it, and for a momentary eternity I hear the language of whatever I'm looking at in conversation with me and everything around us.

I'm intrigued to discover they speak in an archaic English full of "thees" and "thous" and turns of phrase no longer spoken, and yet they each have a unique vocabulary of words, words that swirl around my ears like buzzing bees. The only word I remember later is "honto" which I understand at the time means "follow my lead." It doesn't matter if I remember the words because I know instinctively that only when they are spoken and heard are they important, and nothing is lost because next time it's all different anyway. I realize they are all aware of me and drawn to me because of something I'm doing. In a flash, I know what it is. It's what the bird-man is tied to me with, the attraction to a come-alive person devoid of anything but the wonder of being alive, moving his head in an ecstatic survey of wherever he finds himself.

I'm leaning against the tree trunk going nowhere but I see possible paths leading away, each to a vague jostling of possible events encountered if I choose to go in any of the directions. Each has its unknown but felt attractions, its mysterious timings and experiences and knowings, but none have any more than a momentary lure. A few have disjointed events and discolorations that I recognize as habitual ways for me to go forward feeling moods that try to bury what I now hold so dear. But somebody somewhere has put something in me that makes me cling to what I now know, and I wait. As each extraordinary thing winks out, the transparent softness of the world is only vaguely remembered, the voices of things go mute, the paths before me fade, and I see what I have to do. I have to remember this, keep it alive in me, live it after I become hard again.

I'm coming down to earth where I remember living. I understand now why there was something wrong in how I was living before. The things I chose to value, the directions I went in, the situations I called up in my own intending of things—they all seem like a straitjacket. But not to protect others from me. To hold in the insanity of my own conviction that I had to be in charge, running the show of my life, the only one capable of determining what was best for me. With the straitjacket gone, I see that the world around me is saying "Follow my lead." I see that the best and highest use of this unique point of awareness that is "me" is to choose to follow. As my head continues to turn in the sweep of my surroundings, I realize that everything that has transpired since I stood up has taken only seconds. Something even more interesting than the paths I saw leading away is now coming into view.

My eyes fall on two old Indian men I know sitting a few feet away from where my head was when I was lying down. It seems odd that they have clothes on and I'm naked. I smell something like salmon cooking. They look like miles away down there from the towering height where I'm looking at them. I can read everything about them in a flash of insight. The older one is looking at me with an edge of impatience. These White guys are so plugged up and slow. But ah, now he senses me reading him and chuckles. The younger, more chubby-faced one is startled and relieved to see me standing up, and ah, yes, he cares about me, he's glad to see me alive. What's his name? I can't seem to call up the sounds. In fact, I can't call up even the understanding of what they're saying to each other. The effort makes me dizzy. The thought that I may have brain damage makes me giggle, and I try to talk again. All I can come up with is a put-put-putting sound with my lips. Everything seems way too complex and I give in to a weakened desire to rest, sliding down the rough bark of the tree to sit with a jolt.

The frail one gets up laughing at how I look and goes over to a bright bed of hot coals. Why does the chubby-faced one defer to him? Oh, because he's older. That's how they are—the older you get, the more respect you get. Unlike where I come from . . . and where's that? What people is that? I know but I can't put words on it. I just see the image of the cities, the blank faces, the old people ignored, ridiculed, put away somewhere, and forgotten. The chubby-faced one touches my arm, leans close to my face.

"What's my name?" he says earnestly.

"Chubby face? No. Wait." He's taken aback. The other roars. I wonder who said that.

"I know that. Cl . . . Cl . . . Clay-ton." The sound of my own voice working it out seems to pop something open in my mind. All circuits are on again.

Clayton finally laughed like what I just said was the funniest thing he'd ever heard. Old Willie knelt and handed me the old coffee mug full of warm salmon oil. I didn't share their love of rendered salmon fat skimmed off and drunk straight, but I vaguely remembered they considered it an antidote to any poison in your body, so I drank it off with a grimace. It warmed my insides and reminded me how incredibly hungry I was.

The sun was behind the mountains, light fading. I was beginning to shiver. Clayton helped me stand up again and led me walking somewhere. Looking around made me stumble. It helped to stare at the ground and just focus on where I placed my bare feet.

"Where are we going?" I asked pleasantly.

Clayton had such a fit of laughter he had to let go of me, then grabbed my arm again. He waved toward the sweatlodge a few feet away where Old Willie was pitchforking hot rocks inside.

"This what we call sweatlodge. SWEAT-LODGE!" he pronounced loudly as if I was deaf.

"*T'at'úpa* (great grandparent, oldest of the old relative)," I said, remembering how they addressed Sweatlodge.

"Yah, that's it. Where we go in and thank 'em, that *T'at'úpa*. He the one warm us up, make us feel good to be alive! You remember Sweatlodge, don't you?"

It was odd. I felt like I'd come back to the wrong body. I realized later it was the lingering aftereffects of the old woman still coursing in my blood, but at the time I couldn't understand. Why was I such a pure and powerful force to be reckoned with, but trapped in a used-up, worn-out body barely able to respond to my attempts at the simplest things? I had blinding flashes of headache that lasted only a few seconds, complete lapses when I lost the thread of what I was doing, and if I tried to stay on my feet too long, a crushing fatigue would come over me. The only thing that kept me going was a childlike clinging to how mysterious everything seemed under the veneer of familiarity.

Going back into the sweatlodge was a trial. The smell of my own body was repulsive, no doubt the last residue of corn lily root sweating out of me, which prompted Clayton to open the door briefly several times to clear out the air. Old Willie seemed determined to make it hotter than humanly possible to endure, but as usual, no matter how the steam burned, the two of them sang and switched themselves with fir boughs and joked about things as if they couldn't feel it. Eventually the stink disappeared along with my discomfort and I floated in the familiar pitch-dark shroud of flame where anything seemed equal to anything else. And I was indifferent to what I felt were promptings from the old men to participate more in what was going on—I didn't sing or pray or speak or do anything but sit in mute witness.

In the cool-down at the end, Old Willie spoke directly to me with exhausted slowness. What he said I later heard repeated more or less the same way many times, a sort of final word to those he considered on their own with power and no longer in need of explanations.

"You come back to us, good. What you got come and help you. Whatever how they come, that's just for you, how *shumíx* come for you. Now you know. And now, in the days to come, you know the power come when somethin' happen like the same. Everything narrow down, everything get soft, and you see and hear what don't show like that most time. Kinda like a feelin', maybe hurt your feelings a little, but then you can see somethin' else when he come over you. Maybe you know you can do somethin', or maybe you see who come with power. That's it. There it is. The way the world really is, just power. But we can't live that way all the time. So we come back, and it's done."

Once outside in the dark of night, it seemed like a dreamlike flood of sensations and intricate technical maneuvers to get down the bank and into the river under my own power. I found a pool where I could barely touch bottom, my face out of the water, close to the far bank and out of the main current, where I floated thoughtlessly long after the other two climbed out, dressed, and walked up to the house. Eventually I emerged to sit and drip dry beside the glimmering coals. Managing to find my clothes, dress, and drag up the wet, grassy hill took forever. Inside, I slumped down on Willie's couch where I stared at the floral pattern on his window curtain, ignored by the old men cooking and sitting down to eat.

I woke up the next day about noon in the same position on the couch. I was dreaming about walking across country, trying to get somewhere I needed to be. I ignored attractive things I encountered on the trail, like a gleaming jade-green stone knife that I nearly stepped on crossing a creek, where it lay on the bottom visible under clear water. The various things I saw couldn't tempt me because I needed to get to where I was going. This turned out to be arriving in my body just in time to wake up and open my eyes. It was a reminder of the fragile hold I had on life. It also made me understand why Native elders took such care not to inadvertently startle another person, and why at other times, when someone was out of control, startling them on purpose was used to bring them back to their right mind.

Sitting up more healthy, more fit, more "in" my body than I ever remembered feeling before was a revelation. There were certain raw edges inside, the damage done by whatever had lived so long inside me, left like scar tissue but now growing back together in their proper positions, a few degrees closer to what I sensed as the proper design for a hard being like myself. A deep awareness of things in ways not easily expressed or even having meaning for anyone else gave my presence around the old men an "otherness" I couldn't shake—and didn't try to. Otherwise everything in me worked like brand new and perfectly broken-in. I washed dishes and cleaned the kitchen, went for a long swim in the river, ate with gusto, spoke a few precious words clearly, but there was a definite drifting disconnection, a keeping to myself. Clayton said later they wondered if I wasn't finding the world "too hard"—too brittle and unappealing, and maybe I longed for where I came from, wanted to go back. That's why he handed me a shovel and asked for my help getting his car unstuck.

It took hours of digging in the drying mud and a total concentration on how to get a heavy car up onto the dry sides of the deep ruts. It was a perfect, sunny spring day scented with the balsam of new cottonwood leaves. Both of us soon sweating with the effort, we jacked up the front of the car and toppled it off sideways several times until the front tires stood on hard ground. Then the rear, nearly ruining the jack when we pushed the lifted fenders over and the jack clattered free. It was all muscle and logic, a complete absorption in the elements of a physical situation and how to contrive changing it.

I was more or less my own familiar self when we laughed and clowned and congratulated each other on our success. While Clayton went back to the house, I got in, started the engine and tore off downhill to circle around and find another way up. Unfortunately, the cheatgrass hillside wasn't as dry as it looked and the tires would slip and dig in before I could get all the way on top, so I'd have to back down and try another way. By the time I finally pulled up in front of Willie's house, the formerly white station wagon had become a uniform mudbog brown all the way up to the windows.

Willie had no hose or outside faucet, so I drove to the river bridge where I remembered seeing an old concrete pad by the water's edge. With the bucket and an old shirt I splashed and scrubbed the car clean. When I drove back, I simply loaded my things in the car and waited with the motor running. The tall spruce tree and junipers flanking the walkway to Willie's front porch just seemed like someplace I was finished with. Clayton came out carrying his own gear and nothing was said, we both simply got ready to leave.

Clayton fell asleep on the drive down. The world unfolded in an approaching stream familiar to us reared in industrial civilizations, where we become such experienced multiple machine operators that we rarely notice anything odd about guiding a ton of steel hurtling down a ribbon of asphalt. The magic of it was new all over again for me, and the sacrifice made for shortening time to distant places never more clear. It took all my concentration to make it past the first few semi trucks flattening the air like a wall, and stop being distracted by the faces and stories I glimpsed in the other cars that passed. It took a while to reacquaint myself with the need for sifting and blocking out unnecessary incoming information and focus only on the essentials to keep moving at high speed. Once I regained my old familiarity with being numb to most of what was around me, my thoughts began to take over with a vengeance.

The words "British Columbia" and "Washington state" that were supposed to mark off and contain the fragrant beauty that streamed past seemed like no more than flimsy plastic nametags. The busy business streets of Keremeos seemed like highway litter concentrated and formed into exalted shapes designed to catch and hold the jaded eye. I wondered what would happen if I set myself up on the sidewalks and sold for a pittance the things that really stood for something—spread on a blanket the intricately designed pine cones and perfect shapes of leaves and impossible-to-duplicate constructions of mineralized rocks. The mysterious order of things that humans can only imitate; the magic inherent in how they came to be at all.

The marvel of all the things I see standing out on the wilder stretches of road, lit up in reddish detail from the last light of the setting sun. The very stuff of life on earth—yet what has become for us machine operators nothing but backdrop, ignored, relegated to the same status as the dark of night. Something unknown and vaguely feared unless illuminated in some artificial light that takes away the sting of unknowableness. The things we do that make us feel so clever because it dulls our fear of death. Too bad it's the cleverness of puppeteers, pulling the strings on what we've constructed to dance before our eyes—fooling ourselves into thinking we're like what we see glittering before us, instead of the ignored marvel of who's really doing the doing.

Dark, useless thoughts that faded as I slowed into the line of cars waiting to get through the international border crossing. Something in the eyes of the uniformed U.S. Customs officer gave me pause. I pulled up to a stop where he directed. As he leaned back inside his kiosk to punch in the numbers and letters of Clayton's car license plate, I shivered. Lighten up, dude! It is what it is! At the far reaches of the border crossing's bright overhead lights, I saw the blur of a coyote slinking between buildings. A laugh bubbled up.

"God! Am I glad to be home!" I blurted out to the border guard before he could start his litany of familiar questions.

"Um . . . both American citizens?" he asked, momentarily flustered, but hiking up his weapons belt in the resumption of official authority.

He looked blank and professional and a little too scrubbed as he scanned the inside of the car and studied Clayton yawning and blinking beside me.

"Yeah."

"Just up for a visit?"

"Yeah."

"Are you bringing anything back that you purchased in Canada?" His face was inches from mine, the uniformed invasion of personal space intentional, the intimidation palpable.

"Nothing but this cold. ACHOO!!!"

Coyote power, the one nature power available to all for the asking. The Customs officer was back inside his kiosk in a flash, wiping his face with a tissue, waving us through like lepers.

20

FOR THOSE REALLY NEEDING me to be there, I was as really there as I could be, which not surprisingly had an edge to it. A sense of being too imposing for comfort. More than once Charlene or Stuart or Johnny made it clear that I was "too much." Nothing specific that anybody could put their finger on, just that being in my presence wasn't easy. Something I was clinging to for dear life that unfortunately drew the looks of fear that I remembered from the bad old military days. Only with Clayton or Old Willie, who had their own edge, did I feel that who I'd come back and become was being in my right mind. It never occurred to me to be funny like they were. That came later.

It was impossible to act on the whisperings of power around my own people and still seem okay to them. My own sense of how to live with power was precarious compared to the two old men who seemed at ease in a way I couldn't grasp. I would tune into it when I was around them, but then lose it when off in the man-made mind world of my own people. Instinctively, I began to hide a part of myself from most people's view. Whatever power came up with I learned to present in the ordinary ways people were used to. It didn't do to stand out in threatening ways, and besides, from the beginning Clayton had stressed that it was only practical results that counted. I got good at deflecting the attention away from myself, and just in time since there seemed nothing I could do about how images and voices crowded around, forcing me to see and know things whether I wanted to or not.

When I was back to work walking out the miles of barbed wire fence repairing winter damage and heading for the old wooden cattle guard on Palmer Mountain to meet Stuart Bolster coming the other way, I had a fleeting scenario unfold in my mind's eye. I saw him walking along with steel fence posts over his shoulder, pushing through thick brush below Washburn Lake. The hooked pry part of his fencing pliers snagged on a branch, pulling it out of his tool belt. It hung there as he walked on, unaware. When I met him at the cattle guard he told me he'd somehow lost his fencing pliers, and had already walked back the whole fence line without finding it. While he ate his lunch I went to look and found it exactly where I got a picture of it, still hanging from a limb and hidden in leaves. And when I returned, I handed it to him as if I'd just stumbled upon it accidentally.

Power didn't have anything to do with the part of me that thought and decided about how things worked. Power crept along unnoticed under the floorboards of things, moved behind the curtain of what was in front of me, and only showed up on the periphery of what was at hand. Because our eyes are the main judges of what is real, it was no surprise that so much of what Clayton taught me were ways of noticing what was usually edited out. Slowing down to a halt amidst the minutiae of nature's flood of impressions, cracking open the mind's eye with the unfathomable vastness of *wik'wst,* focusing in the utter darkness of the sweatlodge on the ineffable appearance of spirit lights. I was beginning to see that power was off to the side of what we were trained by habit to narrowly focus upon. That there was vastly more going on in recondite but accessible reaches at the same moment an ordinary event was occurring before my eyes. What my eyes saw now was the "bigger world" that Old Willie spoke of, that our modern conditioning ignored, but was still there for those willing to train "for eyes to see."

The most defining experience I had in those two months before I went on the long wander happened when I heard from Sid Loughren settled in Canada. His letter in block capitals and littered with excessive exclamation points as his only punctuation at least signaled he'd jumped right into another cause with a passion, and I gave in to an urge to go see for myself what all the fuss was about. There was no return address, of course, so I drove up to find the stretch of BC Hydro power line he wrote about. He said he was joining protesters illegally squatting along the right of way cleared through forest, who were trying to prevent by their presence the aerial spraying of herbicides. Instead of cutting back by hand the trees that grew back along cleared power-line swaths, the provincial electrical utility had turned to "Agent Orange," as Sid called whatever chemical they were dropping by helicopter. I figured I would walk the stretch of power line he spoke of in his letter until I found him.

Along the way I drove through the Selkirk Mountains where I'd once lived with the woman who'd meant the most to me in my life, the only woman who enjoyed butchering the game animals I brought home; the one I had a child with, the son who died at birth. The familiar craggy peaks and interior rain forest along the Trans-Canada Highway brought back old memories and feelings—longings that I thought were gone but that came alive with a sharp pain when I saw the places where things happened when we'd been happy together so many years before. The fact that such an unresolved burden was still at work inside me was a shock, and yet I couldn't seem to do anything about a despair that deepened when I strayed from my route and drove the rutted road to find the cabin we once shared. Caved in by heavy winter snows, there wasn't much left to remind me of how we lived there beyond a chipped porcelain wash basin riddled with the bullet holes of someone using it for target practice. But the setting was the same and I wondered why it had such a power to consume me, to hold me in a way that was a little sickening.

Once back on the road it hit me like a rock. This was the kind of thing Old Willie had doctored me for—something in life that I couldn't put behind me, something I myself had welcomed, embraced, let live with me. The dread of life after she left that nothing could touch or alter because it had become so deeply a part of me. Ultimately buried out of sight but still there, festering, coloring every new experience with the taint of not good enough.

Only the death plant had scoured it out of me, given me something to hold in its place. But already I could feel all Willie had done for me was weakening. That I was being drawn to the old scenes and memories to see that it could all come back and take hold of me again, that nothing could protect me from my own inclination to grab onto it and make it mine again. Old Willie had said that he healed many people, but cured only a few. He said that the hardest thing for an Indian doctor to overcome was how those he treated afterward went back to the same kind of heart and mind they had before—that had caused the illnesses and injuries that people came to him with in the first place. He warned me to watch for the signs of what had lived inside me, that it would try to come back, but that my power, renewed and strengthened by the bond we'd forged, would make me see it coming in obvious ways. Willingly accepting the sickness back inside me would become a clear choice, he said, but one nobody, not even a spirit power, could help me with.

I found the power line where Sid said it crossed the highway, parked at a nearby turnout, and set off with a knapsack on my back. It was weird hiking the ruler-straight swath up and down mountains along an overgrown trail through dog-hair thickets of young trees growing back. Overhead a sizzle and snap of massive electrical power running through steel cables was as disturbing as the mood that was consuming me. I walked along obsessing about absurd things—how no woman could ever replace her, how I could have done things differently, how I welcomed the familiar dread enveloping me as something I deserved for not being able to hold on to her.

But then something began to rebel. I remembered how life had been before I met her. That I'd been perfectly fine on my own, making my way with eyes wide open, full of wonder and confidence. And she'd been like that, too—that was how we'd met and why we'd been attracted to each other. We came to each other complete in our own selves . . . and somehow had lost it in our time together, the years that followed. The memory of the bird-man came back, how he looked at me from his little niche in the tree trunk. Why was it such a surprise that what I loved most in others was their own love for themselves?

The realization of what that meant about me, about what I was doing obscuring this precious moment of life with longing for what was gone, slowly sank in. I was an hour into my hike and came to a ridgetop that was dry and rocky, with just a few tall serviceberry and ironwood bushes. From the concrete pad where one of the "monsters from Mars" stood—the steel towers that held up the power lines stretching across country, making them look like giant robots holding up their arms—I could see far ahead. There were bright urban backpacker colors, movements in trees, voices calling. I'd reached the objective of my long road trip and hike, but now I held back. The weight of obsessive thoughts crowding around, ruining the moment, was like a dark cloud hanging over me wherever I went.

Then a memory came back, the moment I stood up from the dead against the tree trunk, flooded with the wonder of still being on earth. The same feeling came over me with a sudden hardness. As if a switch was turned on inside me, I snapped back into wanting only to live. To smell these smells, touch these leaves, feel this wind blowing on me, see this lush and beautiful world spread open before my eyes. The relief of releasing the woman and coming back to myself was immense. I knew instinctively that the earth wanted me to let go of anything that stood in the way of being her man. Itching for whatever was in front of me, I surged onward, descending the other side of the ridge with certainty and poise. I threw myself completely into the mystery and possibility of the moment . . . and the feeling that I would soon see Sid again.

No sooner did I slow to the top of another rise when something happened that stopped me in my tracks. A large, hawk-like blur shot from behind around my left knee and cut in front of me at top speed. My startled eyes locked on and tracked what I suddenly recognized as a peregrine falcon with pumping wings and elegantly splayed tail tilting this way and that through the bushes to my right. Swooping directly at a bluejay that fluttered deep into the safety of deep brush, the falcon veered off and disappeared into the forest. It was over in a matter of seconds and left me dazed, awed, uncomprehending. The falcon had nearly brushed my leg, the sharp turn in front of me a swooshing flap of feathers that stopped my heart. It was so unlikely that a falcon would use me as a screen to attack a bluejay, I felt a bump of recognition. It was a stunning and immediate response from my power, and it shut down any conscious thoughts, leaving only a pinpoint awareness of awe.

It's a strange feeling to drop away from my mind and still find myself aware. Something has been shoved aside, and I feel myself embody the dark man emerging easily. There's incoming sensations, feelings, messages, all wrapped up in a scenario I can vaguely see coming toward me. The bluejay had been pointed out with great force—as great a force as what had come over me when I turned away from what had been sickening me. Now there's a raucous, bad-boy, troublemaker feel coming over me, a very "bluejay" disdain that I surface back into conscious thought with, that focuses on some people, three men, running toward me up the power-line trail. Crashing through bushes in headlong flight from something, right up to where I stand, hard as a rock.

Somehow I'm not surprised that it's Sid Loughren in the lead, sprinting ahead of two young guys, recognizing me and breathlessly urging me to run because the Mounties are right behind them. Too late, I see, as an RCMP constable in sweaty green field uniform races up from behind and grabs one of the young guys, who lets out an involuntary shriek.

"Don't move!" the red-faced Mountie growls at the rest of us, looking around, uneasy at something. Sid immediately snaps into combat mode, but as he tries to get past me I grab his arm and feel him go limp. I start to laugh at nothing—it just bubbles up and feels like someone else doing it. It startles the constable holding the boy's hands behind his back, his free hand trying to open a pair of handcuffs.

"Hey, what's wrong?" I say. "Why are you messing with these guys? They're just lost . . . out hiking and they got lost. I just found them."

Speaking words makes the whole world come brightly into focus. The garish, wide yellow stripes down the side seams of the Mountie's trousers make him look like a nineteenth-century soldier. Sid and his buddies are in camouflage hunting outfits. I'm fascinated by how the constable stares uneasily at me, so distracted he can't get the open cuffs on the boy's wrists, even though he keeps pawing at them. It occurs to me that this is the first time I've experienced the dark man doing something with my fully conscious participation. I keep laughing in a generous, oh-it's-all-just-a-silly-mistake sort of way, but with an edge, because there's a burning in my navel—what it's costing to stay present and follow the lead of what's in front of me. The manhandled boy begins to sob.

"C'mon, they're gonna get away!" I snap with a dry tone of authority. "They need your help! What are you waiting around here for, eh? They're calling for you over there!"

Voices call in the distance. The constable looks at me with vague eyes, his mouth slack, then down at his hands still feebly going through the motions with the handcuffs. Abruptly he shrugs and tucks them back into his belt, then looks up at me and lets out an embarrassed laugh.

"Sorry about that, eh?" he says, suddenly looking very tired.

More calls in the distance turn his head, and he takes off down the power-line trail the way he came. In the silence after his footsteps fade away, the boy sniffs. They're all staring at me.

"What just happened?" Sid says in a small voice.

"Go! Get out of here!" I said.

Sid staggers back like I hit him with my fist. The two guys look from Sid to me, torn. Something loosens inside me and I let some of my warmth for Sid flow out.

"I thought you were an Indian! Be like the trees! Blend in. . . . Disappear. . . ."

Sid looked even more startled.

"Jesus! Is that what my grandpa meant? Well I'll be damned. . . ."

It took another release on whatever I was holding on to, a softening enough to say, "Sid, my brother, now's not the time. . . ." But there's sudden angry shouts turned in our direction. I feel it all slip away.

Laughing like an escaped mental patient, I pounded away at a dead run into the forest, the others close on my heels. After a mile I slowed to let them catch up. All three were grinning ear to ear. I noticed for the first time that the youngest had a face full of freckles, the other had dreadlocks flopping around, and Sid was wearing his Airborne beret. We moved on more quietly. My instinct was to work up and around the mountain in front of us, but Sid kept motioning for me to follow him down a creek. We stopped for a whispered parley.

"We've got to stop meeting like this," I wheezed.

Sid lost it laughing. Then, "Two words!" he gasped. "Follow my lead!"

My ears popped. I'd follow him anywhere.

"That's three words, sergeant, sir."

"We're in my world, now," he said, shining eyes looking around at the unlogged, old-growth forest of Douglas firs towering around us. It took the rest of the day and half the night, but he led us finally to the teepee and minivan in a clearing that he and Isa now called home.

It was like being a teenager again, irrepressibly fixed on a vast world of possibility, my exploratory nose leading me confidently off to see what was on the other side of the hill. No more personal history dragging me down, forcing me into a mold that made next steps in life so predictable, so tame, so deadening. Road trips with no clear purpose, just a scent of something called up by the names of places that came to mind and beckoned. Turning my own power-beam eyes on other places, other people. Already champing at the bit for the long wander without knowing it. Jump-starting it. Doing it in lame, inexplicable ways that after the fact seem to be loaded with meaning and purpose.

The seawater taste of oysters was just what I was craving. Funny how I knew just what I needed to eat, what came to mind to keep me spinning along on an even keel. You'd think in a seaport town like Bellingham I'd just pull into one of the dozens of seafood joints and chow down, but things didn't work for me like that anymore. If I didn't feel something leading the way, I waited. Even out on the rez north of town where a friend of Jim's gave me a place to stay, I wouldn't eat what they had. I went to sleep hungry, listening to the sounds coming through the window—trees dripping in the rain, a drinking party going on next door.

But the sound of banging pots and pans in the wee hours drew me irresistibly to the kitchen where a man had come home with the tide and was striding around in rubber boots, putting water to boil in a huge pot on the stove. Jim's friend's brother, the dark and quiet one. A new friend made, a man who, like his father, a Filipino married into the Lummi tribe, lived by the rhythm of the sea. For whom a two a.m. feast on the night's catch was normal. Listening to him talk to the live crabs and clams he dropped into bubbling water and then telling me you ate when the time came to eat, which had nothing to do with clocks or schedules. That way, he said, the food spoke to you about what it knew about you. Something I heartily agreed with when I discovered his burlap bag full of oysters and took him up on his invitation to eat all I wanted. Two men getting to know each other like two ships passing in the night. The slippery-guts feel of oysters going down. Just what I needed—a certain shallow-sea, muddy-bottom conviction that made me heed the words that came to mind: "Go back. Go back before you lose the thread. Something is waiting for you."

Back to Clayton Tommy in a late June sunset by a withering bonfire of rocks being heated for a sweat at the Woods family sweatlodge. The whole family is going in, even Jim standing there staring blankly into the flames, unaware the heat is crisping the unshirted front of his hairless fat hanging over sweat shorts. Nobody speaks because this is the final goodbye to Grandma, already in the ground, a wrenching turn in the wheel of life for us all. Especially for the teenage girls in old cotton dresses holding each other barefoot and wet-eyed, and for Charlene whose uncontrollable sobs say it all, carried on the wind toward the mountain that always watches and listens from above.

Five days before, Grandma had disappeared, walked away from the doublewide, last seen touching flowers and mumbling on the riverbank. When I pulled up to the Woods place the next day, dazed from my long drive from the coast, there was something wrong with the feel of things. Charlene sat listlessly on the front porch as she spoke to Clayton, her voice after I turned off the engine a distraught mumbling in Salish. I didn't get out. I could see in the way she scratched at her yellow dress that something was very wrong. Clayton shifted on his feet, his hands in his pockets, looking off in the distance, seeing something irrevocable, beyond reach. He turned and seemed to notice my arrival for the first time. His eyes met mine with a palpable sadness I rarely saw.

("I believe I know where she went,") Clayton said at last.

Charlene recognized the look in his eyes and dropped her head to her hands, weeping. Clayton came and stood by my car door, uncharacteristically asking me if I had any cigarettes. I found one in the glove compartment and handed it out the window to him. He lit it and puffed thoughtfully, then waved the smoke all over himself. He came around and got in with me. Neither of us spoke. He gestured for me to drive him someplace and sat smoking as we drove up the old river road.

Motioning for me to pull in at a gate in the barbed wire fence of a White rancher's riverbottom hay field, he pinched out the cigarette stub and crumbled the remaining tobacco in his fingers, letting it drift away in the wind from his hand held out the window. He said to wait for him, got out, opened the gate, and walked slowly off across the tall canary grass swaying in whispery waves. Disappearing over a rise, he was gone a long time and I waited at the wheel, listening to the summer bugs clickering in the hissing grass. Then he came back, opened the gate wide enough to get the car through, got in and directed me driving slowly across the field. We stopped beside some mounds at the edge of a drop-off, looking down on the wetter, lower floodplain where huge cottonwoods grew. In their shadows I saw Grandma curled up as if asleep by a fallen log.

"This what Old Willie tell me that time," Clayton said unexpectedly, somberly. "That my brother, the dead one, say to him, to pass on to me, to prepare me. That in the time of serviceberries this wonderful person go off by herself to where she born, the old *kikwúli* where she come alive on earth." He gestured toward the faint mounds in high grass and weeds beside the car. "Here she go back." He sighed. *"Wai i hwi,"* he added with finality, his voice cracking.

Looking at her so tiny and serene, her hands clasped together where her scarf was tied at her chin, I recalled one of the first things she ever said to me when I showed up at the doublewide with her grandson Jim so many years before. When she was trying to put me at ease, make me feel welcome in the strangely different world of her Indian home under the shadow of Chopaka Mountain.

"Yes, I been lookin' up at that mountain allllll my life. I was born here and here is where I will die. I neeeeever wanted to live anyplace else."

The tears poured down my cheeks. Goodbye Grandma. I'll be coming to see you someday.

Clayton sniffed, took a deep breath, looked at me.

"We gotta be strong for the others. They her blood, all her children. The power gonna hit hard."

As I cleaned up and made room in the back of my old station wagon, Clayton gathered wild rose plants, his hands bleeding from the thorns by the time he had the back of my car strewn with them. There were no bugs on her body and she wasn't bloated at all—she must have been fasting. She was as light as a child as I lifted her into my arms, the initial stiffness of her limbs loosening to hang and sway limply as I carried her up the bank. Her deeply furrowed, nearly ninety-year-old face seemed softened, younger in the bright sunlight. The familiarity of loading a dead body in the back of my car, like a deer I'd killed, brought home to me the finality of how we leave our bodies behind when we die.

The chapel where the wake was held was hardly big enough for the crowd that came to feel the loss together. Johnny Stemilt's Christian-inclined brother showed a charismatic, devout side of himself I'd never seen before, making Johnny take off his cowboy hat with the dangling eagle feather, leading us in singing Salish hymns that had the feel and even sometimes the same melodies of the church songs of my childhood. By midnight everybody had left but the hard-core few of us committed to staying up all night with Grandma's soul still lingering close to her body in the coffin on a table. Jim and I sat together as grief slowly shifted into a vague apprehension at each strange sound or breath of air finding its way into the stuffy room. We passed the sleepless hours distracted by Old Willie's sister Margaret telling the most outrageously obscene and funny stories to keep our attention on continued life. Coyote stories that were bad enough, but by three a.m., the frankly insatiable sexual adventures of Skunk. The atomic Skunk, legend Skunk, the dreadful one of the before time who had power over people almost impossible to overcome. The one who inevitably got thwarted and unleashed his chemical warfare on anybody who got in his way, his power of phew! that was fatal in those days.

When Margaret's throat gave out, Jim told us a nervously self-mocking story from his bachelor days. Seems a White woman asked him if he'd make her something "Indian"—a bag or case for her expensive camera, made from the skin of an animal. But not just any animal, a special animal—her "totem" as she called it—the tanned hide of a skunk. She said she'd always wanted something made from a skunk, and if Jim would make her a camera pouch from a skunk skin, she'd pay him good money for it.

"So me and Kootch are comin' back in his car from Omak one day and we smell it. Phew! Drive through that bad smell of skunk run over. Sure enough road kill skunk, eh? Black and white stripes there on the side of the road, so I say, 'Pull over!' He sees me usin' a rag on my hand to drag that mess to his car, and says, 'No way!'

"But he owes me big time since I gave him the car he's drivin', so he opens the trunk and holds his nose while I lift the thing in and slam it shut. We go on, up the highway, only a few miles, but the smell is creepin' up, creepin' up to where we are in the front seat. It's so bad we're flyin' along with the windows down and our heads way out in the wind to breathe!

"So it's no use, we're gonna die before we get the thing home. Kootch hits the brakes and pulls over, says sorry, he can't take it, he'd rather walk. I say, 'No, wait, dude. I got an idea.' We open the trunk and take 'em out and tie 'em on the outside, with baling wire to the luggage rack on his trunk. See, that way the smell is outside and blown away in the wind. We go on and it works, we don't smell the skunk anymore, and we fly along, gonna make it home just fine.

"Pretty soon we look back and we both lose it laughin' because with his paws tied to the bars, that skunk is stretched out, flappin' in the wind! Like he's Super Skunk and he's flyin', he's chasin' after us! Then a car comes up from behind, overtakin' us. Comes up real close, like wants to pass us. Then suddenly the car falls back, slows wayyyyyy down like somethin' terrible happened! Nobody come close to us after that.

"Finally we get home. I skinned that skunk and buried the rest of 'em in the ground, off in the hills. Way off, ya know? Then I brought that skin back, soaked it in tomato juice. Scrubbed it in soap and water. Took days but finally the smell was gone, only a faint odor if you put your nose right in the hair. Well, I worked it and worked it, and made that bag the lady wanted. Real pretty with the white stripes on black goin' up and down, and the tail hangin' off the bottom. That woman loved it! Gave me two hundred dollars for it and went away happy!

"Well, not long, maybe the next day, I ran into Raymond Stuikin, ya know? I ask how's it going and he says not good, they had to move into town for a while. Seems they woke up one morning to a godaw- ful phew of skunk smell in their house. His grandpa found the remains of a dead skunk behind the water heater. He said they figured the dog must've brought it home. They had to stay with relatives until their house aired out enough. As he's talkin', it occurs to me that Raymond's house is just over the ridge from where I buried the remains.

"And Raymond says to me, 'Ya know what's weird? That skunk had been skinned! Who would skin a skunk?!' All I said was, 'Hmmmm, yah, that really is weird. . . .'"

And then the sweat with all of us—men, women, and children— packed in like sardines so tight nobody had room to escape the burning steam by putting their nose to the floor. So hot with only fifteen rocks that everybody sobbed out every last bit of grief and the women wailed until they were hoarse. The kind of heat that *T'at'úpa* knew we could endure because our pain was stronger than anything the heat could do to us. That was the way sweats were when someone had died—they always burned worse whether you opened the door a lot or not. There was nothing you could do about it.

Yah, that's just the way it is, Clayton says, slumping down beside me on the riverbank when the two of us are alone afterward. Telling me that the sweat would have been easier for me if I'd sweated as soon as I came back from my road trip, instead of waiting for a time like this. I'm so whipped I can hardly move. See, he says, when you go off and spend time away from where your power lives, you pick up all kinds of stuff. Especially in cities, and it clings to you, makes you live in your mind. When you come back, take the time, maybe just a little wipe off, so you can feel in your heart again what's real. Crawl into a hole in the earth for a while, sweat it out of you, let it seep away back into the earth. Then emerge and see the light of day again as it really is. *En'xwlaltán awhá loot cháwtet,* he says over and over: Our being alive is not our own doing. Be ready to live again based on what you perceived in the utter darkness—the flickering motes of light, the voices that spoke—that remind you of being here on earth for some purpose. That ground you in the earth's will for you being here.

The weary mixture of Salish fluency and English oddity of word choice is hard to follow, but I'm sure I heard him right. I've never heard him talk this way before, but it hits me where I know just what he's talking about. And there's something I always wondered about it.

How do I know, I ask him, what that purpose is? What our mother wants me to do, be doing, go toward? Clayton says nothing. I call him uncle and ask him again. How do I know when I'm doing her will for me?

He sighs. It's not that you know, he says. It's more like you're aware every day that you're willing, that you want to do whatever it is. You ask to be able to do it. You ask and you watch and you see what comes, what is presented to you. You get better at being right there, offering yourself to whatever is leading the way.

My ears ring. I've told him nothing of my experience at Old Willie's, but what he said lines up with what I've been doing ever since hearing the words "follow my lead." The inevitable way he fits even this into his lore of living here in the world. The lore of what's true because I experience it myself directly. The little bit of mystery we can convey in words to each other. No conclusions—just commentary, just words that open doors. Seeking life together by going through the same doorways, following the same path.

"Otherwise," he says in his creative English, "to do what we all put here to do—live life to enjoy!"

21

Ｍ Y EXPERIENCE WITH THE Mountie on the power-line swath faded from mind in the press of events. I finally got around to mentioning it to Clayton the morning after the family sweat. Everybody else had left with Jim on a long drive up to the Chilcotin country for a visit with his wife's family, leaving the two of us to the empty silence of the living room couch where we sat sipping the usual thin and watery coffee.

The day after a hard sweat is always drifting and easy—an energized fitness of body that brings back being fully in your own skin, a humble appreciation of what's important in life, a sense of mastery that yet does not focus on getting anything done. Unless you fight it—and that's where the term "sweatlodge hangover" comes from—life is utterly simple again, powered the way it's supposed to be, by easing indirectly into everything at hand. The want to live that's not forced along—that's followed wherever it leads.

Nothing was pressing for either of us that morning. We simply enjoyed each other's company, nibbling on some old donuts because neither of us was hungry. We broke the silence every once in a while with things we remembered about Grandma—funny or remarkable things she did or said. In the Native way, she was never named directly.

"The dead tell me somethin' about you one time," Clayton said. "That once you start talkin' Indian to her, she just tickled to hear the real words come from the mouth of a White man. She say she have to be careful around you when she talk Indian, so she don't hurt your feelings. She say she can see you got somethin', some real old-time power to have the dream and go see it come true.

"She say she always have the hope for Jim to gain power, like his sister, Lucy. But he never see anything, besides ghosts. He have too much of the White mouth, and can't see how the dead reachin' out to him. Why they do that. So she give him somethin' before she go, before she go back. And that is just waitin' for him, that power she pass on. But in another way, she say no need to pass on anything to her adopted grandson. To already have the fine power and make things happen for hisself and others."

He spoke of other things that had been said about me and I realized they'd all been privately discussing the specifics and extent of my power experiences, just like they did with other power people. Evaluating how strong I was "in the power" by the practical results I demonstrated, and how "easy" things came for me in the daily affairs of life. That's when the events on the power line came to mind and I told him about it.

"*Aaaa* . . . I guess you gonna be a Bluejay after all!" he said, bemused. "Pretty hard way to go . . . and hard on others. But maybe that other one, the one who does the grabbin', maybe he can keep 'em in line."

He reminded me how all the Bluejay stories had the unique feature of Bluejay's power cancelling out someone else's power, of stripping whoever Bluejay was using his power on of whatever power they were acting on, exposing them at their weakest to themselves. That's what happened to the Mountie, he said, just like it happened to Eagle and Wolf and Coyote in the different stories. He urged me to notice that Bluejay never used his power on somebody just because they "pissed him off"—that he used it on those who were so "puffed up" with themselves that they were harming others, lording it over other people who didn't go along with them. He called Bluejay "the equalizer," the one everybody liked to hear stories about because he was so seemingly inadequate and ridiculous, but just laughed at himself and didn't care, demonstrating that power had nothing to do with how you appeared to other people. In fact, the main feature of Bluejay in the old animal stories, he said, was that nobody but his wife or closest relative could see anything powerful about him. Even when the time came that he used his power and the results were there for anybody to see, the people seemed dazed, like they couldn't figure out what had happened.

"Just the power for a White man on the earth's side!" Clayton chuckled.

I remembered how he taught me Bluejay songs and sometimes flapped his bluejay feather fan in the sweatlodge; how he called in blue-jays with his gift for bird calls and fed them scraps of food. I told him it seemed strange to me that he had something from Bluejay but never showed the kind of overt use of power like he was pointing out in the stories—at least in my presence. He said it was like he said before, nobody got the same thing. He got something different from Bluejay than I did. He called it "Flock of Bluejays" and said he was given the gift of seeing what was *talht*—true or right. He invoked it in the sweatlodge to keep the "bad hearts" away—people lost in their own hidden desires. And he used it "to watch for a sign of bad heart" in me.

"Huh . . . well, did you see it in me?"

"Yah, a few times," he said coyly.

My curiosity was aroused. "Well, it must notta been too bad, because here we still are."

"Only once," he said, holding up a finger. He said when I showed up after going off to the Yakima country to follow the dream I asked for, came strutting up like a country-western singer in new cowboy clothes, that was the only time he saw me "pretty close to a bad heart."

"But you got the handle on it pretty quick, and now we see the fresh new Bluejay man, have that want to help the people be on the earth's side. Maybe we been tryin' to saddle the wrong horse all along, eh?"

"The wrong horse?"

"Yah, that chicken hawk, the one who grab, he not the one to come on you, maybe. He just the one to walk with you in life, show you how, make the food and point the way. That's not a power I know much, maybe too old, too long-ago kinda gift, for when people just wakin' up to bein' on the earth. For you, for your people tryin' to wake up before too late. Maybe Old Baptiste, he know more about that one.

"But for the power to come on you, to stay hard and use 'em for somethin', sure look like that Bluejay the one. All the same power for a person, but just the one for when you call on 'em. And that Bluejay a good one, one I know about."

He talked about the other kind of stories, not the Animal People stories but the tales handed down that told of Indian people gaining and using gifts of nature power. How the ones that told about people who got something strong from Bluejay showed the uses for that kind of power. People went to somebody who had Bluejay power, he reminded me, to see if the person's power could find something they had lost, or a relative who was missing. Or find out about events happening far away, or in the future.

"Other power can do that, too, sometimes. But that Bluejay, he can find anything!" Clayton said. "Maybe you got somethin' from him like that. The way he show up just the bird in the trees to point out the way, to show you where to find things. Like those bighorns, those deers. Show you just where to go to find 'em. Yah, maybe you been tryin' to call on the wrong one all along!"

I wondered why he thought it was so important to distinguish which power a person was calling on.

"Because this what I been waitin' to see happen all along. That you call on what you got and he come on you. That you call 'em up for somethin', some good reason, some need, and when he come on you, you stay hard, stay awake. To use what you got and come back. All like that is what happen with your friends and the Mountie, but not quite. Just the one thing missing."

"What's that?"

"You didn't call on 'em, did you? He just come on you, show up to your feelings, show up in your time of need, to be used. So I still waitin' to see the power man, call on his power, that he is doin' the choosin' and show that what he got will come when he ask. Then you see why. No way to know but you do it. Then you know."

Clayton was lost in thought. It occurred to me that I had even less to go on with Bluejay than Falcon for calling on him, no memory like I did of the man who grabbed birds out of the air. Just the vague dream image of him coming like an older friend to help me grapple with the deer's antlers. An impression of a badmouthing, undependable jokester who wasn't anything like the solid, forceful, capable man he was with.

Yet there was something attractive about him, made more palpable by the feel of things when I "threw Bluejay words at the Mountie," as Clayton called it. Like I knew more about this Bluejay person than I could consciously call up. It made me wonder how this particular force of nature came to pick me.

Clayton was far more likely, I'd come to notice, to take my questions seriously and talk more at length about something if I asked him in Salish. The way things had to be phrased in his language was far more amenable to talking about power, he'd said. So I phrased my thoughts the best I could:

"*Ha' sch'k̓ínxu, ha' xi stim inchá k̓'stim tul k̠wá'shk̠ai?* ... (How is it, what for do I have something from Bluejay? What for did he choose me? Why not Eagle, or Thunder, or Wolf?)"

Clayton's eyes narrowed.

("Yes, and why not Mosquito, or Skunk, or Rotting Log?") he replied mockingly. I'd unfortunately chosen as alternatives those nature powers known for bestowing great and desirable powers in the stories, and now I had to eat humble pie.

("And that Maggot, eating on the dead bodies, why didn't he choose you? Or that Stinkbug? Now why didn't he notice the handsome White man, the important person so great in his own mind that all the powers of earth fight over who gets to be his partner?")

I had to laugh at myself with him or take even more of it. I said I was just wondering how certain kinds of power came to certain people and not others. He said it really didn't matter, that it was all power whether from the ocean or from the rain puddle that formed in a footprint. There had been great Bluejay men, Bluejay doctors of awesome gift for finding out about things, knowing things, making things happen. And there had been those who only showed Bluejay's obnoxious temperament, pointing out other people's failings and indulging in the opportunistic, self-gratifying ways of bluejays. He said the powers do the choosing, but they knew what they were doing—they knew "how each person grow up different and lean in different ways."

"You in the world so you see all the powers, how they doin' what they doin'—what they show us that we can see. But the certain ones catch your eye. The ones who know that you kinda like they are, and so they set things up for you to see 'em, set things up for you to use 'em. Just like you the man who sneak around in the bush, cross the border, come out from hidin' and grab what you need—another man don't even think to do things like that. Just you, and so we see that *tl'tlak'w,* that falcon who live like that on earth.

"And then you the man who want to find out things, who look around and see what he can know. And just nobody can make him be what he don't want, he just laugh at 'em, the ones who try to tame him. And so we see *kwá'shkai,* that bluejay, the dark one, that is how he live in the world. Whatever how the person is, that's the power that likes to help 'em."

"So it's what I do with it that counts?" I asked.

"Of course. Your power set things up for you to use 'em how you already do things. Make things happen in life so what happen feel like they supposed to be like that. Open the way to go on the path that feel like just yours. Things happen, people show up—or maybe don't happen, or you avoid somethin' bad—just like all set up. That's the power way. To be strong in the power way, well, that's what make the power man with great power.

"And that is why they send 'em on the long wander. The power is strongest in the bush, in the high mountains where nobody go. And even more at night. What you got is tested because no people and nothin' else goin' on. It's all power out there, all move in the power way. And maybe a power man can wander far, far. Why, pretty soon, that is how he stay alive, that is how he can come back. He bring that back with him. That is how he live from then on.

"See, don't matter if you singin' Bluejay, or singin' Wolf, or singin' Stinkbug. On the long wander, it's all power. And out there, you run into a power you can't avoid. The one we all run into, a person of great power who will test your heart. Maybe if you the real thing he might tell you his name, but the Indians just call 'em *sen'kwá'chinux* (the darkness of the night). He the one who live in the dark, who make the world dark. You can't avoid him, he will come to test you. He the one that messes with you, make trouble for you if you only pretend to have power. Lotta people get hurt by him out in the dark, in the timber. Sometimes lose their life. No way to fake power with that one. That's why we say about the real ones: *Ch'maistíselux i sen'koko'ách* (They know something about the night)."

We didn't speak for a long time. In the morning heat-up of a hot day outside, the couch smelled of mildew and baby-diaper changing. I could hear the blackbirds calling as they went about their business out by the river. The day stretched out before me like a pleasant void, anything possible, nothing needing to be done. My thoughts drifted over the things Clayton had said, the promise of things to come in their own time. Then I heard him murmur something, breathe deep, and sigh like he was coming out of a deep reverie, the words hard to make out.

"Hmm?"

"Somethin' is comin'," he repeated.

"Huh."

Another long silence. Then I heard the pickup slow down on the pavement, pull up in front. The clump of cowboy boots on the porch, the sharp White-man pound of fist on the door. Clayton's musical and amused "Come in!" with neither of us budging from our seats. It was Stuart Bolster, blustery deep cigarette voice but somehow subdued as he said his howdys and left his hat on. He'd come to the wake for Grandma, so this was something else.

He said he was looking all over and asking around for anybody who'd seen his youngest son "Boot." A teenager now, Boot had gone off with some buddies to ride the bulls at the Fourth of July Chesaw Rodeo, but then he had disappeared. His buddies said they last saw him get into a pickup they never saw before and ride off with whoever it was. After a day and night of no word from him, his mother was so fearful he'd been abducted she couldn't get out of bed. Stuart wondered with the deeply furrowed brow and sunken eyes of a sleepless night if "you guys know anything about it?" Meaning Clayton, of course, who in Stuart's eyes had some kind of old Indian sixth sense for knowing things that were hidden to anybody else. At the negative shake of our heads, he looked beaten but not defeated. He was up from his chair with a father's resolve to keep looking, said to call him if we "found out anything," and was gone with a slam of his truck door and a squeal of tires on gravel.

There was a faint smile creasing Clayton's faraway look.

"You gonna help him?" I asked.

"No, I think this one come for somebody else," he said, turning his eyes on me. With a shiver, I realized what he was proposing. Everything we'd talked about followed by Stuart showing up in need lined up in my mind. It felt so meant-to-be that the only thing missing was my own decision to accept it and act on it.

"Yeah, I'll do it."

Something dripped on my hands in my lap. A momentary nosebleed I wiped up with my red bandana, startled at such a sudden show of my own blood.

"*Aaaa...*" Clayton said, moved. "That's it. That's the sign. The power ready for you to shine. Come to you doin' the choosin'."

Everything seemed inevitable from then on. Clayton telling me not to drink or eat anything else, gathering up a few things, driving me in his car across the border and up into the high mountains on a hot summer day. Telling me he was taking me to a special spot, the place where his Bluejay power was "from." Saying there were a few last things a power man needed to know about, things he'd show me when the time came. The long drive in a cavalcade of tourist vehicles and heavy trucks heading over the mountains to the coast, Clayton urging me to think about nothing but Boot and the things he was telling me as he drove. That this was a particularly good thing to call your power for, that it was better not to try with something that was about yourself at first—"what you feel strong about just get in the way"—but close enough that "you care, you have the want to help out." That things of personal importance came later, without even asking for it. He said when we got there I should "get on a good trail and follow the power to where it come from," that he'd help me and follow along.

Where the highway turned aside from the river to climb up to the pass, the river came out of a steep-sided, mountainous gorge. Clayton turned off on a dirt track leading down to a picnic area along the river rushing green with snowmelt, and parked well back from the motor homes and barbecues and children in bathing suits screaming how cold the water was. We got out and stretched in the afternoon sun, the limpid mountain air chilly and moist with springlike smells of summer coming late after a winter of heavy snow. There wasn't a cloud anywhere in the sky and the sun was low and brilliant over the western peaks, lighting up the colors of wildflowers tossing in the breeze.

Clayton locked his car, slung his knapsack over one shoulder, and we strolled around in rapt interest for whatever our eyes fell upon. The odd couple drawing the occasional curious stare, saying nothing, following wherever our steps led us.

There were millions of gossamer-winged flies fluttering around, hatched in unison and formed in clouds over the swift water of the river. Red-winged blackbirds darted through the hordes, bills open to the feast. Lush stands of tall grass rustled, willow thickets swam with mosquitoes, osier dogwood held out creamy white clusters of bloom. Balsam-smelling poplars lined the washed-down boulders of the shore. Litter was everywhere—stinking disposable diapers thrown back into the bushes, beer bottles, plastic bags clinging to wild rose with delicate pink petals that fell off as we brushed past. Huge old solitary ponderosa pines with vanilla-scented bark were strewn around the base of trunk with flaked-off fragments that looked like puzzle pieces. There were yarrow plants all fuzzy greenish-white, just beginning to flower, serviceberries still green and hard this far up in the mountains, and elderberries in the full stinkiness of rank bloom. Birds everywhere—robins, blackbirds, tanagers, chickadees—and high in the sky where the pines were releasing pollen from the toss of tiny maroon cones, swallows soared in endless curving dives and climbs. The vivid experience of nature on the day after a sweat that is like waking up on earth for the first time again.

So many directions we could go, ways to explore, things to see, but Clayton was noticeably riding shotgun, letting me choose the way, following close behind me in the narrow spots. Reminding me without a word what we were doing there. Until I felt it—that I was on a good trail, that the direction I was walking was my very own at that moment, in that place. That I was following the lead of something drawing me on—a conviction instantly confirmed by the first strident call of a blue-jay directly ahead, deep in the shadows of the dense fir forest we were entering. Mile after mile of hiking up the left bank of the river, the hummocky flat of bottomland forest giving way to the vertical walls of glacier-scoured mountainside where we followed the faint trails of deer and bear high up and around the craggy headlands. So high, the river was just a ribbon far below, glimpsed through openings in the dark forest of Douglas fir. Until we descended to a wide spot on the river, a meadow of knee-high flowering lushness surrounded by enormous spruce and fir where I made a beeline toward what sounded like a waterfall. The panting, sweaty hike had made me light-headed with hunger and thirst, and I entered the last screen of trees smelling the cool, wet fragrance of mountain water ahead.

All at once I stopped still, stunned by the realization that the rushing sound I'd been hearing was all around and overhead. It was the sound of hundreds of birds singing at once, all bluejays, their raspy-voiced calls and trills and murmurs overlapping into a continuous racket that only sounded like rushing water. Through the trees ahead I could see the river easing by in slow undulations, a slack stretch, making no sound. In the last reddish light before the sun went behind the mountains, I could see bluish bird forms moving everywhere in the trees and on the ground around us.

What were so many bluejays doing in one place? I didn't know what to make of it. I'd seen large flocks of bluejays before, but nothing like this. The nonstop calling made my ears pop. I recognized the low-pitched voices of individual bluejays through the cacophonous blur, the punctuation of imitation hawk whistles, the outcries—always in threes—of strident *kwash! kwash! kwash!* and questioning *shook! shook! shook!* It was deafening and stupefying. It was so unexpected, the hair stood up on the back of my neck, and I simply sat down to listen, amazed.

Clayton sat down behind me and I heard him dig in his pack. I thought he was laughing, as amazed and transfixed as I was, but then recognized he was blending his own bluejay calls into the voices all around us. He put the stick of his bluejay feather fan in my hands and in a low voice said to squeeze the handle between my knees. In a daze, I vaguely listened to his instructions, not wanting to scare the bluejays away and lose the incredible sensation their roar of song was making me feel.

"They not goin' anywhere," he muttered. He was right—the blue-jays kept a discreet distance away, but otherwise seemed to ignore us. Once we stopped moving around they waxed even more loud and unrestrained. Clayton had me relax against the trunk of a huge fir with my legs stretched out, moved the handle of the fan in a little so my thigh muscles held it splayed in front of my knees, and told me to relax completely except where I was squeezing the stick. Under the roar of rich sound, his voice was flat, metallic. He said the part of the body that stored the memory of a person's power was the insides of the thighs, close to the knees, and that was why humans danced, and why the Indians danced their power in the Winter Dances. He said to "squeeze hard on what you got" and concentrate on the sound of "the bluejays singin' their power song" and nothing else. He said the trick to calling on power was to fix my attention on one thing to the exclusion of all else—one persisting sound or one persisting sight that seemed to express my power, that kindled a "religious feeling" of calling into my presence persons greater than myself.

The more I devoted my attention to the sound the bluejays made, the less I was aware of anything else. Once Clayton stopped giving me instructions, there was nothing but the intricate variations of overlapping bluejay voices, raspy and raucous and full of life, flooding into my ears in an ebb and flow like waves that carried me away. I felt like I was floating. The awe I'd been feeling grew into an exultation that seemed unbearable, that made me feel tiny and vulnerable in the face of immense forces at work in the world. I heard Clayton's voice intrude, saying, "Stay hard. . . . Stay here with me. . . . Use your eyes. . . ." I looked around in the roar of sound and saw the tree bark and evening light of where we sat. The same whitish, misty blur as at other times was beginning to blot out my vision directly before my eyes, a vague going slowly blind with my eyes open that made me realize Clayton meant I should use *wik'wst*. My years of training kicked in, my eyes easily unfocused, and a vast panorama appeared, everything in my surroundings frozen in a blurry softness.

Instantly the roar of sound and the view fuse into one. I have a feeling of my body going to sleep—a tingling, sinking away with spasms and jerks that becomes a shaking of my whole body—but I'm still aware with my eyes open. The shaking fades away as I become more accustomed to a hardened feeling of simply holding onto the sequence of things I notice. What I remember later is that I'm aware of only one thing at a time, each following the one before in a seamless flow. I remember Clayton murmuring that "this" is how "they" see the world.

What I see is a blurry vastness that is at the same time exactly where we're sitting in the woods. Somebody is coming and the house lights go up. Things sizzle in the flare-up, and there's a sensation that the whole world can feel my emotions at the discovery that the brightness is caused by some kind of inner light radiating outward from inside the things I see. The world's awareness of my feelings bathes me in something like wind that blows right through me. I know I'm "in the power" and struggle to remember why. There's a sudden strong scent of leather saddles and "boy." I see Boot off somewhere in the distance, sitting in the glow of a greenish light. A voice says, "He's fine. Don't worry about him. He'll be home tomorrow." I wonder who's speaking. There's a glimmering of somebody coming close, a man leaning down to show me some blue beads strung around his neck. "Wear this to keep me close," he says, his voice somehow familiar but not anybody I can identify. I study the string of beads he's holding out in his fingers, realize they're pony beads strung in a certain order, so many dark blue beads and so many light blue beads, each group evenly alternating one after the other.

I hear Clayton's voice intruding again like someone calling from a distance through thick fog, yet I know he's right behind me, to the side of the tree I'm leaning against.

"You see 'em?" I finally make out.

"Yeaaaaaah . . ." I say in a long drone.

He says more. The names he's naming make me see Jim and Charlene and the others in Jim's car, driving somewhere. The voice from before says, "Look what happens." I see the car cross a bridge over a wide river, then pull over with a flat tire. Jim has no spare. He sits down on a rock beside the road. "That's the worst of it. They get there okay, but the two mothers argue." Something about coming right back.

There's more, but things are getting jumbled up. I notice the bluejays getting quiet, the light fading. I'm getting cold. There's still things going on out on the periphery. I can tell they have to do with the things I've wondered about in life, answers shown like dream episodes narrated in the same familiar male voice. One I remember later is animalistic human forms crying in the woods about being ignored by human people, and other White people like me hearing their voices. Women, young girls gaining power, climbing to the tops of the oldest trees and sitting there for months to keep them from being cut down by loggers.

I come to the surface of things where multiple sensations are happening at the same time—the wind picking up in darkening trees, the silence of roosting bluejays fluttering on high limbs, the smell of the river, the feel of squeezing something hard between my knees. I remember the feather fan and look down, but nothing's there. Clayton has removed it and put it away. It's a jarring moment because the actual sensation is like I'm squeezing my thigh muscles together on something much larger, like an oddly shaped rock that moves. It's exactly like holding my legs clamped around a dog that's trying to get away. The instant I see nothing there, the sensation dissipates and my thighs release their tension in a painful cramping of muscles. I sit forward with a deep sigh and massage the soreness of my thighs, aware that I've come back completely to my ordinary awareness of things.

My boots dug into the soft duff as I kneaded cramped muscles. I remembered Old Willie rubbing his thighs the same way after the bear came over him. And I had the same fascination with something peeking out of the surface of what I was sitting on that I had then, this time a dim phosphorescence in the churned-up duff my boots had dug open. My thigh muscles slowly relaxed and I looked around in sleepy, refreshed wonder. I felt a special warmth for the old man sitting quietly beside me. I stretched, yawning, working the kinks out of my back, feeling the most exquisite peacefulness—a sense of utter completion and fulfillment. It was like I had amnesia for anything in my life but what I had just done and the vividness of the immediate moment. It was like I'd been with God and nothing else mattered. I felt like weeping but instead expressed what I was feeling in a soft, sheepish laugh. Clayton stirred beside me.

"See what I mean?" he said in a soft voice, his eyes shining. "No way to say, but the best of a power man, and nobody know but they do it."

What I had seen and heard and smelled when I was in the power was now fleeting and ineffable, but I could dip easily into the memory of it, call any part of it to mind with a rush of vivid detail. It had been so real I was amazed that Clayton hadn't seen the man leaning over to show me his beads.

"When your power come on you, just for you what he show. Same for any power man. This how our mother take pity on us, give us somethin' so we can live the best. Somethin' for the peek at things, to know things in the power way."

Where we sat in the dirt and fir needles under darkening forest trees seemed like the most beautiful place in the world. I felt as if I was sitting directly over the center of the earth. I had a continuous, uninterrupted memory of sitting there ever since we walked up and sat down, the same as Clayton. The coming of night jibed perfectly with my sense of the passage of time. The only difference in our experience of sitting there, our talk afterward revealed, was that I saw and heard and smelled things he didn't. Events as real as sitting there talking to him had happened that he was unaware of. And it was those things that gave where we were sitting a sense of being rooted in eternity.

I told him about seeing Boot and the voice saying, "He's fine. Don't worry about him. He'll be home tomorrow." About the man I saw saying, "Wear this to keep me close." About the vague pictures of things that answered deep wonderings of mine. Clayton asked if I heard him asking my power to look in on the Woods family, look ahead and see what would happen on their trip, "if they get there and come back okay." I said yes and relayed what I was shown and told. Clayton responded with complete acceptance to what I said, as if what I described had already happened. The way he spoke about it made it clear that it was my *shumíx,* my spirit partner, my power—not me— who, by making such revelations, had done something awesome and beyond human capabilities.

"The power man, power woman, they just like somethin' hollow, to fill up with power," he said. "All that we train for, to be empty, to be clean, to be fit for the power to pour in. Just a place for the power to come and do somethin' like through us. Our mother have all the power, *T'at'úpa* watch over us come-alive people, and so they take pity on us, see us train for power and give us the little bit so we know somethin'. You know somethin' now, you feel the power come on you when you call for 'em, and so now your feelings come to the top, eh?"

"Yes. I've never felt this way before."

"But now our thoughts go high on what our power can do. To be humble that our mother take pity on us and this power is her gift. That we are just pitiful people and those powers want to help us. We are nothing compared to those powers, but when they come on us, how high our feelings fly!

"That's the power way, *ixi shumíx tu'últ,* that our thoughts go high on what is *xa'xá,* and not on ourself. So we can live on earth the power man, and not be all puffed up with what our power can do. And that is why we say, '*Wai i hwi,*' 'So be it,' or 'That's it.'"

He picked up some duff and rubbed it between his hands.

"To come back, and that's just the way it is!"

"*Wai i hwi,*" I said.

It was pitch dark when he said it was time "to stop botherin' the blue-jays where they snoozin'." He said we could go to a place nearby where the bluejays knew "we belonged." Upriver about a hundred yards Clayton led the way to where the mountain came steeply down to the edge of river again, an inky blackness where I couldn't make anything out since there was no moon. Along the way he felt for dead branches and broke them off, gathering a bunch in his arms to build a fire. So I gathered branches, too, and stood in the dark while he scuffed around, saying there was a fire pit there somewhere.

He grunted when he found it. As he broke twigs and lit the fire, he told me there were other bluejay places like this one that the old Bluejay doctors talked about. He said bluejays gathered like this only once a year, after nesting, when the young ones were able to fly as well as the adults. The parents brought their young to the great gatherings to meet the flock they were from, to mingle and learn the language before heading off in the world. He said that was why Bluejay doctors used to gather from all over in places like this and train younger ones in how to use their power. He said such things were now only done in secret, in the remotest places.

Smoke billowed up. With bigger and bigger branches laid on, bright flames shot up, finally illuminating our surroundings. The inky blackness turned out to be the underside of an immense piece of mountain rock that had fallen from above in ancient times. We stood at the outer edge, just under the rim over our heads that sloped back twenty feet, forming a dry, airy room. It was another rock shelter, and as usual the faint traces of red ocher pictures of spirit power were defaced with more modern symbols—spray-painted initials, pecked four-letter words, and teenage boys' sexual fantasies obscenely rendered in charcoal.

We found a pile of firewood left by someone far back under the rock where it would stay dry, and gathered more by the light of the fire until we had enough to last the night. Clayton had me fill his fire-blackened tin pot with water from the river, and when I came back he was opening bags of deer jerky, ripe serviceberries, tea, and tobacco. He put the water to boil and I sat waiting with him, famished. He saw me looking at how little he'd brought and shrugged.

"A place like this, have so much power, all we can do is train," he mused.

Once the tea was steeping, he said, "So now we thank 'em, for all they give us." We each tossed a little of everything in the fire and out into the darkness, even drips of tea and pinches of twist. He put the tobacco away and we consumed all that was left. It wasn't much.

We sat feeding the fire as Clayton told me stories about Bluejay power I'd never heard before. Long sagas in the lives of men and women with Bluejay power that enthralled me more than any other "power man" stories he had told because I related so strongly to the familiar inclinations and experiences of the protagonists. The stories also contained bits and pieces of lore specific to Bluejay power that were gems of importance to me, that I grasped immediately as useful ways of dealing with life through Bluejay eyes. They also gave me a framework for understanding what I'd done there that day, opening a place in my mind to accommodate such experiences and have something to build upon.

He talked generally about the power way, touching upon the different things he'd done with me to help me get to the place where I was that night. He said that there were more things to learn about my power, more things to train for, more aspects of using power that came with practice, but that it would mostly be between me and my power from now on. One thing he said I might think about was learning how to say out loud what my power was saying while I was "in the power." That way other people listening would know what the power was saying and I wouldn't have to remember later and explain what I experienced. He said the power would know what I was trying to do and would "speak through me," would be more detailed in words instead of showing me things to see. He said the "way in" to doing it would come with more practice, that I would learn how to let the power come on me only a little, so I would only tremble a little and hear a little buzzing. Then like a distant radio I would hear talking and would let whatever I was hearing come out through my mouth.

He talked about the power way as nothing new, as an ancient and fully developed tradition that a person received in story and example, but that a person had to find out by direct experience how it worked for them personally. He said the power way was only the "hollow thing" that power men made themselves into by training. That it was only "the way in" to power. That it was here—the earth where we found ourselves, the place where we were alive and aware—that had the power. He said it was those who had been here before us—the mountains and the rivers and the trees and the birds and the stars in the sky and even the crackling fire we were staring at—that taught us what we knew. And each power man embodied it, brought it alive in his own lifetime, lived it, followed where it led, and passed on the way of it when the time came.

"But like my elder tell me, this day and time, not many care to know. And like him, some who know hate the White man. Don't want the White man to know. Hide it away from him, how we have our powers. But my power say, 'Look! Look at that White man over there. That's the one gonna follow you around. The smart mouth who love our mother. He know somethin'. He can see us!' And that's just the way it is. *Wai i hwi*."

I slept like a baby in the coziness of reflected heat from the fire. But with nothing more than a flannel shirt and jeans on, I woke up in the wee hours, shivering in the cold. The fire was down to a bed of coals and Clayton didn't stir when I got up and put more wood on. With puffs of breath I blew it up into flames. As it grew into a roaring bonfire again, I remembered I was dreaming about swimming in a river before I woke up. Automatically, I took off all my clothes and tiptoed over to the bank and down into the water. The shock of icy water took my breath away, but I eased under and felt my way around. In the dark, all I could do was form a picture from touch. I was in an eddy formed behind a huge rock, a wide pool outside the main current, with a deep hole way over my head in the center.

I dove down and felt along the bottom, my body going numb in the deep freeze, but it kept going down, down, down. The pressure on my ears grew intense so I shot up and burst out, gasping for air. The flicker of distant firelight on forest trees under a starry sky was beautiful beyond belief. The words *en'hlapomítkxu il siulhk* (to dive in water) came to mind, and all the stories I'd heard about diving for power at night in cold rivers and lakes—or like over on the coast, at night in the ocean—seemed to make sense for the first time.

The mountain wind felt colder than the water, so I dove again, kicking deeper and deeper until I found the very bottom of the pool with my fingers. I felt slippery rocks and strangely shaped objects in soft muck. I began to rise upward in a buoyant underwater sensation of floating suspended, drifting in a slow, circular nothingness until I felt something huge grab my feet. Bumping the giant rock, I felt myself sucked backward out into the main current. Tumbled by the turbulent pounding of the river sweeping me along like a rag doll, I was just as suddenly spit out into the lower end of the pool. I came up gasping for air, swimming away from the clawing fingers of current until I made it back into the center of calm again.

There's a phosphorescent glitter of foam lit up by starlight, and the pallid reflection of stars waving on the glossy surface of river at eye level. The elation I feel is unbearable . . . or is this what it feels like to freeze to death? I ought to know. . . . A laugh bubbles up, loud and shivery and raucous, my voice shattering the mountain stillness. Then there's a sound in the distant trees, a faint, answering call of a bluejay. Clayton always said that a daytime animal making its presence known, calling out in the middle of the night (or vice-versa, a nighttime animal calling out in daytime), was a sign of power moving in the moment. Something to give you pause about what was happening at that moment. Something to grab onto. So I dive down again, down to the bottom of the pool and feel along with my fingers again. Then let myself be sucked back along the slippery-smooth rock, back into the bucking bronco of the main current, riding it like something trying to tear me apart until my lungs are burning from holding my breath so long. Right back into the calm pool again, bursting up into precious gulps of air.

Which of course I have to do again and again, until I'm down on the bottom feeling through the muck and my hand closes around something that feels like a small flat rock with sharp edges. I hold on to it as I'm grabbed and sucked out into the current for one last tumbling ride, then come up, weakly flailing for shore, certain that I can't survive in the water much longer. I drag myself up the bank and stumble toward the fire, so cold and stiff I can hardly keep my feet. The flames have burned down but the heat is intense, instantly thawing and warming my shivering body. I realize I'm still holding what I found at the bottom of the pool. I hold it up to the light. It's a greenish, translucent piece of worked jade, the last pointed inches of an old knife blade or spear point.

Putting more wood on the fire, I danced in place before it, the flames so hot my naked body dried off in no time. As I jogged in place like an idiot bush man, I looked over the fire and saw Clayton awake and up on one elbow, staring at me.

"*Aaaa . . . k'ulsht's i skultemíux ketl' kwá'shkai,*" he said with a smile. ("Ah, the Bluejay man in training.")

He lay back and began to hum something to the rhythm of my alternating footsteps. I recognized the melody of the Bluejay "finding song" he'd taught me years before, and began to sing the words, staring into the fire that was warming me.

We got back the next day and I called Stuart from the pay phone at Sully's Store in Loomis. He answered in his usual brusque, humorous tone. I asked about Boot.

"Yeah, he's here, he showed up this mornin'. He was hangin' out at one of his buddy's. Mad at us, thinkin' he's teachin' us a lesson. But one look at his mother cryin' and he broke down. Said he was sorry. So we don't call him 'Boot' anymore."

His pause for effect was typical. Boot's real name was Henry. I waited for the inevitable punch line.

"No, sir! Now when we call him, we say, 'Hey, Grounded for Life, c'mere!'"

The next day, the Woods family drove up with an exhausted, bleary-eyed Jim at the wheel. He had a brand-new tire on the left rear of his car, where I'd "seen" him have a flat tire. Charlene and Lucy and the girls carried the little ones inside. Jim wryly told a tale of the two mothers-in-law, just fine together in a ceremonial setting, like mixing oil and water as relatives. The old dreamer who knew her son only too well and the old ghost doctor who thought her daughter had married beneath her had dueled with indirect but barbed words for only a day. The little house on the Chilcotin River was too small for the both of them. Charlene had said abruptly, "I want to go home. Now."

"Flat tire?" I asked, kicking the new one.

"Yeah, I picked up a nail comin' over the Fraser River bridge, and had no spare. A tow truck pulled over and the guy had this one on a rim that fit, so he sold it to me."

"But before that, you sat on a rock, wonderin' what to do, eh?"

He looked at me sharply.

"You're creepin' me out, dude. Is that somethin' my uncle said?"

"No, that's somethin' I said."

"Great. Wonderful. Makes my day. As if my mother doesn't say enough about me not havin' anything. Now we got another Clayton

Tommy—taller, and a lot whiter. Why did I ever bring you home with me, anyway?"

He was talking about how we first met, when I picked him up hitch-hiking and he took me home for Clayton's birthday party, years before. "It was my pickup truck," I said. "I was driving. You could've just got out and said so long and thanks for the ride!" I was grinning but he looked at me suspiciously.

"What did the rock look like? That I sat on?"

"White and round. Smooth, like a granite boulder."

"Yep, you got it. Wouldn't you know? Clayton Tommy Junior . . ." He yawned hugely and started to walk away. "Well, I'm gonna crash. Gotta get up and do it again! Later, dude."

22

A FEW DAYS LATER, Clayton Tommy sent me on the long wander. There were certain things he'd taught me specifically to prepare me. The power places I was to see if I could find were described in brief stories he told me over time, which like the other stories he told me, he had me tell back to him until he was sure I'd memorized them correctly. The stories did not contain directions to find the places, only enough detail about the natural features of each spot to know if I'd found the right place. More than anything else, the short, cryptic stories in Salish told of the relation formed between First Hunter and the "person" he encountered at certain places in the long ago. What the person gave to First Hunter as a result of his skill in figuring out the person's particular power was some item that made clear what animal or other force of nature the person was. The way he was tested gave an idea of the dangers encountered at each place. Each story ended with ("He didn't come back") until the last one, which ended ("And then he came back").

So I had my basic itinerary, such as it was. The only hint about what direction I should go was contained in the third story, when First Hunter looked back and saw far to the east, Chopaka Mountain sticking up, glowing red in the sunset. That meant I was going back up into the Pasayten country, the high mountains along the Canada-U.S. border that were still wilderness. And then north, if I was interpreting certain hints correctly in the later stories. But it really didn't matter.

I wasn't going to be following maps or directions or anything of a conscious, thought-out nature to find my way.

Inside the sweatlodge at the Woods place that afternoon, Clayton and I sweated alone to the rumble of distant thunder, an unusually early arrival of hot-weather thundershowers in the mountains. The Similkameen River, flooding with snowmelt through May and June, had dropped to normal levels, signaling that the snow was finally gone in the high country. In the dark burn of steam from splashed, glowing rocks, I was given certain reminders, certain warnings. But beyond the stories of places to find, I was on my own and was expected to follow my power wherever it led.

Never in my life needing a reason to go off in the hills by myself, I now felt more ready than ever to go off into the wilderness. To let time, as the outside world knew it, stand still. My feeling of being more at home in the wild outdoors—that its dangers were nothing compared to, say, driving the freeways of big cities—had always filled me with confidence. But Clayton impressed upon me that seeking with power in the remote places where no humans went was a different proposition. That I was opening myself to things in the natural world that people preoccupied with ordinary matters rarely encountered. He said that what came at me that night in Jersey Bull's pasture was just a taste of what lived in the high mountains. He said to trust and concentrate on what had given me power in life, that it was the best protection I had.

After the first swim in the river, we went back inside the sweatlodge where I began to smell a strong, musky, vaguely familiar odor. Clayton said he'd brought in a little musk, the gland from a grizzly bear, and had wiped it on the hot rocks so I could be sure of recognizing the smell. He said if I smelled it in the far mountains, I would know that I was "in the house of Grizzly Bear." The whole country where they roamed and rubbed themselves, leaving this scent, they considered their own. When I was "in their house" I had to act accordingly. Which meant, unlike people who wore bells or made a lot of noise to warn off grizzlies, that I had only the "saying," the words of the incantation to prepare me for a grizzly showing up. He said grizzlies could feel a person using power to find their way, and that if I encountered one, it would be an opportunity to gain something from them.

After we swam in the river a second time, Old Willie showed up, driven down to see me off by his grandson, Roger Antoine. Roger and I hadn't seen each other in ages and grinned at each other. They both undressed and came in to sweat with us, enlivening the mood of things with their family specialty—relentless, good-natured teasing.

But then they settled down in the pitch-dark burn and Willie's voice began to talk in the indirect way of elders giving advice. He said the long wander was what bears did when first grown up and on their own. He said they sometimes rambled hundreds of miles before they settled in someplace where they liked the food and prospects for mating and hibernation. Another name for the long wander he gave as *en'kxáms i skum'xwíst,* "following the bear's trail." He urged me to be like the bears and do everything I could to avoid people.

Willie sang what he called "callin' on the bear," what turned out to be the same song he sang in his herb room when the bear came over him. I listened closely to the Salish words this time, but I couldn't make out what they meant. He explained the line ("Wherever you go, you will know me") as, "See, that's our mother sayin' that. Wherever a bear go, that's home to 'em. That Bear power, that's what a person want to really know the earth!"

He said the earth gave bears their special gift for finding their way around and knowing where things were because bears had once been human, but chose to "go back to nature." He said they were "only barely the animal," that bears considered humans killing and eating them to be cannibalism, and therefore having a bear as a spirit partner was the most unpredictable and dangerous bond a person could form. He said bears were so aware of us and sensitive to any slight that even the word for "black bear" in Salish (*skum'xwíst*) meant nothing more than "somethin' dark walkin' along."

When he stopped talking, Clayton said now was the time to tell me that I could take along a knife, matches, and dried food on the journey. I'd come prepared to head off with nothing but the clothes I wore. They all laughed at my surprise. Roger said they tested him the same way when he "went walkabout." It was the first time he had ever mentioned it. I tried halfheartedly to get him to say something about his experience, but I knew it was no use. Getting Roger Antoine to tell a straight story was—to use one of his own favorite expressions—like trying to teach a porcupine to sing: It didn't work, and it irritated the porcupine.

"Makes sense if you think about it, though, eh?" he said. "Only somebody who really trust his power be willing to go off with nothin' on a tramp like that."

"Take your rifle, whatever. It's up to you," Clayton added. "Nobody tell a power man what to do. Only his power."

I could tell he didn't expect me to take my rifle, just that such decisions were mine.

"Yah, and don't forget your rubbers!" Old Willie interjected.

"You mean for his feet, to stay dry in the rain?" Roger asked innocently. "Or for the women he's gonna be lookin' for?"

A gale of laughter greeted his words.

"Well, and don't forget," Clayton struggled to say. "Tom don't go nowhere anymore without his prayer beads!"

He was referring to the string of blue beads I now wore around my neck. Roger quickly improvised a story about me just starting off into the mountains and being trailed by a mountain lion, complete with mutterings in fractured Salish like an English-speaking White man trying to pronounce the unfamiliar sounds. It was a brilliant parody of me supposedly terrified and babbling to myself, trying to remember what to do when a lion was closing in with me in mind for lunch. Then he had me turning around to face the lion and counting the rosary, convinced of my doom. The lion sits down facing me, licking its chops, willing to wait for me to finish. But of course, all I'm doing is counting in pidgin Salish, so I get confused, lose track, and have to start all over. This goes on over and over until the lion falls asleep, bored out of his mind by me using my "White man power" to talk endlessly but say nothing of consequence. I was as disabled by laughter as the two old men when Roger came up with his punch line:

"And then he came back!"

It was evening when we climbed out for the last time and swam in the river. After we dressed in silence, Clayton stunned me by giving me his own favorite hunting knife to take along. Roger then gave me a cigarette lighter sheathed in a homemade covering that was beaded in bright red, yellow, and green mountain symbols. Old Willie came back from Roger's car with a big grin of how they'd already worked this out, and handed me a bag of sweet pemmican—the kind he preferred, made from dried, pounded salmon, serviceberries, and fat. I had more than enough now, and it all fit easily in my pockets. Nothing was said, each simply shook hands with me and walked away.

I stood alone in the dusk beside the glow of coals for a long time, thoughtless, waiting. The way was open and all I was looking for was a good trail to be on, my own trail, stretching away before me. Everything faded until there was only the evening songs of robins, their perched, effusive, end-of-day ritual in praise of being on earth, here, now. I floated up in my mind's eye until I could look down on the country where I lived. What I saw was just as Old Baptiste's song had said, *muk'mák'w uhl nish,* nothing but mountains as far as you could see. And in the vast feel of it, a certain place I knew came to mind. Yes, there— that's where I feel something drawing me. That's where I'll head for, I thought, and walked away into the night.

ABOUT THE AUTHOR

Tom Harmer was born in Omaha, Nebraska. He lived for many years on both sides of the Canadian border in British Columbia and Washington state and now makes his home in the woods of northern New Mexico. He is the author of *Going Native*.